DOSSIERS
ICC Institute of World Business Law

Class and Group Actions in Arbitration

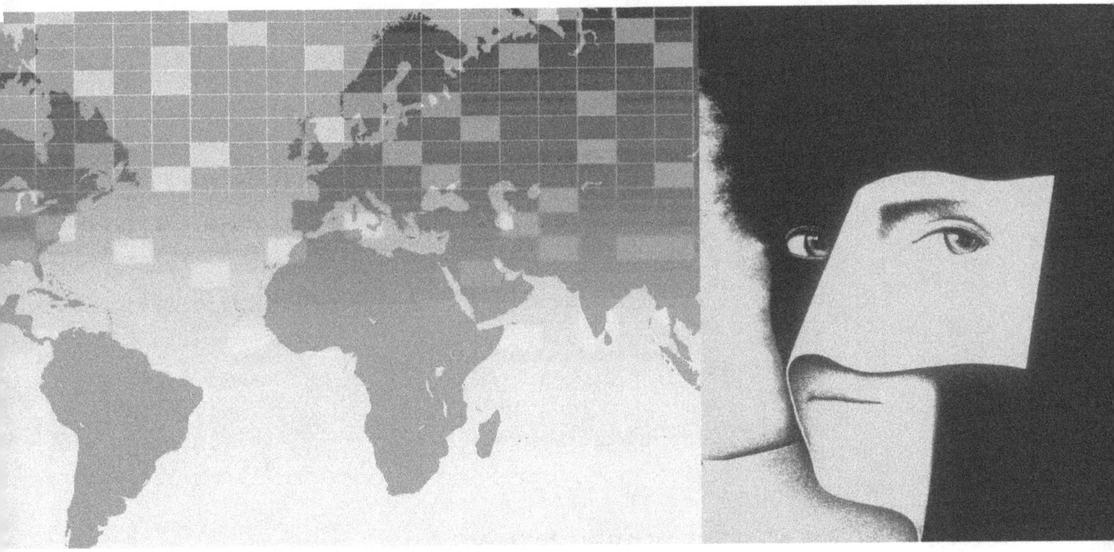

INTERNATIONAL CHAMBER OF COMMERCE
The world business organization

Edited by
Bernard Hanotiau
Eric A. Schwartz

CLASS & GROUP ACTIONS IN ARBITRATION

ICC Services
Publications Department
33-43 avenue du Président Wilson
75116 Paris
France

ICC Publication No. 771E
ISBN: 978-92-842-0414-4

ISBN 978-90-411-8385-9

Contents

FOREWORD

Yves Derains*

For years, arbitral rules were devised for only two parties. The ICC Court of Arbitration was created in 1923, and no provisions regarding arbitration involving more than two parties were introduced in the ICC Rules of Arbitration prior to 1998. Which does not mean that during the preceding 75 years, the ICC Court never dealt with arbitration procedures involving more than two parties. They were seen as exceptions that did not deserve to be specifically addressed by the ICC rules. Some ad hoc solutions were found by adapting the existing rules to problems that the presence of several parties generated.

This slow evolution is fully understandable. The paradigm of an arbitration procedure is a procedure with two parties or two homogeneous groups of parties. The existence of one or several additional independent parties has disruptive effects. It starts with drafting the arbitration clause. It requires a lot of creativity to devise contractual mechanisms that allow all contracting parties to intervene in case a procedure is initiated by one of them against only one other. Then come the problems of constituting an arbitral tribunal, of dealing with cross claims, with requests for disclosure and the use of the same documents directed to parties in different procedural positions, etc.[1] To address all those issues in standard rules of arbitration is a challenge.

With class and group actions, the usual complication of multiparty and multi-contract arbitration is often exacerbated. For instance, how to establish the jurisdiction of arbitrators in a class action procedure where the majority of the parties are signatories of different contracts, with possibly different arbitration clauses and are not even aware of the existence of the procedure? It is a difficulty among many others.

Thus, one may legitimately wonder why to endeavour having recourse to arbitration in resolving disputes for which this institution is not naturally adapted? Would it not be simpler to leave the State courts to deal with class actions and group actions? Organizing class or group arbitration proceedings faces many hurdles. What are the merits of arbitration that would justify crossing them? Maybe there is none. Is 'class arbitration is a worst-of-all-worlds Frankenstein's monster' as the US Chamber of Commerce once described it?[2] But in that case, it would be hard to understand efforts made throughout the word to make class or group arbitration possible. The fact that 180,000 Italian creditors sued Argentina in ICSID on the basis of the BIT between Argentina and Italia is very telling.[3]

Class Action procedures, as developed in the United States Court system and more recently in Canada, are almost nonexistent in Europe. The European Commission has advocated collective redress as an important means of accessing justice, but class actions have found little enthusiasm in

* Founding Partner, Derains & Gharavi, France; Former Secretary General, ICC International Court of Arbitration; Chairman, ICC Institute of World Business Law

the Member States. Class arbitration seems to raise even more hostility, as it is at odds with some basic principles of arbitration.

As already mentioned, one of them is consent, as without consent there is no arbitration. Even if an arbitration clause provides for the possible introduction of class action arbitration before an arbitral tribunal, this resolves only the problem of consent to arbitration in case of a collective dispute. The issue of the consent to be involved in a specific dispute remains unanswered. Opt-in processes may be a solution.

Lack of confidentiality is sometimes presented as another difficulty to accepting class arbitration.[4] Indeed, arbitration is, in principle, a confidential process, and such a principle of confidentiality is seen as one of the main reasons that parties choose arbitration, at least in domestic arbitration. For instance, the principle of confidentiality in arbitration is recalled in article 1464 (4) of the French Code of Civil Procedure, which states that in domestic arbitration the procedure is submitted to the principal of confidentiality unless the parties have agreed otherwise. To the contrary, a class action procedure would necessarily be public, and lawyers have motivation to constitute as wide a class as possible, as they have an interest in raising public awareness on the case as an element of publicity. Here again, an opt-in process would resolve the difficulty, as the party voluntarily entering into class arbitration would implicitly waive any right to confidentiality.

Moreover, it should not be forgotten that the hurdles are not of a procedural nature. No class action arbitration can be exercised through arbitration unless it is established that the subject matter of the dispute is arbitrable (jurisdiction ratione materiae). In several jurisdictions, disputes involving consumers or employees may not be submitted to arbitration, while consumers and labor disputes are the main field of class arbitration in the United States. But it is also true that specific statutes were introduced in some countries to favor consumer protection through arbitration, such as the 2008 Spanish Consumer Arbitration System Statute.

This Dossier of the Institute discusses those complex issues on a comparative law basis. It does so scientifically, by introducing indispensable distinctions among mass actions, in order to avoid confusion between group actions, collective actions and class actions. Each category raises different problems. In group actions, individual claims are merged together on a consensual basis but each individual holder of a claim remains a party. This configuration does not raise insuperable problems to arbitration. Collective actions are also arbitration compatible, as only one representative is acting on behalf of the members of a specific group, with members sharing the same interest. In class actions, members of a class are considered to be party to proceedings at the end of an opt-in or an opt-out process started by a self-designated representative. Here, adaption to the arbitration basics is really problematic.

This book presents the work of the 2015 Annual Meeting of the Institute, under the guidance of Bernard Hanotiau, a prominent member of the Council of the Institute and Eric Schwartz, one of its Vice Presidents. Without their deep knowledge of the subject and their impressive efforts, it would not have been possible to gather so many specialists to produce such an impressive result.

NOTES

1 See *Multiparty arbitration, Dossier VII of the ICC Institute of World Business Law* ICC Product No. 701E, 2010 Edition.

2 Chamber of Commerce of the United States of America's *amicus Curiae* in *Marriott Ownership Resorts, Inc. v Sterman*, No. 15-10627 at 9 (11th Cir. Apr. 1, 2015).

3 *Abaclat and others v Argentine Republic*, ICSID case no. ARB/07/5.

4 Maximin de Fontmichel, «Arbitrage et actions de groupe — les leçons Nord-Américaines», *Rev. Arb.*, Vol.2008/4, pp. 644-645.

Introduction

Bernard Hanotiau, Co-editor*

For the 2015 Annual Meeting of the ICC Institute, the Council of the Institute decided to select the topic of class actions, group actions and mass actions.

Several decades ago, a typical arbitration would involve one claimant against one respondent. This has progressively changed. Over the years, it has appeared that many more cases were involving several claimants against several respondents. Today, one third of all international ICC arbitrations seem to involve multiparty cases, multi-contract cases involving multiple contracts, multiple parties, some of which may sometimes even be non-signatories of the arbitration agreement.

But it does not end there. The evolution has continued and the debate today is whether it would not be possible for a class of people being in the same situation or a group of citizens having the same interest to start one single arbitration procedure as a group or as a class.

It all started in the United States, which used to be the only country in the world whose legislation permitted a class of people having the same rights to defend, to start a class action in court. The system may have some advantages, but over the years it has also attracted a lot of criticism, in particular the fact that those who in the end were the main beneficiaries of the class actions were the lawyers who were making fortunes at the detriment of their clients. This is why banks and other businesses began using arbitration clauses in their standard form contract as a way to reduce the risk of class action litigation. In other words, they thought that by inserting an arbitration clause in their contracts, only individual procedures could be initiated at the exclusion of class actions. But as evidenced by the Supreme Court decision in *Green Tree Financial Corporation v Bazzle*, this proved ineffective. If the relevant arbitration clause is adequately drafted, class-wide arbitration is possible even if it raises a number of delicate issues and practical concerns. Following the *Bazzle* decision, the American Arbitration Association has adopted supplementary rules for class arbitration and we have subsequently seen a substantial development of class-wide arbitration in the United States, and at a same time, a great number of court decisions on issues such as whether silent clauses constitute or not agreement to class arbitration or whether class arbitration waivers are valid or unconscionable.

In Europe, nothing comparable to the American class action existed for a long period of time. But things have changed these recent years, in particular under the influence of the European Union which over the past few years has adopted a global framework for collective redress and alternative dispute resolution in several sectors. In its recommendation of 11 June 2013, the Commission has stated that all member states should have

* Member of the Brussels and Paris Bars; Partner, Hanotiau & van den Berg, Brussels and Singapore; Council Member, ICC Institute of World Business Law

collective redress mechanisms at national level for both injunctive and compensatory relief by 26 June 2015. And in fact, by 2011, 16 member states of the European Union had already implemented collective redress mechanisms. It remains that what has been implemented in several European states is not comparable to what is existing in the United States. Collective redress within the European Union generally takes the form of a group action or a collective interest action and not a class action. In a group action, each member of the group is an individual party to the procedure. In a collective interest action, a party represents a collective interest and only the representing party can be considered as a party to the proceeding. A class action is totally different. The class is structured through an opt-in or an opt-out mechanism, following which all members of the class are considered to be party to the proceeding. The members of the class are represented by a class representative and do not conduct any longer individual claims. Moreover, as will be explained by the speakers on the topic, the legislations on group actions vary considerably from one European state to the other.

Finally, the idea of collective actions has also penetrated the area of investment arbitration. In recent years, we have seen investment treaty tribunals commonly accepting jurisdiction over claims of multiple, unaffiliated parties relating to the same host state measure; but also the emergence of mass claims, the leading case being *Abaclat v Argentina* where, as of the date of its initiation, there were on claimants' side over one hundred and eighty thousand individuals and corporations.

The Institute found therefore that there was great interest in devoting a seminar to the topic of class actions, group actions and mass arbitrations. Is there a place for such proceedings within the framework of the arbitration process? In the affirmative, how can or should such proceedings be organized and conducted? What lessons can be learned from the experience of such cases both in North America and elsewhere and what does the future possibly hold?

To address these issues, we were fortunate to be able to gather a wonderful group of experienced speakers. "*A tout seigneur tout honneur*", the first section was devoted to the North American experience of class arbitration. How has the law and practice concerning class arbitration developed in the United States since the Supreme Court decision in *Bazzle*? And how has the law and practice in this area developed in Canada? And what are the prospects for class arbitration in those two countries in the coming years? Taking into consideration the existing case law, what drafting techniques should be used by the parties wishing to provide for class arbitration in an arbitration agreement? This first session was moderated by John Fellas. The speakers were James Carter, Prof. Christopher Drahozal and Prof. Geneviève Saumier.

The second session focussed on collective arbitration and the European experience. As mentioned above, efforts have recently been made in Europe, in particular in certain countries like Spain and Germany to make collective or group arbitrations possible in certain contexts. What is the nature of those developments and related experience? How do they differ from class arbitration in North America? What other initiatives are being considered in Europe? Are these developments to be welcomed? These questions were addressed by Philippe Billiet, Christian Borris and Prof. Laura Carballo, the moderator of the session being José Miguel Judice.

The first afternoon session was devoted to investment arbitration and the issue of mass arbitrations. What are the jurisdictional and other legal issues that have been raised by these cases? How can they be conducted to ensure due process to all of the parties? What types of disputes may be suited to collective resolution in an investment treaty context and what are the principle obstacles that may be confronted? The speakers of this session, moderated by Eloïse Obadia, were Prof. Zachary Douglas, Carolyn B. Lamm and Prof. Luca Radicati di Brozolo.

The seminar was concluded with the traditional round-table discussion, in this case, on the future of class, collective and mass arbitrations. Are they a marginal phenomenon or has their potential yet to be realized? What are possible solutions to the issues that have been encountered? Can we expect to see more of such arbitrations in the future? These issues were addressed by Sir Franklin Berman, QC, Pierre Dalphond and Elie Kleiman. They were moderated by the leading specialist of class arbitrations, Prof. S.I. Strong.

Finally, the conclusions of the seminar were presented by Eric Schwartz.

The event was a great success due to the efforts of many people who deserve our warm thanks: the ICC Council and, in particular, its president, Yves Derains; Eric Schwartz, who co-organised the seminar; Sybille de Rosny and Katharine Bernet and their whole team at the Institute, who took charge of the organisation; and of course the speakers whose contributions are published in this volume. Their presentations were excellent. They have made a great contribution to the topic.

Chapter 1

Class Arbitration In the United States: Life After Death?

James H. Carter*

After almost a decade of rather vigorous life, class arbitration in the United States came to what was widely assumed would be its end because of decisions by the US Supreme Court in 2010 and 2013. But US class arbitration is not dead, at least not yet.

The boom in US class arbitration was quite recent. It began in about 2003, prompted by the Supreme Court's plurality decision in *Green Tree Financial Corp. v Bazzle*,[1] holding that class-wide arbitration was not precluded when an arbitration clause did not expressly address that subject. Before the *Green Tree* decision, a significant number of business organizations that dealt with the public had decided to include arbitration clauses in their standard form customer or employment agreements. These clauses typically said nothing about possible class claims. After *Green Tree*, arbitrators seemingly were invited to interpret such clauses to permit arbitrations brought by an individual on behalf of a class of all similarly situated persons. Suddenly, companies faced the very real prospect that 'silent' clauses could be latent sources of class arbitrations.[2]

This development prompted two leading arbitration organizations in the United States to publish special rules for class arbitrations, based in large part on US court rules for class actions, and their dockets of class cases increased rapidly. The American Arbitration Association ("AAA") issued Supplementary Rules for Class Arbitration ("Class Rules")[3] in October 2003, and within six years 283 requests for class arbitration had been filed. JAMS thereafter also published Class Action Procedures,[4] which are similar.

The AAA's Class Rules envisage three stages to a class arbitration proceeding, with automatic stays after each of the first two steps to permit any party to seek court review of the arbitrator's decision. The first step is 'clause construction,' in which the arbitrator determines whether the parties' agreement permits the case to proceed on a class basis.[5] A party then may seek confirmation or *vacatur* of the resulting interim award.

In 2009 the AAA submitted a brief as *amicus curiae* to the Supreme Court in the *Stolt-Nielsen SA v AnimalFeeds International Corp.* case,[6] not in support of either party but to provide the Court with neutral data on use of class arbitration. The brief reported that by September of 2009, 135 of the 283 cases filed with the AAA as class arbitrations had resulted in Clause Construction Awards. Of those, 70% held that the clause permitted the arbitration to proceed on behalf of a class. In most cases the agreements in

---

* Senior Counsel, Wilmer Cutler Pickering Hale and Dorr LLP

issue did not refer expressly to class arbitration, so that the arbitrators construed other contract language in reaching their decisions.

If the clause permits class arbitration, the next step is 'class determination,' in which the arbitrator decides whether a particular case is appropriate to certify for resolution on a class basis.[7] This involves considering whether the proposed class members all have entered into agreements containing a similar arbitration clause, whether the proposed class representative and his or her counsel are appropriate to represent class interests and whether the alleged class satisfies requirements of numerosity, typicality and manageability. By 2009, the AAA cases had resulted in 48 Class Determination Awards, each of which was automatically stayed for a second time so that any party could go to court to ask for confirmation or *vacatur*. Exactly half of those awards granted class arbitration status.[8]

Finally, if a class has been certified and no court vacates the Class Determination Award, the case may proceed either to a merits award or to a settlement. However, by 2009, no AAA class arbitration had yet resulted in a merits award.[9]

When the Supreme Court reached its decision in the *Stolt-Nielsen* case in 2010,[10] the result appeared to undermine the *Green Tree* holding. The *Stolt-Nielsen* court decided that a party cannot be compelled to arbitrate on a class basis unless there is a contractual agreement to do so and that an arbitration clause that is silent on the topic of class arbitration does not constitute an agreement to arbitrate class disputes. This significantly slowed but did not stop the trend toward class arbitration, at least in part because whether an agreement is truly 'silent' regarding the parties' relevant intentions is not always clear.

To forestall the use of arbitration on a class basis, after 2003 many businesses began to add language to their standard clauses stating that customers or employees accepting them agreed to resolve any disputes in arbitration but were said to waive any right to bring a claim on a class basis. Some courts, most notably in California,[11] declined to enforce those waivers because they were considered inconsistent with state contract law standards of unconscionability. Their validity thus remained in doubt for a number of years.

But the Supreme Court's 2011 decision in *AT&T Mobility LLC v Concepcion*[12] largely rejected the contractual unconscionability argument, stating that "[r]equiring the availability of class-wide arbitration interferes with fundamental attributes of arbitration and thus creates a scheme inconsistent with the [Federal Arbitration Act]."[13] The Court held that individual US state laws to the contrary are preempted by the federal statute and that class waivers, at least in principle, thus are valid.

In *American Express Co. v Italian Colors Restaurant*,[14] the Supreme Court in 2013 resolved the question of whether such waivers nevertheless might be invalid in practice because they effectively deprive claimants of rights to enforce federal statutes. Claimants' argument in that case was that the recovery in an individual arbitral proceeding likely would be too small to justify asserting complex claims such as those brought under US antitrust laws. The Court rejected that proposition by a 5 to 4 vote, and class waivers thus survived the most significant challenge to their legitimacy.

Class arbitration suffered a second blow in another 2013 decision, *Oxford Health Plans LLC v Sutter*.[15] In that case, the Supreme Court upheld an interim class arbitration decision. It declined to vacate an AAA Clause Construction Award finding a class arbitration appropriate and concluded that the arbitrator had engaged in a legitimate construction of the contract. But the Court distinguished its *Stolt-Nielsen* opinion, in which arbitrators had ruled on class determination issues, and expressly noted that it had not yet decided whether a class determination was a 'gateway' issue normally to be decided in the first instance by a court or an issue to be decided by an arbitrator.[16] The risk that the Court might decide in the future that clause construction should be removed from arbitral competence cast a further shadow on the prospects for class arbitration.

After *Concepcion, Italian Colors* and *Oxford Health*, commentators predicted that waivers of class arbitration rights would become almost universal in standard form contracts, that even 'silent' arbitration clauses without such waivers would not be construed (by an arbitrator or a court) to allow class proceedings and that class arbitration in the United States in short order would become extinct.[17]

1

CONTINUING USE OF CLASS ARBITRATION IN THE UNITED STATES

Yet, somewhat surprisingly, class arbitrations in the United States have gone forward, and new cases continue to be filed. The AAA, the largest US provider organization, publishes its class arbitration docket,[18] including pleadings and awards, so that interested potential or actual class members may follow relevant proceedings. By September 2015, the cumulative class docket had grown to a total of 473 cases. This included 35 new cases filed in 2011, 28 cases filed in 2012, 27 cases filed in 2013, 39 cases filed in 2014 and 32 cases filed in 2015 (through September).[19]

JAMS, which has a smaller arbitration docket, saw 17 cases filed as class arbitrations in 2013, 15 such cases filed in 2014 and another 14 cases commenced on a class basis in the first half of 2015.[20]

There appear to be two principal reasons for the continued, if limited, life for new class arbitrations after what had been presumed to be their death. First, it seems that not all business organizations stampeded to add class arbitration waivers to their standard clauses after the *Italian Colors* decision, so that waiver language is not universal. Second, attempted class waiver language sometimes is not effective to defeat class claims.

In addition, disputes continue to arise and be resolved under older agreements dating from the time before class arbitration waivers came into widespread use. Decisions involving those cases may be of particular interest because some of the cases have reached advanced stages.

a) Arbitration Clauses Without Class Waivers

Older-style clauses without class waivers continue to be used in some consumer agreements. In March 2015 the Consumer Financial Protection Bureau (the "CFPB") released an Arbitration Study (the "CFPB Study"),[21] prepared at the direction of the US Congress, on the use of arbitration in disputes involving consumer financial products or services. The CFPB Study focused on agreements involving credit cards, checking accounts, general-purpose reloadable prepaid accounts, private student loans, payday loans and mobile wireless services, which are only a part of the universe of standard consumer financial transactions in which arbitration is used. In that data set, based on 2010-2012 information provided by the AAA, the use of arbitration clauses varied from almost universal to only about 16% of credit card issuers and only about 8% of banks offering checking accounts. (However, the arbitration users included the credit card issuers and banks with the largest volume of cards and bank deposits.)

The CFPB Study found that when an arbitration clause was present, in about 90% of the cases it included a class arbitration waiver.

While waivers therefore are quite widespread where arbitration is used, this still leaves a considerable universe of around 10% of consumer financial institutions with agreements containing arbitration clauses without class arbitration waivers. The proportion may be similar or larger in other industries in which arbitration clauses are widely used.

b) Ambiguous Arbitration Clauses

Ambiguities are not unheard of in form contracts, and the drafters of some arbitration clauses have found them difficult to avoid. An example is the Macy's department store credit card application accompanied by an amendment providing for a "Credit Protection Program," in use as recently as 2010. The broadly worded arbitration clause governing disputes did not refer expressly to class arbitration but provided for arbitration under AAA rules of "any dispute or controversy" and stated that "the claimant and we agree to consolidate all such disputes." A federal district court in New York held in June 2015 that this "any and all clause" was not a total "silence" as to possible class claims and that the language was sufficient to require that the issue of clause construction and potential class arbitration be referred to an arbitrator.[22]

c) Cases Involving Older Clauses or Older-Style Clauses Still in Use

Older cases dating from pre-class waiver days have continued to work their way through the arbitral process, and they are not all zombies with no real life remaining. A significant arbitral decision in an older AAA case, *Jock v Sterling Jewelers*,[23] dating from 2008, involved employment discrimination issues under federal statutes. In February 2015, after years of interruptions due to various judicial appeals, the arbitrator granted certification to a class estimated to include 44,000 current and former female employees at retail jewelry stores who challenged their employer's pay and promotion practices as inconsistent with federal statutes. The claimants alleged that Sterling Jewelers' work force data showed that women were paid less and promoted less frequently than men and that the disparity could not be attributed to legitimate, non-discriminatory factors. They sought class certification for claims of both disparate impact, based on an asserted company-wide policy, procedure or evaluation method that is discriminatory, and disparate treatment under an alleged gender-discriminatory corporate culture.

In a 118-page award, the arbitrator certified a class only on the disparate impact claims, based on identification of specific challenged policies and procedures. She declined to certify the disparate treatment claims, finding that they did not satisfy the commonality requirement of the AAA Class Rules. The arbitrator nevertheless left open the possibility that claimants might seek an 'opt-in' class for the disparate treatment claim, a remedy that had not been sought.

The case did not end there, however. In November 2015 the federal district court in New York confirmed the award in part but vacated the portion of the award that permitted members of the class to opt out of declaratory and injunctive relief.[24] Further proceedings are possible.

In July 2015 the US Court of Appeals for the Fourth Circuit affirmed a lower court decision confirming a class arbitration award on the merits, *Jones, et al. v Dancel, et al,*[25] in favor of 487,066 consumers using 'credit repair' services. That case began as a court action seeking enforcement of a federal statute, among other claims. The matter was referred to AAA arbitration in 2006 and only recently has come to an end. The arbitrator certified a nation-wide class of consumers, a district court confirmed the Class Determination Award, and the court of appeals affirmed. Some of the defendants then entered into class-wide settlements, approved by the arbitrator, which resulted in an award of US$2.6 million in attorney fees to counsel for the claimants. The case proceeded to a merits hearing against the remaining defendants.

On the merits, the arbitrator found that the defendants had failed to make certain disclosures to consumers mandated by statute but declined to award actual damages. Instead, the arbitrator awarded punitive damages, as allowed under the statute, of about US$2 million. Rather than distribute a tiny portion of that amount to each consumer in the class, the arbitrator invoked the *cy pres* doctrine and distributed the damage award in equal portions to two consumer protection organizations: the National Consumer Law Center and the National Association of Consumer Advocates. The courts affirmed that outcome.

2 A NEW FRONTIER: CLASS ARBITRATION UNDER CORPORATE CHARTER OR BYLAW PROVISIONS?

Corporate governance disputes between shareholders or between a company and its officers, directors or shareholders are subject to arbitration agreements in various jurisdictions, but arbitration of these disputes historically has been disfavored by courts and regulatory authorities in the United States.[26] That has changed in recent years with respect to closely held corporations and, to some extent, publicly traded corporations, although the Securities and Exchange Commission maintains an informal policy discouraging the registration of securities whose governing documents include a mandatory arbitration provision.[27] There is thus only limited history in the United States of arbitration under corporate bylaw provisions requiring its use for shareholder disputes.

That may be changing, however. The bylaws of CommonWealth REIT, a publicly traded Maryland real estate investment trust that owned properties in 31 US states, include a provision stating (with emphasis added):

> Any disputes, claims or controversies brought by or on behalf of any shareholder of the Trust... *either on his, her or its own behalf, on behalf of the Trust or on behalf of any series or class of shares* of the Trust or shareholders of the Trust against the Trust or any Trustee, officer, manager... agent or employee of the Trust, including disputes, claims or controversies relating to the meaning, interpretation, effect, validity, performance or enforcement of

> the Declaration of Trust or these Bylaws (all of which are referred to as 'Disputes') or relating in any way to such a Dispute or Disputes shall, on the demand of any party to such Dispute, be resolved through binding and final arbitration in accordance with the Commercial Arbitration Rules (the 'Rules') of the American Arbitration Association ('AAA') then in effect, except as those Rules may be modified in this Article XVI. For the avoidance of doubt, and not as a limitation, *Disputes are intended to include* derivative actions against Trustees, officers or managers of the Trust and *class actions by shareholders* against those individuals or entities and the Trust. For the avoidance of doubt, a Dispute shall include a Dispute made derivatively on behalf of one party against another party.[28]

Such a clause reflects the fact that a corporation might consider it advisable to resolve derivative or shareholder claims on a class basis rather than be subjected to multiple disputes over the same events. These sorts of claims could be particularly amenable to class treatment because of their common origin in discrete corporate events with similar impact on all shareholders, and prospective respondents could want them resolved in arbitration rather than litigation.

Two investment funds that had purchased 9.8% of CommonWealth REIT's shares commenced litigation in a Maryland court in 2013 seeking declaratory and injunctive relief to prevent certain alleged 'value-destroying' and self-interested conduct by CommonWealth, its trustees and REIT management. In response, the defendants initiated arbitration under the bylaw provision, and a Maryland state court confirmed the bylaw's enforceability. The court reasoned that the funds had constructive knowledge of the bylaw provision and consented to arbitration because each CommonWealth share certificate included a legend stating, *inter alia*, that "the holder of this Certificate ... agrees to be bound by all of the provisions of the ... Bylaws..."[29] The Maryland court, echoing the US Supreme Court's *Italian Colors* decision, did not see an obstacle in the fact that a claimant in arbitration might not be able to recover attorney fees in as large an amount as it could in a derivative claim in court, nor did the court consider such a result to be certain.

In a second case involving the same CommonWealth REIT bylaw provision, in 2014 a federal district court in Massachusetts followed the Maryland decision enforcing the arbitration obligation.[30] It did so both because the court found that the Maryland decision constituted a *res judicata* ruling on the subject and also because, even in the absence of such preclusion, the Massachusetts judge would have found the bylaw arbitration provision to be enforceable. Accordingly, disputes under that particular bylaw involving derivative or class claims are arbitrable.

Mandatory arbitration under corporate governance provisions also has featured in US litigation in another context. In July 2015 a US court gave effect to a requirement that shareholder claims be arbitrated under the law of Brazil. Holders of Petrobras American Depository Shares brought class action securities litigation in New York arising from a Petrobras bribery scandal. In addition to US securities law claims, the plaintiffs asserted causes of action under Brazilian law on behalf of Brazilian purchasers of Petrobras securities either on the New York Stock Exchange or the Sao Paulo stock exchange, BM&F Bovespa. The defendants contended that the Brazilian law claims were subject to mandatory arbitration pursuant to Petrobras' bylaws in accordance with the rules of BM&F Bovespa's Market

Arbitration Chamber ("CAM"), which specializes in disputes involving corporate and securities laws. CAM's Arbitration Rules make no express reference to class arbitration, but they provide for joinder of parties and consolidation of proceedings.[31]

The US district court in New York considered expert testimony concerning 2001 amendments to the Brazilian Corporate Law pursuant to which companies such as Petrobras included mandatory arbitration clauses in their bylaws and noted that "over 160 Brazilian companies have adopted bylaws mandating arbitration of shareholder disputes." The court did not order arbitration of the claims under US securities laws, but it dismissed the Brazilian law claims on behalf of purchasers of Petrobras securities in Brazil on the basis of the company's bylaw arbitration provision.[32] The decision appears to indicate additional recognition by a US court that mandatory arbitration under corporate bylaws, where provided for under governing law, is not inherently inconsistent with US public policy.

The line of authority supporting arbitration of class claims under corporate charters and bylaws in the United States has been questioned, primarily on the basis that corporate governance documents do not constitute agreements of the type regulated by ordinary contract law.[33] Nevertheless, recent cases suggest that class arbitrations in the United States may continue in the corporate setting in at least some contexts.

3 THE CFPB 2015 ARBITRATION REGULATORY PROPOSALS

In October 2015 the CFPB issued proposals, on the basis of its earlier CFPB Study, for rules to regulate use of arbitration in consumer financial transactions.[34] If put into effect, the proposals could have sweeping consequences for future class arbitrations.

The CFPB considered three possible approaches to arbitration clauses in US consumer financial transactions: that they be banned, that they be freely allowed, or that some middle ground be found. The CFPB propounded a complicated compromise solution: that such clauses be required to state that they do not compel the consumer to give up the right to participate in a claim for relief on a class basis, which at the consumer's election could be either in a court or in a class arbitration. Arbitration clauses could continue to require that any individual claim be brought in arbitration, but the CFPB proposed that such a clause could not be invoked as a defense to a class claim in court unless and until class certification is denied or the class claims are dismissed by the court.

In addition, the CFPB proposed that regulated financial services entities within its jurisdiction be required to submit copies of all initial arbitration claim filings and written awards in consumer finance arbitration proceedings, whether individual or on a class basis, to the CFPB for analysis and possible publication. The CFPB's proposals are now subject to a period of comment and review, after which they might be enacted in the proposed or a different form.

The CFPB assumed in making its proposals that most businesses would prefer that any class claim against them be brought in court rather than in arbitration and that they therefore might restrict their use of arbitration altogether rather than risk class arbitrations; but that hypothesis remains to be tested if the proposals become a formal set of rules. The proposal that all consumer financial arbitration demands and arbitral decisions be published, if put into effect, also could result in broad changes in the transparency of such proceedings.

The CFPB Study found, and its rule proposals assume, that final judgments on the merits in class litigation are extremely rare and that class actions in court are essentially engines for settlement. Class arbitrations also have led to settlements, and businesses subject to CFPB jurisdiction may find it necessary to choose whether they prefer to face settlements in class claims in courts or before arbitrators.

4 WHAT HAVE WE LEARNED?

The Supreme Court discussed the benefits and drawback of class arbitration, albeit briefly, in the majority and dissenting opinions in the *Concepcion* case. Writing for the majority, Justice Scalia stated that class arbitration is inconsistent with basic goals of the Federal Arbitration Act because in his view it is slower than standard, individual party arbitration, more costly, "more likely to generate procedural morass than final judgment" and more formal. He also wrote that class arbitration increases the risk to defendants of large, potentially devastating losses because of the absence of multilayered judicial review, which occurs in arbitration only under deferential standards, is "unlikely to have much effect" and "makes it more likely that errors will go uncorrected."[35] The result was said to be "*in terrorem*" settlements.

In dissent, Justice Breyer compared data available for class arbitrations and class actions in litigation, writing that arbitration at least appears to be the quicker of the two mechanisms and that businesses have been shown willing to use arbitration for disputes with large financial stakes (although the examples cited did not involve class arbitration).[36]

With the benefit of additional experience with class arbitration, is it accurate to conclude that this mechanism fits poorly within the FAA scheme because its high stakes make procedural informality and lack of appellate review particularly risky? Can it properly be said, as the Chamber of Commerce of the United States has asserted, that "Class arbitration is a worst-of-all-worlds Frankenstein's monster" because "It combines the enormous stakes, formality and expense of litigation ... with exceedingly limited judicial review of the arbitrators' decisions"?[37]

We do know from recent examples that class arbitrations can lead to sophisticated determinations, orderly settlements and merits awards that courts review with care. There has been no detailed analysis of those results, outside of the limited data on consumer financial disputes studied by the CFPB, and most of the judicial energy devoted to class arbitration thus far has been spent on issues preliminary to a final award. Since class arbitration is continuing, it may be possible in due course to compare actual results with the two Supreme Court opinions in *Concepcion* to evaluate the accuracy of their views on class arbitration and the role judicial review will play.

NOTES

1 U.S. 444 (2003).

2 See William H. Baker, Class Action Arbitration, In INTERNATIONAL COMMERCIAL ARBITRATION IN NEW YORK (James H. Carter and John Fellas, eds.) 319, 336-340 (2010).

3 *Available at* **https://www.adr.org/aaa/faces/rules/searchrules/rulesdetail.**

4 *Available at* **http://jamsadr.com/rules-class-action-procedures.**

5 AAA Class Rule 3.

6 Brief of American Arbitration Association as Amicus Curiae in Support of Neither Party, Case No. 08-1198 (Sept. 4, 2009). The data in the AAA's brief were not cited in the *Stolt-Nielsen* opinions but were referred to by both the majority and the dissenting justices in *AT&T Mobility LLC v Concepcion*, 131 S.Ct. 1740, 1751, 1759 (2011).

7 AAA Class Rule 5.

8 AAA Brief, *supra* n 6 at 22.

9 Id. at 23.

10 U.S. 662 (2010).

11 E.g., *Discover Bank v Superior Court*, 36 Cal. 4th 148, 30 Cal. Rptr.3d 76, 113 P.3d 1100 (2005).

12 U.S. 333, 131 S.Ct. 1740 (2011). Four years later the Supreme Court again rejected an attack on class waivers, which was based on the argument that a reference in the clause to "the law of your state" referred to pre-*Concepcion* California law permitting an unconscionability analysis. *DirectTV, Inc. v Imburgia*, 577 U.S. ___ (2015).

13 S.Ct. at 1748.

14 S.Ct. 2310 (2013).

15 S.Ct. 2064 (2013).

16 S.Ct. at 2068 n 2.

17 E.g., John M. Townsend, *The Rise and Fall of Class Arbitration*, 2011 AMERICAN YEARBOOK ON ARBITRATION AND LAW 395 (2011).

18 *Available at* **https://www.adr.org/aaa/faces/services/disputeresolutionservices/casedocket?_afrLo.**

19 Information on file with the author. In the cases filed in 2014, clause construction resulted in three class claims contested but approved, four classes stipulated and 10 denied. In the cases filed in 2015, the results to date are one class claim approved, one class stipulated and two denied.

20 Information on file with the author.

21 Consumer Financial Protection Bureau, Arbitration Study: Report to Congress, Pursuant to Dodd-Frank Wall Street Reform and Consumer Protection Act Sec. 1028(a), *available* at **http://www.consumerfinance.gov/reports/artbitration-study-report-to-congress-2015.**

22 *Edwards v Macy's, Inc.*, 2015 U.S. Dist. LEXIS 86816 (S.D.N.Y. June 30, 2015). Following the decision, the defendants agreed to waive their right to arbitration and proceed with the case before the court. Edward M. Spiro and Judith L. Mogul, *Class Arbitration—Dying but Not Dead*, New York Law Journal Aug. 18, 2015, n 16.

23 AAA Case No. 11-20-0800-6655. See Samuel Estreicher and Kristina A. Yost, *"Jock": Employment Class Arbitration Allows Disparate Impact Claims,* New York Law Journal April 10, 2015.

24 U.S.Dist. LEXIS 154209 (S.D.N.Y. 2015).

25 F.3d 395 (4th Cir. 2015).

26 Gary B. Born, INTERNATIONAL COMMERCIAL ARBITRATION §6.04[K] (2d ed. 2014).

27 See Carl W. Schneider, *Arbitration in Corporate Governance Documents: An Idea the SEC Refuses to Accelerate*, 4(5) INSIGHTS 21 (May 1990).

28 *Corvex Management LP v CommonWealth REIT*, 2013 Md. Cir. Ct. LEXIS 3, 6 (2013); a subsequent related case is *Katz v CommonWealth REIT*, No. 24-C-13-001299 (Cir. Ct. Balt. Feb. 19, 2014).

29 Md. Cir. Ct. LEXIS at 27-30.

30 *Del. County Employees Ret. Fund v Portnoy*, 2014 U.S. Dist. LEXIS 40107 (D. Mass. 2014).

31 *Available at* http://www.bmfbovespa.com.br.

32 *In re: Petrobras Securities Litigation*, 2015 U.S. Dist. LEXIS 99322 (S.D.N.Y. July 30, 2015).

33 *E.g.*, Ann M. Lipton, *Manufactured Consent: The Problem of Arbitration Clauses in Corporate Charters and Bylaws*, 104 GEORGETOWN LAW JOURNAL ___ (2015) (forthcoming), *available at* http://papers.ssrn.com/sol3/papers.cfm?; Christos Ravanides, *Arbitration Clauses in Public Company Charters: an Expansion of the ADR Elysian Fields or A Descent Into Hades?*, 18 AMERICAN REVIEW OF INTERNATIONAL ARBITRATION 371 (2009).

34 Consumer Financial Protection Bureau, Small Business Advisory Review Panel for Potential Rulemaking on Arbitration Agreements: Outline of Proposals Under Consideration and Alternatives Considered (Oct. 7, 2015), *available at* http://www.consumerfinance.gov/f/201510_cfpb_small-business-review-panel-packet-explaining-the-proposal-under-consideration.pdf. Separately, the National Labor Relations Board maintains that class action arbitration waivers in employment contracts violate the National Labor Relations Act and will not be enforced; but several courts have rejected that interpretation.

35 S.Ct. at 1751-52.

36 S.Ct. at 1760.

37 Brief for Chamber of Commerce of the United States of America as Amicus Curiae in Support of Plaintiff-Appellants, *Marriott Ownership Resorts, Inc. v Sterman*, No. 15-10627 at 9 (11th Cir. Apr. 1, 2015).

Chapter 2

Class Arbitration in the United States

Christopher R. Drahozal*

Class arbitration in the United States dates back more than 30 years.[1] But it did not become common until after the United States Supreme Court's 2003 decision in *Green Tree Financial Corp. v Bazzle*,[2] which many construed as approving of the practice. After *Bazzle*, the American Arbitration Association (AAA) promulgated rules governing class arbitration proceedings,[3] and the number of class arbitration cases filed with the AAA peaked at 57 in 2006. In recent years, however, the Supreme Court has reined in the use of class arbitration, both by enhancing the enforceability of contractual waivers of class arbitration and by clarifying the standard for construing an arbitration clause that does not address the availability of class arbitration.

This paper provides an overview of class arbitration in the United States. Part 1 sets out background on the practice, including a description of the Supreme Court's decision in *Bazzle*. Part 2 discusses the Court's subsequent class arbitration decisions, as well as noting a recent regulatory development by the Consumer Financial Protection Bureau. Finally, Part 3 examines how parties have responded to the Supreme Court's developing class arbitration jurisprudence. It looks at changes both in the AAA's class arbitration docket and in the contracting practices of franchisors and consumer financial services companies in the United States following the Court's class arbitration decisions.

1 BACKGROUND

Class arbitration became common in the United States not because of a desire to have arbitrations resolved on a class basis but because of a desire not to have court cases resolved on a class basis. In the late 1990s, banks and other businesses began using arbitration clauses in their standard form contracts as a way to reduce the risk of class action litigation.[4] Consumers and others whose contracts included arbitration clauses could not be a party to a class action in court — they had agreed to arbitrate all disputes instead. As a result, by using arbitration clauses in their contracts, businesses could reduce the risk of being subject to class actions in court.

Only some, but not all, of the contracts addressed the availability of class relief in arbitration. For those contracts that did not do so, plaintiffs' lawyers began seeking to have arbitrations administered on a class basis. Although federal courts generally refused to order arbitrations to proceed on a class basis, some state courts were more willing to order class arbitration.[5]

* John M. Rounds Professor of Law and Associate Dean for Research and Faculty Development, University of Kansas School of Law. I am a special advisor for the Consumer Financial Protection Bureau (CFPB) in connection with its work on consumer financial services arbitration. The views stated in this paper are mine and should not be attributed to the CFPB or the United States.

The issue reached the US Supreme Court in *Bazzle*.[6] In *Bazzle*, the South Carolina Supreme Court had ordered the parties to proceed to class arbitration under an arbitration clause that did not address class arbitration. Before the US Supreme Court, the result was a badly splintered decision. The plurality of the Court (four Justices in an opinion authored by Justice Breyer) vacated the decision below, deciding that the arbitrator, and not a court, must determine whether an arbitration clause forbids class arbitration. Justice Stevens would have affirmed the South Carolina Supreme Court's decision as correct as a matter of law, but concurred in the judgment to provide a fifth vote for the outcome. Chief Justice Rehnquist, joined by two other Justices, dissented arguing that the issue was one for the court to decide and that the South Carolina Supreme Court's decision was inconsistent with the parties' arbitration agreement. Justice Thomas dissented, reiterating his view that the Federal Arbitration Act (FAA) does not apply in state court.

As stated by John Townsend, following the decision in *Bazzle* the AAA "realized that the Supreme Court had opened the door for arbitrators to certify class proceedings without specific judicial direction," and promulgated its class arbitration rules as noted above.[7] The resulting growth of class arbitration led directly to the Supreme Court cases described in the next section.

2 LEGAL DEVELOPMENTS UNDER US LAW

This section summarizes legal developments in the United States subsequent to the US Supreme Court's decision in *Bazzle*, focusing primarily but not exclusively on decisions by the Supreme Court

a) US Supreme Court Cases

Fundamentally, the availability of class arbitration is a matter of contract. Parties might expressly preclude any dispute from being resolved on a class basis, expressly agree that any dispute will be arbitrated on a class basis, or might not address the issue in their arbitration agreement. This section traces developments in how courts deal with these varying types of agreements under US law.

i. Agreements Expressly Precluding Class Arbitration

Businesses responded to the growth of class arbitration after *Bazzle* by increasingly including provisions waiving the availability of class arbitration in their arbitration clauses. The enforceability of those class arbitration waivers was challenged on two grounds. First, parties challenged class waivers as unconscionable under state contract law. Second, parties challenged class waivers as invalid because they precluded the effective vindication of federal statutory rights.

The Supreme Court sharply limited the use of unconscionability doctrine to invalidate arbitration clauses with class waivers in *AT&T Mobility LLC v Concepcion*.[8] In *Concepcion*, the Court reversed a Ninth Circuit decision that had held an arbitration clause with a class waiver unconscionable under California law, finding California law preempted by the FAA. The Court identified a number of ways in which class arbitration differs from bilateral arbitration: it "sacrifices the principal advantage of arbitration — its informality — and makes the process slower, more costly, and more likely to generate procedural morass than final judgment"; it "*requires* procedural formality"; and it "greatly increases risks to defendants."[9] Because of these differences, the Court concluded that "[r]equiring the availability of classwide arbitration interferes with fundamental attributes of arbitration and thus creates a scheme inconsistent with the FAA."[10]

Thereafter, the Supreme Court also limited the use of the effective vindication doctrine to invalidate arbitration clauses with class waivers in *American Express Co. v Italian Colors Restaurant*.[11] The plaintiffs in *Italian Colors* challenged the enforceability of the arbitration agreement (with class waiver) in their contract with American Express on the ground that litigating their antitrust claims would be too expensive without the ability to aggregate each (relatively small) individual claim in a class action. As a result, according to the plaintiffs, the arbitration clause precluded them from effectively vindicating their federal statutory rights under the Sherman Act. The Supreme Court rejected the claim, reasoning in important part that because class actions were not available when the Sherman Act was enacted, the lack of class relief could not deny plaintiffs the ability to effectively vindicate their federal statutory rights.[12] Although the holding in *Italian Colors* was narrow, it has been applied more broadly such that at present arbitration clauses with class waivers are generally enforceable under the FAA.

ii. Agreements Expressly Authorizing Class Arbitration

In the United States, pre-dispute agreements expressly permitting class arbitration are rare to the point of being nonexistent. I have seen two agreements from affiliated franchisors that expressly authorized class arbitration on one narrow issue, but that is all.[13] More common are post-dispute agreements in which parties stipulate that the arbitration can proceed on a class basis, but those agreements may well reflect the parties' expectation of how arbitrators would have interpreted their arbitration agreement rather than any agreed preference for class arbitration.

Some have suggested that the Supreme Court's decision in *Concepcion* might cast doubt on the enforceability of agreements expressly providing for class arbitration.[14] Those suggestions are really criticisms of the Court's analysis, I think, rather than reflecting any true likelihood that an agreement expressly authorizing class arbitration would be held unenforceable under the FAA. Indeed, the Court in *Concepcion* emphasized the non-consensual nature of the class arbitration resulting from the Ninth Circuit's decision (referring, for example, to procedures states "superimpose on arbitration"), while stating that the FAA "requires courts to honor parties' expectations."[15] As such, *Concepcion* likely would not preclude courts from enforcing an agreement expressly authorizing class arbitration (as unlikely as it is that parties would enter into such an agreement).

iii. Agreements Neither Expressly Precluding nor Authorizing Class Arbitration

The remaining set of arbitration agreements are ones that neither expressly authorize nor expressly preclude class arbitration.[16] As noted above, in *Bazzle* a plurality of the Supreme Court held that whether such an agreement permits class arbitration is a question for the arbitrator rather than the court to decide. But because the *Bazzle* decision comprised only a plurality of the Court, doubt remained about the precedential value of the decision.

The Supreme Court revisited such agreements in *Stolt-Nielsen S.A. v AnimalFeeds Int'l Corp.*[17] and *Oxford Health Plans LLC v Sutter.*[18] In *Stolt-Nielsen*, the Court vacated an award construing an arbitration agreement as permitting class arbitration when the parties had stipulated that the agreement was 'silent' on the practice. While the outcome in *Stolt-Nielsen* — adopting a default rule that arbitration clauses in commercial shipping contracts do not authorize class arbitration — may be sensible, the decision itself is problematic in a number of respects, most of which are not relevant to this paper.[19] The key points in the decision for my purposes here are twofold. First, the Court cast serious doubt on (if not rejected outright) any precedential value of the plurality opinion in *Bazzle*, although it did not itself resolve the 'who decides' question because the parties had agreed post-dispute to have the arbitrators decide.[20] Second, the Court held that the standard for deciding the issue is "whether the parties *agreed to authorize* class arbitration," and on the facts of the case, "where the parties stipulated that there was 'no agreement' on this question, it follows that the parties cannot be compelled to submit their dispute to class arbitration."[21]

In *Oxford Health Plans*, the Court likewise did not resolve the 'who decides' question, again because the parties had agreed post-dispute to have the arbitrators decide.[22] Unlike in *Stolt-Nielsen*, however, the Court in *Oxford Health Plans* deferred to the arbitrators, who had construed the arbitration agreement as authorizing class arbitration. The Court limited *Stolt-Nielsen* to cases in which an award "lack[s] *any* contractual basis for ordering class procedures," and made clear that when a court decides whether to vacate an arbitration award, "the question for a judge is not whether the arbitrator construed the parties' contract correctly, but whether he construed it at all."[23]

Currently, courts are divided on whether the arbitrator or the court decides whether an arbitration agreement authorizes class arbitration. Some courts continue to follow the plurality opinion in *Bazzle* and hold that it is an issue for the arbitrator to decide.[24] Other courts follow what they see as suggestions from the more recent Supreme Court decisions that the issue is one for the court to decide.[25] The division likely will remain until the Supreme Court steps in to resolve the issue.

b) Regulatory Note

On May 5, 2016, the Consumer Financial Protection Bureau (CFPB) issued a notice of proposed rulemaking setting out a proposed rule regulating the use of predispute arbitration clauses in consumer financial services contracts.[26] The proposed rule followed upon the CFPB's release in March 2015 of an extensive study of the use of arbitration to resolve consumer financial services disputes.[27] Having completed the study, the CFPB has the authority to "prohibit or impose conditions or limitations on the use" of predispute arbitration agreements in a broad range of consumer financial services contracts, "if the Bureau finds that such a prohibition or imposition of conditions or limitations is in the public interest and for the protection of consumers."[28]

The CFPB's proposed rule consists of two elements. First, it "would prohibit covered providers of certain consumer financial products and services from using an agreement with a consumer that provides for arbitration of any future dispute between the parties to bar the consumer from filing or participating in a class action with respect to the covered consumer financial product or service."[29] Second, it "would require a covered provider that is involved in an arbitration pursuant to a pre-dispute arbitration agreement to submit specified arbitral records to the Bureau," which would monitor those proceedings and possibly make the records public.[30]

The proposed rule still must go through a notice-and-comment review process before it becomes final. Nonetheless, one law firm has advised financial services clients that they should "strongly consider" including arbitration clauses in their contracts now so that the clauses will be grandfathered if and when the CFPB issues a final rule on the subject.[31]

3 RESPONSES TO LEGAL DEVELOPMENTS

This section tracks how parties have responded to the changing legal landscape governing class arbitration in the US It first looks at changes in the AAA's class arbitration docket, and then examines changes in contracting practices based on data from US franchise and consumer financial services agreements.

a) AAA Class Arbitrations

Unlike its commercial arbitration rules, the AAA's class arbitration rules provide for the arbitration demand and any awards to be made publicly available on the AAA web page.[32] Although case information on the AAA web page has been unreliable at times, it nonetheless provides some insights into AAA cases and practice. In addition, the AAA itself has on occasion released information about its class arbitration docket.

Figure 1 provides information on AAA class arbitration filings over time.[33] Filings peaked (at 57) in 2006, and (generally) declined until 2013, when only 25 class arbitrations were filed. But in 2014 filings jumped back up to 43, with 23 filings through early October 2015.[34]

Although somewhat dated, data on the types of parties filing class arbitrations come from the AAA's amicus brief in *Stolt-Nielsen*.[35] While most of the claims seeking class arbitration were brought by consumers (106, or 37%) or employees (96, or 34%), a surprising number involved business claimants (81, or 28%), typically small businesses. Perhaps that number is not so surprising given that three of the four most recent Supreme Court cases dealing with class arbitration also involved business claimants: *Stolt-Nielsen* (shippers), *Italian Colors* (businesses that accept credit cards), and *Sutter* (doctors). The upturn in class arbitration filings in 2014 appears largely due to a growth in the number of employees (often from California, because of particular California causes of action) filing class arbitrations. Of the 43 filings in 2014, at least 26 were by employees, including 16 by employees in California.

Figure 1. AAA Class Arbitration Filings 2003-2015 (through 10/14/15)

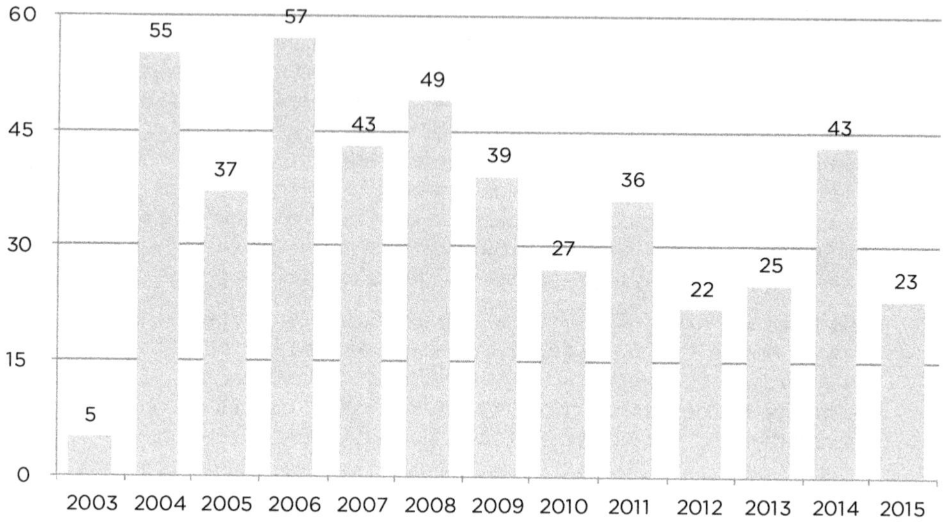

The AAA does not accept filings under an arbitration clause including a class arbitration waiver, unless a court ordered the case to arbitration.[36] As a result, many of the class arbitrations were filed based on arbitration clauses that did not address class arbitration. Prior to *Stolt-Nielsen*, arbitrators overwhelmingly construed such clauses as permitting class arbitration (the standard under the AAA class arbitration rules): only 5% of clause construction awards found that the clause did not permit class arbitration.[37] Since *Stolt-Nielsen*, in which the Supreme Court held that arbitration clauses must authorize (rather than just permit) class arbitration, that proportion has increased dramatically. Of the cases filed from 2012-2015 in which arbitrators have issued clause construction awards, 21 of 39 (or 54%) construed the clause as not authorizing class arbitration.[38]

b) Contracting Practices

Some commentators have argued that, in response to *Concepcion* and *Italian Colors*, essentially all businesses will adopt arbitration clauses with class arbitration waivers. Brian Fitzpatrick, for example, has contended:

> [I]n many cases, these waivers are tantamount to insulating businesses altogether from liability for the small-stakes injuries they cause. Why wouldn't every business want such insulation? I think every business would.[39]

Similarly, Myriam Gilles, in a prediction that predates *Concepcion* and *Italian Colors* but that she has reiterated since, has stated:

> I regard it as inevitable that firms will ultimately act in their economic best interests, and those interests dictate that virtually all companies will opt out of exposure to class action liability. Why wouldn't they? Once the [class] waivers gain broader acceptance and recognition, it will become malpractice for corporate counsel not to include such clauses in consumer and other class-action-prone contracts.[40]

And, indeed, anecdotes provide some support for this view, as press reports have identified several large software or technology companies that adopted arbitration clauses with class waivers following *Concepcion*.[41]

The available empirical evidence, however, does not yet support such a view. Bo Rutledge and I examined changes in the use of arbitration clauses following *Concepcion* in two samples of franchise agreements and found that "the use of arbitration clauses in franchise agreements has increased since *Concepcion*, but not dramatically, and most franchisors have not switched to arbitration."[42] In a sample of 67 leading franchisors, "the use of arbitration clauses increased from 40.3% of franchisors immediately before *Concepcion* to 44.8% by 2013."[43] In a broader sample of franchisors, "the net use of arbitration clauses increased only slightly after *Concepcion*, with 62.6% of franchisors using arbitration clauses before *Concepcion* and 63.6% after the decision."[44]

Similarly, in its study of consumer financial services arbitration, the CFPB found only a "slight upward trend" in the use of arbitration clauses in credit card agreements following *Concepcion*, although a somewhat larger change in the use of arbitration clauses in deposit account agreements (at least between 2012 and 2013).[45] For the credit card issuers in the CFPB's sample every year from 2010 through 2013, "the number of issuers using arbitration clauses increased from 53 as of year-end 2010, to 54 as of year-end 2011, to 55 as of year-end 2012, to 58 as of year-end 2013."[46] The CFPB's data on deposit account agreements was less comprehensive, but the Bureau reported an increase of seven (out of 88 in the sample) such agreements using arbitration clauses between 2012 and 2013, but no new large banks (of a more limited sample of 57) adding arbitration clauses between 2013 and 2014.[47]

It is too soon to tell whether the limited move to arbitration since *Concepcion* will increase (because standard contract terms are sticky but will change eventually) or tail off (because parties that have not switched to arbitration prefer to have their disputes resolved in court).

4 CONCLUSION

While US law on class arbitration has been in flux, recent Supreme Court decisions have resolved many uncertainties, generally in ways unfavorable to class arbitration. The most significant remaining legal question is whether arbitrators or the court decide if an arbitration agreement that does not expressly address class arbitration nonetheless authorizes the practice. The Supreme Court's increasing skepticism of class arbitration (and class actions) appears to have led to some decline in the frequency of class arbitration filings, although not as much as might have been expected. And, conversely, the use of arbitration clauses has increased following the Court's decisions, although not as dramatically as some predicted.

NOTES

1 Jean R. Sternlight, *As Mandatory Binding Arbitration Meets the Class Action, Will the Class Action Survive?*, 42 Wm. & Mary L. Rev. 1, 41 n.149 (2000).

2 539 US 444 (2003).

3 Am. Arb. Ass'n, Supplementary Rules for Class Arbitration (Rules Effective Oct. 8, 2003, Fees Effective Jan. 1, 2010), https://www.adr.org/aaa/ShowPDF?url=/cs/groups/commercial/documents/document/dgdf/mda0/~edisp/adrstg_004129.pdf [hereinafter AAA Class Arbitration Rules].

4 *Ross v American Exp. Co.*, 35 F. Supp. 3d 407, 414-30 (S.D.N.Y. 2014) (describing meetings during 1999-2003 of 'Arbitration Coalition' of financial institutions and law firms to discuss arbitration clauses and class actions), *aff'd*, 2015 WL 7292176 (2d Cir. Nov. 19, 2015) (summary order); *see, e.g.*, Edward Wood Dunham, *The Arbitration Clause as Class Action Shield*, 16 Franchise L.J. 141, 141 (1997); Alan S. Kaplinsky & Mark J. Levin, *Excuse Me, but Who's the Predator? Banks Can Use Arbitration Clauses as a Defense,* 7 Bus. L. Today, May/June 1998, at 24, 26; J.T. Westermeir, *How Arbitration Clauses Can Help Avoid Class Action Damages: Strategies for Managing Risks of Litigation,* 14 Computer L. Strategist, Sept. 1997, at 1, 1.

5 *Compare Iowa Grain Co. v Brown*, 171 F.3d 504, 510 (7th Cir. 1999) (finding no authority to order class arbitration); *Champ v Siegel Trading Co.*, 55 F.3d 269, 274-77 (7th Cir. 1995) (same) *with Keating v Superior Court*, 31 Cal. 3d 584, 609-14 (Cal. 1982) (finding authority to order class arbitration), *rev'd on other grounds sub nom., Southland Corp. v Keating*, 465 US 1 (1984); *Bazzle v Green Tree Fin'l Corp.*, 569 S.E.2d 349, 359-62 (S.C. 2002) (same), *vacated*, 539 US 444 (2003).

6 539 US 444 (2003).

7 John M. Townsend, *The Rise and Fall of Class Arbitration*, *in* AAA Yearbook on Arbitration and the Law 395, 398, 399-401 (Ben H. Sheppard, Jr. & Stephen K. Huber eds., 23rd ed. 2011) (also describing the AAA class arbitration rules).

8 563 US 333, 351 (2011).

9 *Id.* at 348-50.

10 *Id.* at 344.

11 133 S. Ct. 2304 (2013).

12 *Id.* at 2311 ('[T]he individual suit that was considered adequate to assure "effective vindication" of a federal right before adoption of class-action procedures did not suddenly become "ineffective vindication" upon their adoption.').

13 Christopher R. Drahozal, *"Unfair" Arbitration Clauses*, 2001 U. Ill. L. Rev. 695, 731 & n.265.

14 Gary Born, *The US Supreme Court and Class Arbitration: A Tragedy of Errors*, Kluwer Arbitration Blog (July 1, 2011), **http://kluwerarbitrationblog.com/blog/2011/07/01/the-u-s-supreme-court-and-class-arbitration-a-tragedy-of-errors/.**

15 *Concepcion*, 563 US at 351.

16 For a more detailed description, see Christopher R. Drahozal, *The Supreme Court and Class Arbitration: There and Back Again*, *in* Contemporary Issues in International Arbitration and Mediation: The Fordham Papers 95 (Arthur Rovine ed., 2015).

17 559 US 662 (2010).

18 133 S. Ct. 2064 (2013).

19 *See* Christopher R. Drahozal & Peter B. Rutledge, *Contract and Procedure*, 94 Marquette L. Rev. 1103, 1144-53 (2011).

20 559 US at 680.

21 *Id.* at 687.

22 133 S. Ct. at 2068 n.2.

23 *Id.* at 2069, 2071.

24 *E.g.*, *Edwards v Macy's Inc.*, 2015 WL 4104718, at *11 (S.D.N.Y. June 30, 2015) ('[I]t is clear that the issue of whether the language quoted above authorizes class-wide arbitration is for the arbitrators in the first instance, not for the court.'); *Williams-Bell v Perry Johnson Registrars Inc.*, 2015 WL 6741819, at *6 (N.D. Ill. Jan. 8, 2015) (same); In re: A2P SMS Antitrust Litig., 2014 WL 2445756, at *12 (S.D.N.Y. May 29, 2014) (same); *Lee v J.P. Morgan Chase & Co.*, 982 F. Supp. 2d 1109, 1113-14 (C.D. Cal. 2013) (same); see also *Robinson v J & K Admin. Mgmt. Servs., Inc.*, 2016 WL 1077102, at *4 (5th Cir. Mar. 17, 2016) ('[I]f parties agree to submit the issue of arbitrability to the arbitrator, then the availability of class or collective arbitration is a question for the arbitrator instead of the court.').

25 *E.g.*, *Del Webb Communities, Inc. v Carlson*, 2016 WL 1178829, at *4 (4th Cir. Mar. 28, 2016) ('We ... hold that whether an arbitration clause permits class arbitration is a gateway question of arbitrability for the court.'); *Chesapeake Appalachia, LLC v Scout Petroleum*, LLC, 809 F.3d 746, 753 (3d Cir. 2016) (same); Opalinski v Robert Half Int'l Inc., 761 F.3d 326, 335 (3d Cir. 2014) (same), *cert. denied*, 135 S. Ct. 1530 (2015); *Reed Elsevier v Crockett*, 734 F.3d 594, 598 (6th Cir. 2013) (same), *cert. denied*, 134 S. Ct. 2291 (2014); *see also* Claudia Pharaon, *The Extent of Arbitrators' Power to Order Class Arbitration*, 31 Arb. Int'l 589, 610 (2015) ('The Supreme Court has suggested that it will likely treat the question of the availability of class arbitration as one of arbitrability to be resolved by national judges in the future.'); Kevin P. Sack, *Plurality Influence:* Reed Elsevier *and the Precedential Value of* Bazzle *on Class Arbitrability*, 2014 J. Disp. Resol. 379, 393 (2014) ('Because lower courts should give greater deference to the marked indications of the Supreme Court majority than to the plurality of the past, *Reed Elsevier* achieved the preferable result, which will likely align with a future Supreme Court decision resolving this current circuit split.').

26 Consumer Financial Protection Bureau, Arbitration Agreements: Proposed Rule with Request for Public Comment (May 5, 2016), *available at* **http://files.consumerfinance.gov/f/documents/CFPB_Arbitration_Agreements_Notice_of_Proposed_Rulemaking.pdf** [hereinafter CFPB Proposed Rule].

27 Consumer Financial Protection Bureau, Arbitration Study: Report to Congress, Pursuant to Dodd-Frank Wall Street Reform and Consumer Protection Act § 1028(a) (Mar. 2015), *available at* **http://files.consumerfinance.gov/f/201503_cfpb_arbitration-study-report-to-congress-2015.pdf** [hereinafter CFPB Arbitration Study].

28 Dodd-Frank Wall Street Reform and Consumer Protection Act § 1028(b). In addition, '[t]he findings in such rule' must be 'consistent with the study.' *Id.*

29 CFPB Proposed Rule, *supra* note 26, at 1.

30 *Id.*

31 Mark J. Levin, CFPB Issues Proposed Rule to Prohibit Class Action Waivers in Consumer Arbitration Agreements, CFPB Monitor (May 5, 2016), https://**www.cfpbmonitor.com/2016/05/05/cfpb-proposes-rule-to-prohibit-class-action-waivers-in-consumer-arbitration-agreements/** ("In the meantime, companies that do not presently use arbitration agreements in their financial services contracts should strongly consider adding them, since agreements entered into before a final rule becomes effective are grandfathered under existing law which is favorable to class action waivers.").

32 AAA Class Arbitration Rules, *supra* note 3, Rule 9(a) & (b).

33 Data on filings from 2012 through October 2015 come from the AAA web page. Am. Arb. Ass'n, Search Case Dockets and Awards, https://**www.adr.org/aaa/faces/services/disputeresolutionservices/arbitration/classarbitration/casedocketsearch** (last visited Oct. 14, 2015). Data for prior years come from

Gregory A. Litt & Tina Praprotnik, *After* Stolt-Nielsen, *Circuits Split, but AAA Filings Continue*, Mealey's Int'l Arb. Rep., July 2012, at 1; *see also* William K. Slate II & Eric P. Tuchmann, *Class Action Arbitrations*, 11 Int'l Arb. L. Rev. 50, 53 (2008) (reporting data 'for the period October 8, 2003 through January 1, 2008') ('Filings by year are as follows: 2003, 6 cases filed; 2004, 65 cases; 2005, 47 cases; 2006, 58 cases; 2007, 41 cases.').

34 To the extent there is a lag in posting class arbitrations to the AAA web page after filing, the graph may underestimate the number of filings for 2015.

35 Brief for American Arbitration Association as Amicus Curiae in Support of Neither Party at 23-24, *Stolt-Nielsen S.A. v AnimalFeeds Int'l Corp.*, 559 US 662 (2010) [hereinafter AAA Amicus Br.].

36 Am. Arb. Ass'n, AAA Policy on Class Arbitrations (July 14, 2005), https://www.adr.org/aaa/ShowPDF?doc=ADRSTG_003840.

37 AAA Amicus Br., *supra* note 35, at 22.

38 *See supra* note 33. Of the 18 clause construction awards holding that the arbitration clause authorized class arbitration, in one the arbitrators followed a prior interpretation of the clause by a court and in another they construed the clause as authorizing collective arbitration under the Fair Labor Standards Act but not class arbitration more broadly. Another clause construction award, not included in the totals reported in the text, construed the company's pre-2011 clause (which did not include a class waiver) as authorizing class arbitration but its post-2011 clause (which included a class waiver) as not authorizing class arbitration.

39 Brian T. Fitzpatrick, *The End of Class Actions?*, 57 Ariz. L. Rev. 161, 190 (2015).

40 Myriam Gilles, *Opting Out of Liability: The Forthcoming, Near-Total Demise of the Modern Class Action*, 104 Mich. L. Rev. 373, 377 (2005); *see also* Myriam E. Gilles & Gary Friedman, *After Class: Aggregate Litigation in the Wake of* AT&T Mobility v Concepcion, 79 U. Chi. L. Rev. 623, 627 (2012).

41 *See* Peter B. Rutledge & Christopher R. Drahozal, *"Sticky" Arbitration Clauses? The Use of Arbitration Clauses After* Concepcion *and* Amex, 67 Vand. L. Rev. 955, 1001 tbl. 3 (2014).

42 *Id.* at 961.

43 *Id.* at 990. 'Of the four franchisors that have switched to arbitration since *Concepcion*, three had used arbitration clauses at some point prior to the decision and switched back afterwards, while the fourth used arbitration to resolve some disputes before *Concepcion* and expanded its use to all disputes afterwards ....' *Id.*

44 *Id.*

45 CFPB Arbitration Study, *supra* note 27, § 2, at 12.

46 *Id.* § 2, at 12-13.

47 *Id.* § 2, at 16.

Chapter 3

Mass and Class Claims in Arbitration

A Canadian Perspective

Geneviève Saumier*

Looking to Canada to provide perspective on mass and class arbitration can provide unique insights for Europeans who may otherwise assume that the US model is representative of the North American approach to arbitration.[1] Indeed, Canada does not have any equivalent of the Federal Arbitration Act[2] that has been in force in the United States for close to a century and that has had a significant unifying impact on the regulation of arbitration in that country. Instead, arbitration in Canada is governed by provincial law, allowing for diverse responses to challenges posed by arbitration. The only external constraint on provincial power rests in the overriding effect of international obligations flowing from the New York Convention,[3] ratified by Canada in 1986. While the Supreme Court of Canada has been instrumental in supporting arbitration in the country, often following judicial trends from south of the border, its jurisprudence can be, and has been, overridden by divergent legislative policies of individual provinces.

While the topic for this paper concerns consolidation in arbitration, I cannot proceed without a few words regarding arbitration and consolidation of claims generally. I will thus provide a brief overview of the legislative context in Canada regarding arbitration and consolidation of claims before turning to the critical issue of mass and class arbitration.

1 THE LEGISLATIVE FRAMEWORK FOR ARBITRATION IN CANADA

The most significant difference between Canada and the United States when it comes to arbitration is the absence of an equivalent in Canada to the Federal Arbitration Act. Indeed, there is no nationally applicable federal law of arbitration in Canada and provinces essentially retain legislative competence over arbitration.[4] Still the framework for arbitration remains largely uniform across the country, given each province's agreement to implement the New York Convention and to follow the UNCITRAL Model Law.[5] Nevertheless, absent a pre-emptive federal power over arbitration, provincial legislatures retain significant autonomy to define arbitrability or to adopt other limitations to arbitration and neither the federal Parliament nor the Supreme Court have any power to decide otherwise.

For the longest time, provincial legislatures did not intervene to modify the liberal regime for arbitration in place since Canada's accession to the New York Convention. In so doing, they were in sync with the Canadian Supreme Court who, when called upon to interpret arbitration legislation, adopted a

* Professor, Faculty of Law, McGill University. This paper is an updated version of a paper originally published in (2014) 8:3 World Arbitration and Mediation Review 351, that was itself an expanded version of a presentation at the ITA-ASIL Conference on Mass and Class Claims in Arbitration held on 9 April 2014 in Washington DC.

pro-arbitration stance. This included most famously the recognition that claims based on regulatory law were not outside the purview of arbitration, in a manner analogous to the US Supreme Court decision in *Mitsubishi v Soler*.[6]

In the landmark judgment *Les Éditions Chouette v Desputeaux*,[7] the Supreme Court of Canada held that claims involving a decision in respect of copyright could be subject to arbitration. In so doing, it refused to apply a statutory provision in the Civil Code of Quebec that excludes certain matters from arbitration, namely "status and capacity of persons, family matters or other matters of public order."[8] Favouring an expansive role for private consensual arbitration, the Supreme Court focussed on the narrow scope of the notion of "public order" as exemplified in its use as an exception to the recognition of arbitral awards. This strict interpretation of "public order" as applied to arbitrability was reinforced in a subsequent case concerning the arbitration of consumer claims in which the Supreme Court of Canada can again be seen to follow the US Supreme Court's lead.

This occurred in *Dell Computer Corp. v Union des consommateurs*,[9] where the Supreme Court was forced to address the potential clash of policies between arbitration and class actions. The case involved a consumer claim against Dell. The company was seeking to avoid judicial proceedings by invoking the arbitration clause contained in the online contract concluded with the consumer. The very existence of this clause is attributable to another development in US arbitration law and practice that migrated north: the inclusion of pre-dispute mandatory arbitration clauses in consumer contracts.[10] While the US jurisprudence validating these clauses is directly linked to the text of the Federal Arbitration Act,[11] the Supreme Court of Canada arrived at the same result despite the absence of an equivalent statutory mandate. Instead, the Supreme Court of Canada relied on its own general pro-arbitration jurisprudence as well as legislative silence regarding any guaranteed access to courts for consumers.[12] In a companion case, the Supreme Court also held that any argument based on unconscionability was a question for the arbitrator and thus could not be invoked before a court to avoid the reference to arbitration.[13]

The arrival of pre-dispute mandatory arbitration clauses in consumer contracts led some Canadian provinces to reconsider their liberal approach to arbitration.[14] Departing from the Supreme Court's view that arbitration of consumer claims is not problematic, provincial legislatures took advantage of their unfettered constitutional power to legislate. Three provinces currently prohibit pre-dispute mandatory arbitration clauses in contracts that fall within the purview of their consumer protection legislation while a fourth subjects such clauses to governmental approval.[15] As a result, consumers in Quebec, Ontario, Saskatchewan and Alberta, (representing over 70% of Canada's population) have a statutory right of access to courts, including to class actions, notwithstanding the inclusion of an arbitration clause or a class action waiver in their contract.

Even outside those provinces, recent decisions may suggest a softening of the pro-arbitration stance. In *Seidel v Telus*[16], the Supreme Court of Canada heard a consumer complaint against a cell phone company regarding airtime billing.[17] The defendant sought to avoid the judicial class proceedings in British-Columbia by invoking the arbitration clause contained in the service contract. Given the Court's decision in *Dell Computer*, it seemed likely that the defendant would be successful, barring some distinct statutory wording to the contrary that would distinguish the two cases. In fact, the defendant was largely successful since the Court referred most of the plaintiff's claims to arbitration in a few sentences.[18] The Court did refuse the reference to arbitration in reference to the specific claim for injunctive relief provided for by one section of the BC consumer protection statute. It did so largely on the view that the remedy being sought was in pursuit of a public interest objective, and that the judicial forum was the only appropriate one to grant relief of that nature.[19] Still, even on this narrow point, the Court's reasoning in *Seidel* is difficult to reconcile with the decisions in *Desputeaux* and *Dell Computer*, based as it is on statutory interpretation that was rejected in those earlier cases.[20] (It is worth noting that it has taken five years for the claim that was not sent to arbitration to be certified.[21])

The Ontario Court of Appeal has even expressed scepticism with regard to arbitration clauses outside the consumer context. In *Griffin v Dell Canada*,[22] the Court refused to send a group of non-consumer purchasers to arbitration, questioning the defendant's motivation in invoking the arbitration clause, which the Court described as "an attempt to exploit the inefficiency of arbitrating individual claims" and essentially immunize itself from any potential liability.[23] An appellate court in Manitoba relied on *Seidel* to refuse to send a consumer to arbitration, even for those claims that were not based on statute, arguing that it was more efficient for all of the claims to be resolved in a single proceeding.[24] The Supreme Court refused leave to appeal in both of these cases, thus choosing not to intervene to resolve a growing inconsistency in the interpretation of its jurisprudence by provincial courts. These examples suggest that given the option, some courts in Canada, including its highest court, may give precedence to policies other than arbitration, even absent clear legislative language to that effect.

The resistance to mandatory arbitration is directly related to the policy favouring access to courts by way of class actions. Indeed, the Canadian cases involving challenges to arbitration almost invariably involve a defendant seeking to avoid certification of a class action. It is therefore useful to briefly review the law concerning the aggregation of claims in Canada before turning to the issue of consolidation in arbitration.

2 OVERVIEW OF MASS/CLASS CLAIMS IN CANADA

As in the United States, class actions in commercial matters are an important procedural vehicle for relief in mass claims in Canada.[25] Similar to the situation with arbitration, class action legislation arrived much later in Canada than in the United States and has been widely adopted only in the last two decades.[26] Again like arbitration, legislative competence vests with provincial legislators and there is no uniform regime that is applicable across the country. Still, the basic approach in all provinces is very similar, with few substantive variations of any great import.[27] Another feature of class actions in Canada is the absence of a general requirement that common issues predominate over individual issues.[28] As a result, mass tort claims routinely proceed to court on a class action basis even if individual damages assessments will have to take place at a separate stage.[29]

Mass and class claims face challenges in Canada because of its particular court structure and the absence of a multi-district consolidation system to deal with interprovincial or national classes. In terms of the court structure, Canada has no equivalent to the US Federal Court system. [30] Instead, most claims proceed through the various provincial courts according to provincial rules of civil procedure including provincial statutes governing class proceedings.[31] The Supreme Court of Canada can grant leave to hear cases on any matter coming from the appellate court of a province — as such, it can render decisions on procedural or substantive issues, of private or public law. The binding nature of any judgment may be limited to the province from which the appeal arose if it involves a question of provincial law. On the other hand, if that interpretation involves general principles, such as whether arbitration should pre-empt class actions in the absence of legislative text to the contrary, it will be effective across the country.[32] In addition to, or perhaps because of, the absence of a court structure allowing for multi-jurisdiction actions, Canada also lacks any equivalent to the US Judicial Panel on Multidistrict Litigation.

The effect of these separate and autonomous provincial courts, intersecting only at the level of the Supreme Court, is often a complex web of competing parallel or overlapping class actions.[33] This is obviously inefficient and is the source of wasteful litigation as courts in different provinces struggle to deal with the situation.[34] The Supreme Court of Canada has refused to address the problem when given the opportunity to do so. In *Canada Post v Lépine*, the Court placed responsibility squarely on the provincial legislatures: "More effective methods for managing jurisdictional disputes should be established in the spirit of mutual comity that is required between the courts of different provinces in the Canadian legal space. It is not this Court's role to define the necessary solutions."[35]

Despite this admonition, there has been no attempt to negotiate a political agreement between provincial legislatures regarding multijurisdictional class actions. The Uniform Law Conference of Canada did put forward a suggested amendment to its model class proceedings statute for adoption by provincial legislatures.[36] This amendment made use of the doctrine of *forum non conveniens* as a tool allowing courts to use their discretion to stay class proceedings in favour of a court in another province, based on a set of listed criteria. This approach has not been very successful, however, attracting only two ratifications since its adoption in 2006. [37]

More recently, in 2011, a judicial protocol to assist with the management of multijurisdictional class actions was proposed by the Canadian Bar Association.[38] The protocol is meant to harness existing court discretion in the management of class proceedings and therefore not involve any legislative amendments. The protocol contemplates two measures. First, a Notification List of counsel involved in identical or similar actions and second, coordination of settlements through Multijurisdictional Class Settlement Approval Orders. The first measure is connected to another CBA initiative, the Canadian Bar Association Class Action Database established in 2007. Endorsed by most courts in Canada, the database is "designed to give lawyers and the public easy access to court documents submitted with regard to class action lawsuits currently underway across the country." The second measure is directed at allowing and coordinating joint settlement hearings by courts in different provinces, as well as with US courts.[39] This non-legislative approach has proven to be more attractive, has been adopted by courts in several provinces,[40] and appears to have been successful in those proceedings, admittedly few in number, that have relied upon it.[41]

When the cross-border dimension involves the United States, the picture is slightly different. Admittedly, there are few examples of mass or class claims proceeding in Canada purporting to include a North American class including both Canadian and American members. One well-known example was a securities class action against IMAX that went forward in Ontario prior to a settlement being reached in a parallel claim brought in the US. The Ontario court eventually agreed to exclude any American members of the Canadian action, holding that their claims were best dealt with under the US settlement.[42] In related proceedings, the court had considered the ABA/CBA *Protocol on Court-to-Court communications in Canada-US Cross-Border Class Actions*, but held that it did not address the issue before it, therefore identifying some shortcomings in that approach.[43] In an earlier case, parallel actions in six Canadian provinces and in the US led to an eventual settlement proposal in the US action that purported to extend to the Canadian class members. On a joint motion, the parties sought to discontinue all of the Canadian actions, which was granted on the basis that the US settlement was advantageous to the Canadian class members.[44] These examples indicate that there is no single way to deal with cross-border class actions, whether to maintain separate actions or to proceed by way of a global action or settlement. On the other hand, they do demonstrate that courts are able to deal with overlapping or parallel cross-border actions in a reasonable and efficient manner, even without any prescribed framework imposed by statute or rules of court.

Still, these two examples may not be typical or be replicated in the future. Apparently up to 40% of all class claims brought in Canada have a cross-border dimension with the US.[45] This refers of course to the common existence of parallel claims in US and Canadian courts against the same defendant regarding the same claim. But it also refers to increasing collaboration between Canadian and US counsel, particularly on the plaintiff side. While the original claim is most often initiated in the US, the fact that Canadian class action criteria is less demanding than its US counterpart might reverse that trend for certain types of mass claims that are less likely to be certified in American courts. Given this context, it is at least arguable that a more predictable and potentially efficient means of addressing mass and class claims might be through class arbitration, to which I now turn.

3 CONSOLIDATION IN ARBITRATION

Whether the challenges associated with mass and class claims could be resolved by class arbitration is a topic that has received little attention in Canada. Few lawyers or judges seem attuned to the opportunities class arbitration may provide, particularly to avoid the vexing problems associated with multijurisdictional class actions in Canada or in the Canada-US context.[46] What then explains the absence of any move in that direction in Canada? Is there a statutory bar to it? Judicial reluctance? Practical impediments? These three possible explanations will be examined in turn.

Perhaps not surprisingly, Canadian arbitration statutes, like American ones, are silent with respect to the question of consolidation.[47] For consolidation to be admitted immediately, therefore, it would have to be consistent with general principles of arbitration and be feasible under existing arbitration rules, whether these are drawn from state procedural law or private institutional arbitration service providers. In terms of general principles, since private arbitration is based on consent, claims based in contract are the likeliest candidates for class arbitration.[48]

One significant challenge in Canada regarding consolidation of contract claims in arbitration is the presence of statutory prohibitions against pre-dispute mandatory arbitration clauses in consumer contracts in a growing number of provinces. Where merchants are denied the ability to impose arbitration as a method of dispute resolution, consumers in those provinces may be limited to judicial methods of claims aggregation. In other words, in those provinces, consumers might only be able to pursue a consolidated claim in court. The rationale for statutory intervention is based on access to justice objectives and the concern that merchants are seeking to immunize themselves from non-economically viable claims, thereby potentially avoiding obligations imposed by mandatory state consumer protection law. If class arbitration can be structured to provide an alternative means of achieving these legislative objectives, the current prohibition could be subject to reconsideration. Indeed, no provincial government has declared consumer claims to be inarbitrable; rather they have sought to guarantee access to a consolidation mechanism. If class arbitration provides such a mechanism then limiting consumers to judicial class actions becomes a potential obstacle to access to justice and therefore difficult to justify.[49]

Beyond the realm of consumer contracts, however, there is no statutory priority given to judicial aggregation mechanisms. Given the pervasiveness of standard form contracts even in the B2B context, the potential for the development of class arbitration in Canada remains. Again, the issue of consent will be central and the challenge will be interpreting the arbitration clause that is silent as regards consolidation. The US Supreme Court has been inconsistent on this question and it is not readily evident where Canadian courts would go. It is worth repeating that the US jurisprudence is deeply rooted in the Federal Arbitration Act and its very strict exceptions to the enforcement of arbitration clauses. Without any equivalent statutory language in Canada, its courts could follow a different path. Whether that would support consolidation following *Green Tree Financial v Bazzle,*[50], reject it following *AT&T v Concepcion,*[51] or leave it to the arbitrator to decide following *American Express v Italian Colors Restaurant,*[52] is difficult to predict although some insight is available from the few existing relevant cases.

On more than one occasion, class counsel has indicated to a court in Canada that it would be prepared to participate in class arbitration.[53] In one of those cases, the judge appeared to see no statutory bar to such a possibility, stating that it would be up to the arbitrator to determine whether consolidation was appropriate.[54] In another case, the court did not object to the idea of class arbitration but thought it needed legislative support.[55] Finally, in a third case, the court used the defendant's rejection of class arbitration to support its refusal to refer the parties to arbitration:

> I would have found Dell's position much more persuasive had Dell been prepared to submit to an arbitration that would allow for the efficient adjudication of the claims on a group or class basis. However, in oral argument, Dell's counsel confirmed that his client ... would resist any attempt before an arbitrator to join together the claims of a group or class of consumers. In my view, this provides further evidence, if further evidence is required, that Dell does not genuinely seek to have the claims advanced against it determined by way of arbitration. Dell is simply seeking to exploit the inefficiency of arbitrating individual claims.[56]

It is worth noting that in that case the arbitration clause relied on by the defendant expressly excluded consolidation. This decision, therefore, stands in sharp contrast to the US Supreme Court's own in *AT&T v Concepcion* where the exclusion of consolidation was not sufficient to strike down the arbitration clause as unconscionable. This marks a significant difference between Canada and the US after *AT&T v Concepcion*. If consolidation waivers can be successfully challenged in Canada, defendants may reconsider their desire to avoid class arbitration if the alternative is a class action.

The Supreme Court of Canada has not dealt with the issue of class arbitration, though it has referred to the private and autonomous nature of arbitration on several occasions, suggesting that it may not be a forum appropriate for the type of oversight and publicity necessary for an opt-out consolidation mechanism.[57] On the other hand, the Supreme Court has held that any argument that an arbitration clause is invalid or unenforceable on grounds of unconscionability is usually to be directed in the first instance to the arbitrator rather than the courts.[58] If this view were to prevail even in the face of a consolidation waiver in the arbitration clause, it might well open the door for class arbitration since the arbitrator would be well placed to decide whether the dispute could be resolved on that basis, assuming that the waiver of consolidation was deemed invalid without impugning the validity of the reference to arbitration. For such a result to occur, however, the arbitrator would have to consider the feasibility of a class arbitration procedure, a separate question to which I now turn.

Class arbitration raises numerous practical questions given the procedural complexities involved particularly with an opt-out system.[59] The notice requirement challenges the possibility of confidentiality, usually expected with arbitration. Scrutiny of the settlement and of legal fees to ensure fairness to absent class members and to control for the risk of collusion between legal counsel also goes beyond the typical role of arbitrators. Finally, the binding nature of the eventual award, even on absent class members, requires an expansive interpretation of consent. All of these issues are addressed in class action legislation including the conferral of a special supervisory role on courts. [60] Arbitration law (whether in Canada or the US), silent regarding consolidation, obviously does not provide equivalent procedural safeguards. Given this regulatory gap, the US experience with the class arbitration mechanism offers many answers that should be readily transferable to Canada.

The protocols developed by US arbitration institutions provide ready-made and tested templates for the administration of class arbitrations.[61] Because of the significant similarity between US and Canadian law on arbitration and on class actions, one could even imagine a wholesale import with only a few modifications to conform to local exigencies. Despite this promise, no Canadian arbitral institution appears to offer any consolidation procedures nor seems to be considering them.[62] Absent some local demand for these specialized services, they may not be offered, thus delaying the potential for class arbitration in Canada.

Two factors might raise the profile of class arbitration in Canada and lead to a change. First, with the still large number of pending class arbitrations in the US, there is the potential for eventual recognition proceedings in Canada. Given existing Canadian law on the recognition of foreign arbitral awards, this should not be a problem. First, Canada's adhesion to the 1958 New York Convention means that it is bound to recognize foreign arbitral awards with very limited exceptions.[63] Second, courts in Canada have admitted that US class action settlements could be binding against Canadian class members.[64] Since the procedural safeguards provided under, for example, the AAA class arbitration procedure, are analogous to those guaranteed by class action legislation in the US and in Canada, there is every reason to believe that Canadian courts would be prepared to recognize an arbitral award that conformed to those safeguards.

A second factor that may lead to change resides with Canadian practitioners themselves. Class arbitration may be attractive to these lawyers because of its jurisdictional advantages in cross-border cases. Indeed, as private arbitration is non-territorial or anational,[65] none of the constitutional obstacles to the jurisdiction of provincial courts over non-resident class members arise in the arbitration context. In the non-consumer context, this provides a significant incentive to plaintiff counsel who need only institute one arbitration process instead of multiple parallel judicial actions across Canada. Moreover, that single proceeding option also avoids the risk of competing parallel or even overlapping judicial actions. With regard to claims arising from consumer contracts, this opportunity is diminished by the statutory monopoly granted to courts for consolidated proceedings in certain provinces but it is not excluded for the remaining provinces. There are thus market incentives to pursuing the class arbitration option and arbitral institutions should be alert to this potential and offer the necessary procedural rules to enable it.

In sum, regardless of the current lack of evidence indicating the emergence of class arbitration in Canada, history suggests that innovative procedural mechanisms to deal with mass and class claims that are developed in the US have a tendency to migrate northward. With broadly similar rules governing arbitration and class actions in the two countries, there is no reason to believe that class arbitration faces any insurmountable obstacle in Canada. In fact, without the strictures of the US Federal Arbitration Act and its vigorous application by the US Supreme Court, one might say that Canada is more fertile ground for consolidation in arbitration. While the lack of uniformity in provincial treatment of mandatory arbitration in certain fields may be seen as a challenge, this same diversity is what may allow class arbitration to be tested in some parts of the country. Should it prove to be successful, this could lead to changes in legislative policy elsewhere in pursuit of alternatives avenues for access to justice. The availability of specialized arbitration rules is a critical element and if no Canadian institution is prepared to design its own, parties may well refer to existing American models. None of this is likely to happen overnight, of course. But unless the alleged death of American class arbitration renders it unfit for export, I expect that class arbitration will make an appearance somewhere in Canada within the next decade.

NOTES

1 I use "North America" as a shorthand for Canada and the US and as a reflection of the common law tradition largely prevalent in both countries, a fact that distinguishes Mexico within that region.

2 *Federal Arbitration Act*, 9 USC § 1 (1925).

3 *Convention on the Recognition and Enforcement of Foreign Arbitral Awards*, Convention on the Recognition and Enforcement of Foreign Arbitral Awards, 10 June 1958, 21 UST 2518, 330 UNTS 3 (entered into force 10 August 1986, accession by Canada 12 May 1986) [the New York Convention].

4 John E.C. Brierley, "Canadian acceptance of international commercial arbitration" *Maine Law Review* 40 (1988) 287 at 290. However, the federal *Commercial Arbitration Act*, RSC 1985, c 17, also modelled on the UNICTRAL Model Law applies to limited matters of federal jurisdiction, including suits against the federal Crown and its Crown corporations and in maritime or admiralty matters. See also Strong, SI, "Resolving Mass Legal Disputes through Class Arbitration: The United States and Canada Compared" *North Carolina Journal of International Law & Commercial Regulation* 37, (2012), 921 at 932-933.

5 Gerald W Ghikas, "The UNICTRAL Model Law in Canada" in Association for International Arbitration ed, *The UNICTRAL Model Law on International Commercial Arbitration: 25 years* (Antwerp: Maklu, 2010) at 14-15.

6 *Mitsubishi Motors Corp. vSoler Chrysler-Plymouth, Inc.*, 473 U.S. 614 (1985).

7 [2003] 1 SCR 178.

8 Article 2639 C.C.Q.

9 2007 SCC 34 [*Dell Computer*].

10 Jean R Sternlight, "Mandatory Binding Arbitration Clauses Prevent Consumers from Presenting Procedurally Difficult Claims" *Southwestern University Law Review* 42, (2012-2013), 87 at 88-89. See also Theodore Eisenberg, Geoffrey P Miller and Emily Sherwin, "Arbitration's Summer Soldiers: An Empirical Study of Arbitration Clauses in Consumer and Nonconsumer Contracts" *University of Michigan Journal of Law Reform* 41 (2008) 871 at 882-85; Geneviève Saumier, "Consumer Arbitration in the Evolving Canadian Landscape" *Penn State Law Review* 113 (2009) 1203.

11 These clauses were upheld by the U.S. Supreme Court in cases as early as 1995 in *Allied-Bruce Terminix v Dobson*, 513 U.S. 265 (1995) and as recently as last December in *DirecTV v Imburgia*, 577 U.S. __ (2015).

12 See Strong, SI, "Class Arbitration Outside the United States: Reading the Tea Leaves", in Bernard Hanotiau and Eric A Schwartz, eds, *Multiparty Arbitration: Dossier VII of the ICC Institute of World Business Law* (ICC Publication No 701, 2010) at 5.

13 *Rogers Wireless v Muroff*, [2007] 2 SCR 921 at paras 15-16. See case comment by Frédéric Bachand and Pierre Bienvenu, "L'arrêt Dell et le contrôle de la compétence arbitrale au stade du renvoi à l'arbitrage" 37,(2007), *Revue générale de droit* 477.

14 The Quebec legislation was enacted during the Dell Computer litigation but the Supreme Court held that it did not retroactively apply to the contracts at issue in that case.

15 Quebec Consumer Protection Act, RSQ c. P-40.1, art. 11.1; Ontario Consumer Protection Act, S.O. 2002, chap. 30, s. 7(2); Saskatchewan Consumer Protection and Business Practices Act, SS 2014, c. C-30.2, s. 101; Alberta Fair Trading Act, RSA 2000, c. F-2, s.16. There is no available record of requests by merchants to have their arbitration clauses approved under this statute. In *Young c. National Money Mart Company*, 2013 ABCA 264, the consumer proved that the merchant had submitted its clause but that it had not been approved. Leave to appeal to the Supreme Court was dismissed.

16 *Seidel v Telus Communications*, [2011] 1 SCR 531 [*Seidel*].

17 For a detailed discussion of the case see Shelley McGill, "Consumer Arbitration after *Seidel v Telus*" *Candian Business Law Journal* 51, (2011), 187.

18 Ibid. at para 5 : [T]o the extent Ms. Seidel's complaints shelter under s. 172 of the *BPCPA* (and only to that extent), they cannot be waived by an arbitration clause and her court action may continue, in my opinion. As to her alternative complaints, whether under other sections of the *BPCPA*, the now repealed *Trade Practice Act*, or at common law, the Telus arbitration clause is valid and enforceable." (references omitted). This is a point that most commentators appears to neglect.

19 Ibid. See summary of reasons at para. 40 of the majority decision. There was an unusually sharp dissent penned by the judges who had authored the reasons in *Desputeaux* and *Dell Computer*.

20 Frédéric Bachand, "The Supreme Court of Canada: Pro-Arbitration No More", online: Kluwer Arbitration Blog <http://kluwerarbitrationblog.com/blog/2011/03/31/the-supreme-court-of-canada-pro-arbitration-no-more/>.

21 *Seidel v Telus Communications Inc.*, 2016 BCSC 114.

22 2010 ONCA 29 (Ont. C.A.). Leave to appeal to the Supreme Court dismissed. *Griffin* was recently followed in *Wellman and Corless v TELUS and Bell*, 2014 ONSC 3318.

23 Ibid. at para. 60. The Quebec Court of Appeal did not follow this line of reasoning in similar circumstances, sending the corporate clients to individual arbitration despite the fact that consumers were entitled to proceed by way of a class action: *Telus Mobilité c. Comtois*, 2012 QCCA 170.

24 *Briones v National Money Mart Company et al.*, 2014 MBCA 57 (Man. C.A.); leave to appeal to the Supreme Court of Canada dismissed.

25 Michael Eizenga, Danny H Assaf, and Emrys Davis, "Antitrust Class Actions: A Tale of Two Countries" *Antitrust* 25, (2010-2011), 83 at 83-84; contrast the Canadian position in *Pro-Sys Consultants Ltd v Microsoft Corporation*, 2013 SCC 57 (CanLII) at paras 99-105 with the US position in *Comcast Corp v Behrends*, 569 US -, 133 S Ct 1426 (2013), Scalia J for the Court at 6-7.

26 It was introduced first in Quebec in 1976, then in Ontario in 1992, in B.-C. in 1996 and only in this century in the remaining provinces, save one. McCarthy Tétrault, *Defending Class Actions in Canada* (Toronto: CCH, 2011) at 4-5

27 Ibid at 6-12.

28 Ibid at 13-14 and 177-178. The criteria is not mentioned in most statutes while it is specifically excluded in the B.C. version (*Class Proceedings Act*, RSBC 1996, c 50 at s 4(1)(c)).

29 Admittedly most certified class actions are settled without a trial, as is the case in the US. See Jamie Cassels and Craig Jones, *The Law of Large-Scale Claims: Product Liability, Mass Torts, and Complex Litigations in Canada*, (Toronto: Irwin

Law, 2005) at 340-341; Catherine Piché, "A Critical Reappraisal of Class Action Settlement Procedure in Search of a New Standard of Fairness" *Revue de droit d'Ottawa* 41:1, (2010), 112.

30 The Canadian Federal Court is a court of limited statutory jurisdiction that hears claims against the Crown (though not exclusively) or in particular matters of federal law such as maritime, immigration, income tax, and intellectual property. See : Peter W Hogg, "Federalism and the Jurisdiction of Canadian Courts" *University of New Brunswick Law Journal* 30, (1981), 9 at 17.

31 The Supreme Court did hold, in *Western Canadian Shopping Centres v Dutton*, 2001 SCC 46 (CanLII), that courts in Canada could devise a class proceeding mechanism even in the absence of specific statutory provisions — since then, however, every province save Prince-Edward-Island has adopted a class proceedings statute. See McCarthy Tétrault, *supra* note 26 at 5.

32 That is precisely what occurred with the *Dell Computer* decision, *supra* note 9 at paras 41-42. This is akin to the effect of the U.S. Supreme Court's decision in *AT&T v Concepcion* that defined the allowed interface between State law doctrines of unconscionability and s. 2 of the Federal Arbitration Act while ostensibly deciding a California case. See Michael J Yelnosky, "Fully Federalizing the Federal Arbitration Act" *Oregon Law Review* 90, (2011-2012), 729.

33 Because most class actions are brought to provincial courts, there is a potential constitutional issue relating to a court's ability to bind non-resident class members especially where the claim is against a foreign defendant and thus the jurisdiction of the court is established on the basis of a connection between the cause of action and the court seized of the action. Whether such multijurisdictional class actions are constitutional is debated in the literature but the Supreme Court has not yet addressed the issue. Compare Peter W. Hogg & S. Gordon McKee, "Are National Class Actions Constitutional?" (2010) 26 Nat'l J. Const. L. 79 and Janet Walker, "Are National Classes Constitutional? A Reply to Hogg and McKee" (2010) 48 Osgoode Hall L.J. 95.

34 Janet Walker, "Recognizing Multijurisdiction Class Action Judgments within Canada: Key Questions — Suggested Answers" *Canadian Business Law Journal* 46, (2008), 450 at 460.

35 2009 SCC 16 at para 57. See Geneviève Saumier, "Competing Class Actions across Canada: Still at the Starting Gate after *Canada Post v Lépine*?" *Canadian Business Law Journal* 48, (2009), 462.

36 *Uniform Class Proceedings Act (amendment) 2006*, online: Uniform Law Conference of Canada < **http://www.ulcc.ca/images/stories/Uniform_Acts_EN/Uniform_Class_Proceedings_Amendment_En.pdf>.**

37 See s. 6.1 of Saskatchewan's *Class Actions Act*, SS 2001 Chapter C-12.01as amended by SS 2007, ch. 6 and ss 5(6)-5(8) of Alberta's *Class Proceedings Act*, SA 2003, ch. 16.5 as amended by SA 2010 c15 s5. See also the recent modifications to Quebec's Code of Civil Procedure (s. 577) that entered into force this year.

38 *Canadian Judicial Protocol for the Management of Multijurisdictional Class Actions*, adopted 13 August 2011 (available at **www.cba.org).**

39 To that end, the CBA adopted the ABA's Protocol on Court-to-Court Communications in Canada — U.S. Cross-Border Class Actions.

40 See for example, 2013 *Civil Practice Directive #3 of the Court of Queen's Bench for Sakatchewan*;

41 The settlement approval protocol was applied in *Markus v Reebok*, [2012] J.Q. no 7304 (Quebec S.C.), *Honhon v Canada (A.G.)*, 2013 QCCS 2782, *Eidoo v Infineon Technologies AG*, 2013 ONSC 853, *Mackie v Toshiba*, 2013 ONSC 5665

and in the three parallel actions in *Osmun v Cadbury Adams Canada Inc.*, 2012 ONSC 3837, *Main v Cadbury Schweppes plc*, 2012 BCSC 1062 and *Roy v Cadbury Adams Canada inc.*, 2012 QCCS 1606; the general protocol was adopted as applicable to the action in *St-Marseille v Procter & Gamble inc.*, [2012] J.Q. no 3384 (Quebec S.C.) and *Option Consommateurs v Infineon Technologies*, [2012] J.Q. no 17071 (Quebec S.C.); it was also referred to in *Silver v Imax Corp*, 2012 ONSC 1047 at paras 71-73 and in *Lebrasseur v Hoffmann-La Roche*, 2011 QCCS 5457.

42 *Silver v Imax Corp.*, 2013 ONSC 1667 (CanLII) (leave to appeal denied in 2013 ONSC 6751). In January 2016, a settlement was approved. It provides for slightly higher recovery per shareholder than the US settlement. See *Silver v Imax Corp.*, 2016 ONSC 403.

43 *Silver v Imax Corp.*, 2012 ONSC 1047, at para. 70-71.

44 *Wong v TJX Companies*, 2008 CanLII 3421 (Ont. S.C.).

45 Jennifer Lewington, "Cross-border playbook" (26 November 2013), online: National magazine <http://www.nationalmagazine.ca/Articles/November/Cross-border-playbook.aspx>

46 The literature is sparse and seems to be exclusively produced by practitioners: W.K. Winkler, "Class Proceedings and ADR: Synergies in a Civil Action" *Advocate's Society Journal* (2001), 3; D. Bisson & S. Finn, "A Disputes Alternative to Alternative Dispute Resolution — A Discussion of Class-Wide Arbitration and its Relevance for Quebec Class Action Litigants and Practitioners" *Canandian Bar Review* 82, (2004), 309; B. Casey, "Class Action Arbitration Should be Available" (2006) 25(44) Lawyers' Weekly 1; J.S. Leon, E.R. Hoaken & R. Huang, "Class Arbitration in Canada: The Legal and Business Case" *Canadian Class Action Review* 6, (2010), 383; M. Schafler & A. Pasalic, "Is Canada Ready for Class Arbitration?" (Paper presented at ADRIC 2013 — Gold Standard ADR, 25 October 2013), [unpublished].

47 Strong, SI, "Resolving Mass Legal Disputes through Class Arbitration: The United States and Canada Compared" *North Carolina Journal of International Law & Commercial Regulation* 37, (2012), 921 at 949-950.

48 However, as it is possible to agree to arbitration once a dispute has arisen, there is no necessary bar to class arbitration of non-contractual claims. In fact, it is not uncommon for mass claims to be resolved through a settlement which itself provides for arbitration to administer the funds to be distributed to individual claimants. Once these claimants are bound to the settlement terms, including the arbitration mechanism, it may be that certain types of claims or categories of claimants could be aggregated within the arbitral procedure. Admittedly, this is a different scenario from the one usually assumed when talking of class arbitration — the idea is usually to replicate within arbitration the opt-out class action mechanism.

49 See Leon et al, *supra* note 46 at 416. This was also put forward to the Supreme Court by the London Court of International Arbitration, who was granted intervener status in the *Dell Computer* case. The Supreme Court did not address the argument or the issue in its judgment. See Leon et al., *ibid.* at 397.

50 539 U.S. 444 (2003) [*AT&T v Concepcion*].

51 I mention *AT&T v Concepcion* here rather than *Stolt-Nielsen v Animal Feeds*, 130 S. Ct. 1758 (2010), because the former went even further, enforcing a "no consolidation" clause because, *inter alia*, it was not allowed under the FAA. See *AT&T v Concepcion*. It is not clear yet what impact this decision will have on class arbitration in the US. See J.R. Sternlight, "Tsunami: AT&T Mobility v Concepcion Impedes Access to Justice" *Oregon Law Review* 90, (2012), 703.

For a different view see Strong, SI, "Does Class Arbitration 'Change the Nature' of Arbitration? Stolt-Neilsen, AT&T and a Return to First Principles" 17 *Harvard Negotiation Law Review* 20, (2012), 1.

52 133 S. Ct. 2304 (2013).

53 *Kanitz v Rogers Cable Inc.*, (2002) 58 O.R. (3d) 299 (Ont. S.C.); *Griffin v Dell Canada Inc*, 2010 ONCA 29; *MacKinnon v National Money Mart Co*, 2009 BCCA 103. In all three cases the defendant refused the request.

54 *Kanitz v Rogers Cable Inc.*, ibid. at para 55.

55 *MacKinnon v National Money Mart Co*, *supra* note 53 at para 33.

56 *Griffin v Dell Canada Inc*, *supra* note 22 at para. 60, per Sharpe J.A.

57 *Seidel v TELUS Communications Inc*, 2011 SCC 15 (CanLII), Binnie J for the majority at paras 3 and 7. See also *Dell Computer Corp v Union des consommateurs*, 2007 SCC 34 (CanLII), Bastarache and LeBel JJ in dissent at para 142.

58 *Rogers Wireless v Muroff*, *supra* note 13. This is on the assumption that the argument is one of fact or of "mixed fact and law." If the question were purely one of law, then the Supreme Court admitted that a court could decide it.

59 For a full discussion of the procedural issues in class arbitration, see Strong, SI, "From Class to Collective: The De-Americanization of Class Arbitration" *Arbitrational Journal* 26, (2010), 493 at 509-523.

60 Canadian practitioners writing about class arbitration call for an expanded role for courts, which is not currently possible under existing arbitration law. See Leon et al., *supra* note 46 at 417; Schafler & Pasalic, *supra* note 46 at 18-19.

61 See for example the American Arbitration Association Supplementary Rules for Class Arbitrations (**www.adr.org.**).

62 For example, the recently updated rules of the ADR Institute of Canada, in force since December 2014, do not mention consolidation (see **www.adric.ca**). A discussion with the president of a leading arbitral institution in Canada yielded the explanation that "there is no demand for it." This raises the traditional chicken-and-egg query: perhaps there is no demand because there are no procedures?

63 Due process and public policy concerns in international class arbitrations are likely not enough to overcome the presumption in favour of the enforcement of awards under the New York Convention, especially in jurisdictions open to class actions in domestic matters: Strong, SI, "Enforcing Class Arbitration in the International Sphere: Due Process and Public Policy Concerns" *Journal of International Law* 30, (2008), 1 at 95-100.

64 *Currie v McDonald's Restaurants of Canada Ltd.*, [2005] 74 OR (3d) 321 (Ont. C.A.) (leave to appeal to S.C.C. denied); *Silver* v *Imax Corp.*, [2011] O.J. No. 656 at para. 130 (leave to appeal to C.A. denied). For a comment on the *Currie* case see G. Saumier, "USA-Canada Class Actions: Trading in Procedural Fairness" *Global Jurist Advances* 5(2), (2005), 1.

65 This is agreed to in strong terms by both the majority and the dissent in the *Dell Computer* case.

Chapter 4

Collective Arbitration in Europe

The European Way Might Be the Best Way

José Miguel Júdice*

1 INTRODUCTION

Collective redress is an important means of access to justice and has been on the agenda of the European Commission from quite some time.[1]

As it is well known, the modern economy can sometimes create situations where a large number of people are harmed by the same illegal practices (mass harm situation). By allowing "many similar legal claims to be bundled into a single court action", collective redress promotes greater access to justice (particularly in cases where the individual damage is low and potential claimants would not consider it would be worth pursuing an individual claim) and contributes to the efficient administration of justice (following reasons of procedural economy).[2]

However, at the same time, collective redress can potentiate abusive law suites, as evidenced by the American system of class actions. Hence the reason why class actions are usually viewed in the United States has a synonym of controversy: in a highly controversial way, they are as criticized by some as they are acclaimed by others.

Given the advantages and popularity of arbitration, it is natural to wonder whether it is conceivable to combine collective redress with arbitration (the so-called 'collective arbitration');[3] particularly in the wake of the reference that the European Commission made to alternative dispute resolution procedures — where arbitration clearly fits — in its Recommendation of 11 June 2013 on collective redress (see paragraph 16 of the preliminaries and paragraph 26 of the Recommendation).[4]

Two questions are generally posed when addressing the possibility of combining class actions or collective redress with arbitration. First, is it possible? Second, how should it be organized and conducted?

These are the two main questions we will analyse in the present article, from a European perspective on the subject.

2 IS COLLECTIVE ARBITRATION POSSIBLE? AN OPTIMISTIC VIEW ON THE SUBJECT, GIVEN THE FLEXIBILITY AND EVOLUTION OF ARBITRATION

This is the first question and it is a question that makes sense, because as the United States Supreme Court held (in what concerns the combination

* Head of PLMJ ARBITRATION and member of the ICC Institute of World Business Law. I wish to thank António Pedro Pinto Monteiro (Senior Associate in PLMJ ARBITRATION) as without his cooperation it would not be possible to prepare this text.

of class actions with arbitration), "class-action arbitration changes the nature of arbitration."[5]

Given the controversy of the subject, the easiest and more conservative solution would be to take a negative approach and, as we will see, there are certainly many reasons for that. We prefer, however, a more optimistic view, considering the well-known flexibility and evolution of arbitration.

It is important to recall that, throughout the years, arbitration has proven itself to be a very flexible dispute resolution method. Constantly facing new realities and challenges, arbitration managed to adapt to certain situations that, at first sight, would seem impossible to adjust to.

Being a very old form of dispute resolution, we can say that arbitration has come a long way. From its very distant roots (so remote they seem almost impossible to trace) to more recent years, the evolution of arbitration is absolutely astonishing and undeniable.[6]

Such evolution, of course, was not (and is not) easy. There have been many obstacles along the way, some roads going nowhere, which sometimes make us wonder about the efficiency of arbitral tribunals to handle certain disputes. Nevertheless, the truth is arbitration has constantly kept pushing its boundaries to new territories, defying those who have little or no faith in the arbitral system.

For instance, 20 years ago many people certainly didn't think that arbitration was able to face and solve issues of competition, tax or labor law, intellectual property, bankruptcy or insolvency, bribery and corruption, etc. In many civil law jurisdictions even national public law issues are not arbitrable. And today — albeit with a few limits — we have seen that, in several countries, some of these disputes can be arbitrable.

And what about the possibility of arbitral tribunals to order interim measures and *ex parte* preliminary orders? What about third party intervention, consolidation, etc.?

Twenty years ago, many authors believed this could never be possible in arbitration. Well, the passing of time has proven otherwise.

When confronting the possibility of combining class actions or collective redress with arbitration, we should not simply exclude such possibility. Of course, given the many difficulties on the subject, it would be easy to have a negative approach. However, as mentioned above, this might not be the wisest approach.

One thing that the (long) evolution of arbitration has demonstrated is that we should never say never in arbitration; we should not underestimate the flexibility of this dispute resolution method and its constant capacity to surprise us. The American case law has already proven this, demonstrating that class arbitration is possible — despite the many difficulties the subject has lately been facing in the United States (we refer, particularly to i. *Stolt-Nielsen S.A. v AnimalFeeds International Corp.*, ii. *AT&T Mobility LLC v Concepcion*, iii. *Oxford Health Plans LLC v Sutter*, and iv. *American Express Co. v Italian Colors Restaurant*).[7]

Therefore, the main question at this moment should not be *if* class or collective arbitration is possible, but *how* it should be organized and conducted. This is clearly the key question and that which we will try to answering in the next chapter, by focusing on the opt-in/opt-out distinction.

3 HOW SHOULD COLLECTIVE ARBITRATION BE ORGANIZED AND CONDUCTED? THE 'OPT-IN' VS. 'OPT-OUT' SYSTEM

As stated above, this is the key question. This is where class or collective arbitration face major difficulties.

Among the different issues that could be analyzed, we will focus on its main topic: the opt-in vs. opt-out system. As a matter of fact, and in our opinion, choosing one or the other might hold the key to truly unlock collective arbitration in Europe.

As is well known, in an opt-out system (like the American class action model) "victims of a defendant's conduct are *automatically included* in litigation over that conduct, unless they take steps to exclude themselves from that lawsuit".[8] All individuals will be bound by the judgment, except for those who expressly opted out.

Differently, in an opt-in system, claimants will have to take affirmative steps to be represented in the group, meaning that only those who opted in will be bound by the judgment. This is the model which the majority of the European countries are familiar to (Portugal is one of the few exceptions).[9]

This distinction is important because, as we will see below, the opt-in system might be the decisive factor in construing a reliable and efficient collective arbitration model.

3.1. The Consensual Nature of Arbitration and the Problem with the 'Opt-Out' System

Consent is the cornerstone of arbitration, the *pierre angulaire de l'arbitrage*.[10] This is quite obvious and yet, when addressing class or collective arbitration, many authors seem to forget it.

When analyzing the possibility of combining class actions or collective redress with arbitration, this is something that cannot just simply be ignored.[11] After all, consent is a prerequisite for arbitration[12] and its importance should never be underestimated.[13] The consensual nature of arbitration is at the heart of the arbitral system and represents the fundamental difference from state court proceedings[14] (this is the reason why many authors consider, for instance, that mandatory or compulsory arbitration is not real arbitration).[15]

That being said, it is not difficult to see the conceptual difficulties that may arise here. As some authors correctly observe, at first sight arbitration and class actions do not seem compatible with one another.[16] In fact, they seem to be mutually exclusive processes, in the sense that they seem to mutually exclude one another.

This is mainly due to the opt-out system, which contravenes the consensual nature of arbitration. It is difficult to sustain that someone could be bound by an arbitration agreement and be automatically included in the arbitration process, due to the sole fact that such person did not expressly opt out, with all the known difficulties to do so or even to be aware of that possibility in due time.

The opt-out system is, in our opinion, the center of the many procedural problems that class or collective arbitration are facing. We refer not only to the problem concerning the consensual nature of arbitration, but also to three other related issues:

a) The *res judicata* effect — with the opt-out system there is a risk that someone would be represented without him being aware of it, with the relevant consequence of being bound by the judgment, since he/she hasn't opted out;[17]

b) confidentiality — the opt-out system seems to compromise one of the most important advantages of arbitration.[18] Potential class members must have the opportunity to opt-out, which implies some (relevant) degree of public disclosure. This need of disclosure is much higher in an opt-out system, because as Professor Strong rightly observes "failure to opt out leads to the extinguishment of a claim, whereas failure to opt in allows an individual claim to survive, even if the party cannot take advantage of a positive result arising out of the initial proceeding".[19] Hence the reason why providing adequate notice to potential claimants is so vital in an opt-out proceeding;[20] and

c) recognition and enforcement uncertainties under the New York Convention[21] — with an opt-out system, a variety of objections could be invoked to oppose the recognition and enforcement of a class or collective arbitration award, such as: i. article V, paragraph 1 (b) [the non-present class member can always argue that he was not given *proper notice* of the arbitration]; ii. article V, paragraph 1 (d) [there can also be problems with *lack of consent*, when interpreting the agreement of the parties]; and iii. article V, paragraph 2 (b) [*public policy* can always be tricky on this subject, particularly in a continent, such as Europe, where class actions or collective redress do not have a strong tradition and where the majority of countries follows and opt-in model].[22]

All things considered, it is really not surprising that the future of class arbitration remains unsettled in the United States and it could soon become a "relatively unusual creature," "theoretically possible, but rare as a practical matter".[23]

In our opinion, as we will see in the next chapter, if Europe wants to create a reliable and efficient collective arbitration model it must avoid the referred problems and try another approach, an opt-in approach.

3.2. The 'Opt-In' System as the Key to Unlock Collective Arbitration in Europe

3.2.1. European Collective Redress: A Different Answer to the American Class Actions

As mentioned before, collective redress has been on the agenda of the European Commission for quite some time.

The recent development consists of the 11 June 2013: a) Communication "Towards a European Horizontal Framework for Collective Redress" [Communication from the Commission to the European Parliament, the Council, the European Economic and Social Committee and the Committee of the Regions, COM(2013) 401 final]; and the b) Commission Recommendation on common principles for injunctive and compensatory collective redress mechanisms in the Member States concerning violations of rights granted under Union Law (2013/396/EU).

To put it in a few words, collective redress is "the EU answer to the US class action"[24] and, with all due respect, it is a better answer.

First of all, it is a necessary answer, because there is no uniformity in the Member States regarding the procedural mechanisms to deal with mass claims. National mechanisms vary considerably on this subject.[25] It is therefore quite understandable that the Commission felt the need to recommend collective redress principles to Member States.

It is also a different answer. Perhaps the most distinct feature of the emerging EU regime is the distance from the American class action.[26] The European Commission has made it clear that it took no inspiration from US-style class actions. On the contrary.

In a Memorandum issued on the 11 June 2013, the Commission unequivocally stated that "the European approach to collective redress clearly rejects the US style system of *class actions*."[27]

But that is not all. The aversion towards US class actions is also quite clear under the referred Communication and Recommendation (likewise from 11 June 2013). In the first one, for instance, we can read that:

> For the Commission, any measures for judicial redress need to be appropriate and effective and bring balanced solutions supporting European growth, while ensuring effective access to justice. Therefore, they must not attract abusive litigation or have effects detrimental to respondents regardless of the results of the proceedings. Examples of such adverse effects can be seen in particular in 'class actions' as known in the United States. The European approach to collective redress must thus give proper thought to preventing these negative effects and devising adequate safeguards against them.
>
> Class actions in the US legal system are the best-known example of a form of collective redress but also an illustration of the vulnerability of a system to abusive litigation. Several features of the US legal system have made class actions a particularly powerful instrument that is, however, feared by those on the defending side, namely trade and industry as it can be used as a forceful tool to compel them to settle a case, which may not necessarily be well founded. Such features are for instance contingency fees of attorneys or the discovery of documents procedure that allows 'fishing expeditions'. A further important feature of the US legal system is the possibility to seek punitive damages, which increases the economic interests at stake in class actions. This is enhanced by the fact that US class actions are legally 'opt-out' procedures in most cases: the representative of the class can sue on behalf of the whole class of claimants possibly affected without them specifically requesting to participate. In recent years, US Supreme Court decisions have started to progressively limit the availability of class actions in view of the detrimental economic and legal effects of a system that is open to abuse by frivolous litigation.[28]

The Recommendation further develops the above-mentioned ideas, creating a different model that clearly distinguishes itself from class actions. Many of the collective redress principles recommended by the Commission prove this. We refer particularly to the:

a) *prohibition of punitive damages* ("the compensation awarded to natural or legal persons harmed in a mass harm situation should not exceed the compensation that would have been awarded, if the claim had been pursued by means of individual actions. In particular, punitive damages, leading to overcompensation in favour of the claimant party of the damage suffered, should be prohibited");[29]

b) *limits on contingency fees*, which are not accepted as a general rule ("the Member States that exceptionally allow for contingency fees should provide for appropriate national regulation of those fees in collective redress cases, taking into account in particular the right to full compensation of the members of the claimant party");[30]

c) *limits on third party funding* ("the Member States should ensure, that, in addition to the general principles of funding, for cases of private third party funding of compensatory collective redress, it is prohibited to base remuneration given to or interest charged by the fund provider on the amount of the settlement reached or the compensation awarded unless that funding arrangement is regulated by a public authority to ensure the interests of the parties").[31]

Among the different features that mark the difference between the European collective redress model and the American class actions, one assumes particular relevance in the context of this article: the opt-in system.

3.2.2. The European Way: 'Opt-In' System

The European Commission has chosen an opt-in system,[32] which is quite understandable if we consider the fact that the opt-out system does not work well in EU jurisdictions. Take the Portuguese case for instance.

Portugal has what might be called a class action mechanism (the so-called popular action — *"acção popular"*)[33] and, as referred before, is one of the few European countries that actually follows an opt-out procedure. Such procedure, however, combined with the *res judicata* effect, has been heavily criticized by some authors.[34] The regime can have severe consequences on the holders of homogeneous individual interests who have not exercised the right to exclude themselves from representation — in principle, they will not be able to file another action with the same object, if the defendant is acquitted.[35] The main problem is that the law does not require personal identification of those to whom the writ of summons is directed (which, of course, would be very difficult or even impossible). The summons is made via one or various announcements made public through the media or through public notice, which may not be sufficient to reach its intended recipients. And the risk is even higher since anyone (any citizen, as well as certain associations and foundations) can file a popular action[36] — the legitimacy criterion is quite broad. Therefore, there is the possibility that someone is being represented in a popular action without even knowing it, with the relevant consequence of being bound by the judgment, since he hasn't opted out.[37] It is also important to recall that the Popular Action Law does not foresee an adequacy of representation criteria like the one contemplated in the Rule 23, (a), of the American Federal Rules of Civil Procedure.[38]

As a result, the opt-out procedure has received many critics in Portugal and after so many years does not work well at all. The same can be said about the popular action *per se*, which is not very common in Portugal.[39]

The opt-in choice by the European Commission is therefore quite understandable and was to be expected. Still, it was a thoughtful decision.

As the Commission reasoned, "a significant number of stakeholders, in particular businesses, strongly oppose the 'opt-out' model, arguing that it is more prone to abuse and that it may be unconstitutional in some Member States, or at least incompatible with their legal traditions. On the other hand, some consumer organisations argue that 'opt-in' systems may fail to deliver effective access to justice for all consumers who have been harmed. In their view, the availability of 'opt-out' is therefore desirable, at least as an option in appropriate cases and subject to approval by the court. (...) The 'opt-in' system respects the right of a person to decide whether to participate or not. It therefore better preserves the autonomy of parties to choose whether to take part in the litigation or not. In this system the value of the collective dispute is more easily determined, since it would consist of the sum of all individual claims. The court is in a better position to assess both the merits of the case and the admissibility of the collective action. The 'opt-in' system also guarantees that the judgment will not bind other potentially qualified claimants who did not join. The 'opt-out' system gives rise to more fundamental questions as to the freedom of potential claimants to decide whether they want to litigate. The right to an effective remedy cannot be interpreted in a way that prevents people from making (informed) decisions on whether they wish to claim damages or not. In addition, an 'opt-out' system may not be consistent with the central aim of collective redress, which is to obtain compensation for harm suffered, since such persons are not identified, and so the award will not be distributed to them".[40]

All things considered, the Commission chose the opt-in approach. And it has chosen wisely.

It is true that an opt-out system permits to aggregate (at least formally) a more significant number of persons. This has traditionally been an important advantage of this model, compared to the opt-in principle.[41] However, in this era of information that we (fortunately) live in, where many people have easy access to the internet and social networks, and where potential claimants are much more well informed of their rights, the advantages of the opt-out system, in our opinion, are not as significant as they once might have been.

An opt-in system, today, can also gather a significant number of persons and potentiate an effective access to justice for all consumers who have been harmed, avoiding, at the same time, litigation abuse.

More importantly, the opt-in system is more coherent with the possibility of combining collective redress with arbitration and may also prevent some of the problems class arbitration faces in the United States.

For instance, with an opt-in model there is no risk that someone would be represented without him being aware of it. The *res judicata* is, therefore, not an obstacle.

There are also fewer problems with confidentiality. The need to provide adequate notice to potential claimants is not as vital as in opt-out proceedings. If someone did not opt in, there is still a possibility to file an individual claim.

The same can be said about the recognition and enforcement of collective arbitration awards under the New York Convention. The problems previously described as a consequence of the opt-out system simply do not apply to an opt-in model.

Finally, and most importantly, an opt-in system is more consistent with the consensual nature of arbitration and with arbitration *per se*.

Therefore, it is time to answer the question we posed on the title of this third chapter: "How should collective arbitration be organized and conducted?" The answer is: by an opt-in system.

The opt-in principle might be the necessary key to unlock collective arbitration in Europe and to create a reliable and efficient model of collective arbitration.[42] A model that can have a real future and not an uncertain future, as class arbitration is facing in the United States at the moment.

4 CONCLUSION

The conclusion of this text is favorable to a system (the opt-in one) that it is better suited for the arbitration process when compared with the alternatives. It assumes that arbitration may be more efficient and better prepared as the choice of a skilled Tribunal for the complexities of this system suits better the needs than the traditional national courts.

However, this conclusion does not mean that the combination of arbitration with collective redress and class actions case is not a land to be discovered and only afterwards organized. One may by optimistic and even revolutionary about the beauties of arbitration, and this is our case. But one way of killing the conditions for the spread of a culture that favors optimism and innovation, is to be naïf to the point of forgetting the complexities of the application of the model to a very different kind of dispute, where consent is not always absolutely clear, the rules of the process need to be tailored and the role of public entities (like, for instance, the Public District attorneys in Portugal) is difficult to be integrated as their experience in relation to arbitration is very limited, to say the least.

Another problem that appears in the critical path of the system is the relation between situations in which responsibility is born from a contract and other in which *responsabilité délictuelle* or tort is the source of the problem.

This, and other equivalent problems, exist. As before with multiparty situations, "group of companies" issues, tax arbitration and even public law arbitration, experience shows that pessimism can be been destroyed as the dawn smog disappears gradually when the sun comes strong and warm.

NOTES

1 See Gorywoda, Lukasz, "The Emerging EU Legal Regime for Collective Redress: Institutional Dimension and Its Main Features", *in Cross-Border Class Actions. The European Way*, 2014, pages 173-188, Harbour, Laurel / Evans, John / Poisson, Erwan / Fléchet, Camille, "Representative actions and proposed reforms in the European Union", *in World Class Actions. A Guide to Group and Representative Actions around the Globe*, 2012, pages 144-168, Wrbka, Stefan, "European consumer protection law: Quo vadis? — thoughts on the compensa-

tory collective redress debate", Uytsel, Steven van, "Collective actions in a competition law context — reconciling multilayer interests to enhance access to justice?", both articles published *in Collective Actions — Enhancing Access do Justice and Reconciling Multilayer Interests?*, 2012, pages 23-56 and 57-92, and Marisi, Flavia, *Il Class Action Arbitration — La sua evoluzione negli Stati Uniti e la sua possibile introduzione nell'Unione Europea*, 2011, pages 200-211. Regarding the evolution of collective redress mechanisms in Europe, see Hodges, Christopher, *The Reform of Class and Representative Actions in European Legal Systems. A New Framework for Collective Redress in Europe*, 2008, pages 9 and following, and Luther, Jörg, "The constitutional impact of class actions in European legal systems", *in The Law and Economics of Class Actions in Europe: Lessons from America*, 2012, pages 309-313.

2 European Commission Communication [COM(2013) 401 final], page 4.

3 On the distinction between "class arbitration", "*mass arbitration*" and "*collective arbitration*", see Strong, SI, *Class, Mass and Collective Arbitration in National and International Law*, 2013.

4 Commission Recommendation on common principles for injunctive and compensatory collective redress mechanisms in the Member States concerning violations of rights granted under Union Law (2013/396/EU).

5 *Stolt-Nielsen S.A. v AnimalFeeds International Corp.*, 130 S. Ct. 1758 (2010). See Rubino-Sammartano, Mauro, *International Arbitration: Law and Practice*, 3rd edition, 2014, pages 183-184.

6 Regarding the historical origins of Arbitration and its evolution through the years, see, for instance, Born, Gary, *International Commercial Arbitration*, vol. I, 2nd edition, 2014, pages 6-70, Blackaby, Nigel / Partasides, Constantine / Redfern, Alan / Hunter, Martin, *Redfern and Hunter on International Arbitration*, 6th edition, 2015, pages 4-6, Baptista, Luiz Olavo, *Arbitragem Comercial e Internacional*, 2011, pages 21-26, and Mendes, Armindo Ribeiro, "A uniformização do direito da arbitragem através da adopção da Lei-Modelo da CNUDCI sobre a arbitragem comercial internacional", *in V Congresso do Centro de Arbitragem Comercial — Intervenções*, 2012, pages 223 and following. Despite the very distant roots of arbitration, it can be said that it was particularly after the end of the Second World War that arbitration began its fast growth until today (Bernardini, Piero, *L'arbitrato nel commercio e negli investimenti internazionali*, 2nd edition, 2008, page XI) — this evolution was, without a doubt, more accentuated in the last thirty years (see Fouchard, Philippe / Gaillard, Emmanuel / Goldman, Berthold, *Fouchard Gaillard Goldman On International Commercial Arbitration*, 1999, page 1).

7 Regarding these case law, see, for instance, Born, Gary, *International Commercial Arbitration*, vol. I, *cit.*, pages 1514-1523, Strong, SI, *Class, Mass and Collective Arbitration..., cit.*, pages 12-14, 106-110, 206 and following, 361-362, Park, William W., "La jurisprudence américaine en matière de «class arbitration»: entre débat politique et technique juridique", *in Revue de l'Arbitrage*, volume 2012, no. 3, 2012, pages 507-538, and Orgel, Marc, *Class Arbitration — Von der Gruppenklage zum Gruppenschiedsverfahren und zurück? Eine Untersuchung zum US-amerikanischen Schiedsverfahrensrecht*, 2013, pages 317 and following.

8 Hausfeld, Michael D. / Ratner, Brian A., "Prosecuting class actions and group litigation", *in World Class Actions. A Guide to Group and Representative Actions around the Globe*, 2012, page 546. See also Sousa, Miguel Teixeira de, *A legitimidade popular na tutela dos interesses difusos*, 2003, page 209.

9 European Commission Communication [COM(2013) 401 final], page 11. See also Hodges, Christopher, *The Reform of Class and Representative Actions in European Legal Systems..., cit.*, page 119.

10 These are among the several expressions that many authors usually refer to describe the importance of consent in arbitration. See, for example, Mantilla-Serrano, Fernando, "Multiple parties and multiple contracts: divergent or comparable issues?", and Youssef, Karim, "The limits of consent: the right or obligation to arbitrate of non-signatories in group of companies", both articles published *in Multiparty Arbitration*, Dossier VII, 2010, pages 25 and 72, Hanotiau, Bernard, *Complex Arbitrations: Multiparty, Multicontract, Multi-issue and Class Actions*, 2005, pages 32-33, Craig, W. Laurence, "Introduction", and Park, William W., "Non-signatories and international contracts: an arbitrator's dilemma", both articles published *in Multiple Party Actions in International Arbitration*, 2009, page lvii and pages 3-4, Caron, David D. / Caplan, Lee M., *The UNCITRAL Arbitration Rules — A Commentary*, 2nd edition, 2013, page 54, Steingruber, Andrea Marco, *Consent in International Arbitration*, 2012, page 1, and Diallo, Ousmane, *Le consentement des parties à l'arbitrage international*, 2010, page 7.

11 As the United States Supreme Court clearly stated in the referred *Stolt-Nielsen S.A. v AnimalFeeds International Corp.*, *"arbitration is a matter of consent"*.

12 Blackaby, Nigel / Partasides, Constantine / Redfern, Alan / Hunter, Martin, *Redfern and Hunter on International Arbitration*, *cit.*, page 85.

13 *Vide* Diallo, Ousmane, *Le consentement des parties à l'arbitrage international*, *cit.*, page 7.

14 See Voser, Nathalie, "Multi-party disputes and joinder of third parties", *in 50 Years of the New York Convention, ICCA Congress Series*, no. 14, 2009, page 350, and Fouchard, Philippe / Gaillard, Emmanuel / Goldman, Berthold, *Fouchard Gaillard Goldman On International Commercial Arbitration*, *cit.*, page 1.

15 *Cfr.* Jarrosson, Charles, "L'arbitrage et la Convention européenne des droits de l'Homme", *in Revue de l'Arbitrage*, vol. 1989, no. 4, 1989, pages 581 and following, Besson, Sébastien, "Arbitration and Human Rights", *in ASA Bulletin*, vol. 24, no. 3, 2006, page 398, and Silva, Artur Flamínio da, *A Resolução de Conflitos Desportivos em Portugal: entre o Público e o Privado*, 2016, and "A arbitragem desportiva em Portugal: uma realidade sem futuro? — anotação ao acórdão n.º 230/2013 do Tribunal Constitucional", *in Desporto & Direito*, ano X, no. 28 (Setembro/Dezembro), 2012, pages 68 e 69.

16 See Tuchmann, Eric P., "The administration of class action arbitrations", *in Multiple Party Actions in International Arbitration*, 2009, page 327, Monteiro, António Pedro Pinto, "Anotação ao acórdão *Green Tree Financial Corp. v Bazzle*, Supreme Court of the United States, 23/06/2003 — class arbitration", *in 100 Anos de Arbitragem — os casos essenciais comentados*, Coleção PLMJ, no. 9, 2015, pages 248-251, Brozolo, Luca G. Radicati di, "Class Arbitration in Europe?", *in Cross-Border Class Actions. The European Way*, 2014, page 214, and García, Ana Montesinos, "Últimas tendencias en la Unión Europea sobre las acciones colectivas de consumo. La posible introducción de fórmulas de ADR", *in REDUR* — Revista electrónica del Departamento de Derecho de la Universidad de La Rioja, no. 12, 2014, page 105.

17 See García, Ana Montesinos, "Últimas tendencias en la Unión Europea...", *cit.*, pages 105-106.

18 Although not an absolute principle, confidentiality is usually considered one of the biggest advantages of arbitration — see Poudret, Jean-François / Besson, Sébastien, *Comparative Law of International Arbitration*, 2007, pages 315-320, Lachmann, Jens-Peter, *Handbuch für die Schiedsgerichtspraxis*, 3rd edition, 2008, pages 41-45, Matray, Didier / Matray, Gautier, "La rédaction de la convention d'arbitrage", *in La convention d'arbitrage. Groupes de sociétés et groupes de contrats — Arbitrageovereenkomst. Vennootschapsgroepen en*

groepen overeenkomsten, no. 9, 2007, page 23, and Correia, A. Ferrer, "Da arbitragem comercial internacional", *in Temas de Direito Comercial e Direito Internacional Privado*, 1989, pages 174-175.

19 Strong, SI, "From Class to Collective: The De-Americanization of Class Arbitration", *in Arbitration International*, vol. 26, no. 4, 2010, page 513. Regarding this mater, see also Kuck, Lea Haber / Litt, Gregory A., "International Class Arbitration", *in World Class Actions. A Guide to Group and Representative Actions around the Globe*, 2012, page 729, and García, Ana Montesinos, "Últimas tendencias en la Unión Europea...", *cit.*, pages 106-107.

20 See Hausfeld, Michael D. / Ratner, Brian A., "Prosecuting class actions and group litigation", *cit.*, pages 547-548.

21 See Strong, SI, *Class, Mass and Collective Arbitration..., cit.*, pages 346-357, Kuck, Lea Haber / Litt, Gregory A., "International Class Arbitration", *cit.*, pages 732-736, and Nater-Bass, Gabrielle, "Class Action Arbitration: A New Challenge?", *in ASA Bulletin*, vol. 27, no. 4, 2009, page 686.

22 Regarding the importance and role of public policy in arbitration, see Monteiro, António Pedro Pinto, "Da ordem pública no processo arbitral", *in Estudos em Homenagem ao Prof. Doutor José Lebre de Freitas*, vol. II, 2013, pages 589-673.

23 Born, Gary, *International Commercial Arbitration*, vol. I, *cit.*, page 1523.

24 Gorywoda, Lukasz, "The Emerging EU Legal Regime for Collective Redress..., *cit.*, page 173. On the concept of collective redress, see Hodges, Christopher, *The Reform of Class and Representative Actions in European Legal Systems...*, *cit.*, page 3.

25 See Issacharoff, Samuel / Miller, Geoffrey P., "Will aggregate litigation come to Europe?", *in The Law and Economics of Class Actions in Europe: Lessons from America*, 2012, pages 48-65, and Gorywoda, Lukasz, "The Emerging EU Legal Regime for Collective Redress..., *cit.*, pages 181-184.

26 See Gorywoda, Lukasz, "The Emerging EU Legal Regime for Collective Redress..., *cit.*, page 186.

27 European Commission Memo, available at **http://europa.eu/rapid/press-release_MEMO-13-530_fr.htm;%20http://europa.eu/rapid/press-release_IP-13-525_en.htm.**

28 European Commission Communication [COM(2013) 401 final], pages 3 and 8.

29 Paragraph 31 of the European Commission Recommendation (2013/396/EU).

30 Paragraph 30 of the European Commission Recommendation (2013/396/EU) — see also paragraph 29.

31 Paragraph 32 of the European Commission Recommendation (2013/396/EU) — see also paragraphs 14, 15 and 16.

32 Paragraphs 21 to 24 of the European Commission Recommendation (2013/396/EU).

33 Law no. 83/95, of 31 August 1995 (Law of Popular Action) and article 52, paragraph 3, of the Portuguese Constitution. As some authors correctly observe, the Popular Action Law was in some points influenced by the American class actions. *See* Martins, António Payan, *Class Actions em Portugal? Para uma análise da Lei n.º 83/95, de 31 de Agosto — Lei de Participação Procedimental e de Acção Popular*, 1999, page 26 (and also the Forward of Júdice, José Miguel), Sousa, Miguel Teixeira de, *A legitimidade popular na tutela dos interesses difusos*, *cit.*, page 119, Fábrica, Luís Sousa, "A Acção Popular no Projecto de Código de Processo nos Tribunais Administrativos", *in Cadernos de Justiça Administrativa*, no. 21, 2000, page 17, and Grinover, Ada Pellegrini, "A ação popular portuguesa: uma análise comparativa", *in Lusíada — Revista de*

Ciência e Cultura, 1996, page 246. For an analysis of the Popular Action Law, *see* also Monteiro, António Pedro Pinto / Júdice, José Miguel, "Class Actions & Arbitration in the European Union — Portugal", *in Estudos em Homenagem a Miguel Galvão Teles*, vol. II, 2012, pages 190-199, Monteiro, Nuno Líbano / Monteiro, António Pedro Pinto, "Portugal", *in Getting the Deal Through — Class Actions 2016*, pages 59-61, Gouveia, Mariana França / Garoupa, Nuno, "Class Actions in Portugal", *in The Law and Economics of Class Actions in Europe: Lessons from America*, 2012, pages 342-350, and Pimentel, João / Júdice, José Maria, "Portugal", *in The International Comparative Legal Guide to Class & Group Actions 2014. A practical Cross-Border Insight into Class and Group Actions Work*, 6th edition, pages 140-145.

34 *See* Freitas, José Lebre de, "A Acção Popular no Direito Português", *in Estudos sobre Direito Civil e Processo Civil*, vol. I, 2nd edition, 2009, pages 215-219 and "A acção popular ao serviço do ambiente", *in Lusíada — Revista de Ciência e Cultura*, 1996, pages 238-241, Martins, António Payan, *cit.*, pages 112-117 and 128, Ascensão, José de Oliveira, *Direito Civil. Teoria Geral*, vol. III, 2002, pages 117-118, and Fábrica, Luís Sousa, "A Acção Popular no Projecto...", *cit.*, pages 17-18.

35 As a matter of fact, an opportunistic group defined by quickness and lack of skills could compromise a better representation by lawyers more prepared and specialized.

36 *See* Freitas, José Lebre de, "A Acção Popular no Direito Português", *cit.*, page 217.

37 The risk is even higher if the class action is filed by lawyers not really trustworthy.

38 *See* Martins, António Payan, *Class Actions em Portugal...*, page 112, and Grinover, Ada Pellegrini, "A ação popular portuguesa...", *cit.*, page 250.

39 As some authors observe, "the effectiveness of class action litigation in Portugal is dubious to say the least" (Gouveia, Mariana França / Garoupa, Nuno, "Class Actions in Portugal", *cit.*, page 349).

40 European Commission Communication [COM(2013) 401 final], pages 11 and 12.

41 On the distinction between the "opt-in" and "opt-out" system, see Hodges, Christopher, *The Reform of Class and Representative Actions in European Legal Systems...*, *cit.*, pages 118-130, Hausfeld, Michael D. / Ratner, Brian A., "Prosecuting class actions and group litigation", *cit.*, pages 545-551, Issacharoff, Samuel / Miller, Geoffrey P., "Will aggregate litigation come to Europe?", *cit.*, pages 59-65, and Sousa, Miguel Teixeira de, *A legitimidade popular na tutela dos interesses difusos*, *cit.*, pages 209-214.

42 Demonstrating its preference for an "opt-in" system, see also García, Ana Montesinos, "Últimas tendencias en la Unión Europea...", *cit.*, page 105, and Billiet, Philippe / Association for International Arbitration (AIA), "General Conclusion", *in* Philippe Billiet (editor), *Class Arbitration in the European Union*, 2013, page 233.

Chapter 5

Collective Redress and Class Arbitration in the EU[1]

Philippe Billiet*

1 INTRODUCTION

If we look at the roots of regulated collective redress in the European Union, we can trace them back to 17th-century England. Collective redress is a concept that derived from England's "Bill of Peace",[2] where multiple parties sharing common interests (a 'multitude') could go to court and have their cases resolved by the Courts of Chancery. The concept was later modified and brought to the US, where the American understanding of collective justice gave it new rise, amounting to US class actions. Modern class arbitration has existed in the US for over 20 years now, and has been shaped mainly through arbitration case law.[3]

Given the growing interest in large-scale group injuries all over the world, the increasing involvement of non-US parties in international class arbitration[4] and the engagement of national and EU officials in discussions on collective redress in Europe,[5] it is worth analyzing whether US-style class arbitration, or a European corollary thereof, should be adopted in European jurisdictions.[6]

Hereby it must be noted that numerous alternative forms of collective redress exist, such as group actions, collective interest actions, enhanced *res judicata* effects, etc., which may already have shaped one or more European jurisdictions. It may therefore be that the European forum is not open for one single approach to collective redress or would rather welcome only one or more of the alternative forms.

This article aims to provide an overview of the currently existing means for collective redress in a selected number of European jurisdictions and to provide a *prima facie* reflex as to what extent there may be room for class arbitration in those jurisdictions. In the case that the answer to the latter was negative, it is worth looking at the level in which foreign class arbitration awards could at least enjoy recognition and enforcement in the European Union.

It exceeds the scope of this article to render a complete and profound analysis on the forms of collective redress in all European jurisdictions. For such overview, we recommend *P. Billiet, Y. Derains, B. M. Cremades, G. Crespi Reghizzi, I. Hunter, L. Flannery, J-M Judice, L. Kecskes, H. Bagner, A. J. Belohlavek, S. Ribbeklint, P. Ewerlöf, J. Skadhauge, L. Wallacher, R. Cortes, A. P.P. Monteiro, A. Descombes & M. Dragoni in Class arbitration in the*

* Partner, Billiet & Co, Belgium; Director, AIA; Lecturer, Brussels VUB University, Advisory board member (Brussels Diplomatic Academy). Contact details: philippe.billiet@billiet-co.be. Particular thanks go to Ewa Kurlanda and Polina Gryganska for their assistance in the prepatarion of this article.

European Union, Philippe Billiet (editor) & Association for International Arbitration (AIA) (co-editor), 2013, Maklu, 241 p.

A further limitation exists in that only particular observations in relation to the selected jurisdictions will be presented. This article therefore emphasizes characteristics without aiming to be exhaustive in relation to selected jurisdictions.

Last but not least, every European jurisdiction provides already for a minimum possibility for group actions by allowing Parties' claims or defences to be joined under certain conditions and by allowing claims to be transferred to other persons by contract, following which the assignee subrogates in the rights of the assignor and may ultimately have collected a bundle of independent claims in a single lawsuit. The present article will not focus on these basic sources of potential group actions but will only focus on enhanced group actions and other particular forms of collective redress in the selected jurisdictions.

2 COMMON TYPES OF COLLECTIVE REDRESS IN THE EU

Collective redress within the European Union usually takes the form of a group action or a collective interest action. The latter is often referred to as a representative action.

In a group action several persons form a group of parties as their individual claims merge together. This usually happens through a consensual joinder of claims. Each member of such a group is and remains an individual party to the procedure. A default ruling may be rendered against (only) those parties that have not appeared in court.

A collective interest action (also known as a representative action) on the other hand exists when a party 'represents' a 'collective interest' (e.g. the interests of its members), while only the representing party (as opposed to the persons whose interests are represented) can be regarded as a party to the proceeding. The beneficiaries are usually not required to participate in the trial. Stringent conditions may exist as to who can be a representing entity.

A class action is neither a group action nor a collective interest action. Indeed, as opposed to a collective interest action, the class is construed through an opt-in or an opt-out mechanism, following which all members of the class are considered to be party to the proceeding. As opposed to a group action, the members are represented by a so-called class representative and conduct no longer mere individual claims. Their claims can be described as procedurally merged into one class, consisting of numerous member parties to the proceeding.

The European legal tradition, as will be explained further, is not much familiar with class actions and certainly not with class arbitrations.[7]

3 CLASS ARBITRATION IN THE UNITED STATES

Class arbitration is very popular in the United States. The number of US class arbitration cases is expanding at a rapid rate, amounting to over 430 cases today.[8] The increase in numbers occurred especially after leading US arbitration institutions such as AAA and JAMS decided to adopt specific rules on class arbitration.[9]

Consequently, it can be said that US class arbitration now has a fixed pattern and is *grosso modo* subject to the following three-step approach:

1. The clause construction stage: the arbitrator determines whether the arbitration agreement permits the arbitration to proceed on behalf of or against a class.[10] A distinction is to be made between: a) an arbitration agreement explicitly authorizing class arbitration, b) an arbitration agreement explicitly prohibiting class arbitration, and c) an arbitration agreement silent on the possibility of class arbitration. Unfortunately, the latter scenario has divided US adjudicators.[11]
2. The class certification stage: the arbitrator is guided to allow the class certification only where the arbitral clause was deemed to allow class arbitrations or where a court has ordered that class arbitration may be maintained.[12]
3. The final award: the arbitrator renders a final award on the merits, which is reasoned and defines the class.

Very few US class arbitrations actually result in a final award on the merits. Indeed, the vast majority of cases are settled, withdrawn or dismissed. Opponents deduct from statistics that class arbitrations frustrate the efficiency that arbitration procedures are meant to offer, whereas proponents point out that class treatment enhances communication and negotiation, ultimately leading to high settlement rates.

The argument of the proponents is of particular interest, considering that European bodies are often found to 'steer' the ongoing debate on new forms of collective redress towards means for settling mass claims in an amicable manner.

4 EUROPEAN LAW TRADITIONS AND CLASS ARBITRATION

Consultations conducted by three separate EC Directorates General have been found to demonstrate a widespread hostility within European Member States towards US-style class actions. [13] Some features of the US system have even been described as a "toxic cocktail" and widespread agreement seems to exist among stakeholders that they should be avoided at all cost in any European response to improve access to collective remedies.

The constitution of a class through opt-out mechanisms (that may even lead to situations where persons don't even know that they are member to a class) is contrary to European law traditions. European legal thinking indeed emphasizes party autonomy, the voluntary character of alternative dispute resolution methods, party equality, the right to present the case, and individual control over substantive rights and procedure. Nevertheless, EU style class arbitrations that would reflect European legal thinking should not *a priori* be excluded.

In addition to concerns in relation to US class actions, it seems that Europe also takes a different view to arbitration as compared to the US perspective. The current EU perspective may even include a paradox. Indeed, on the one hand we observe the rise of consumer-ODR and consumer-ADR in Europe,[14] while on the other hand arbitration clauses in a consumer contract are still regarded as 'unfair' towards consumers.[15]

Last but not least, civil law traditions take an accusatorial approach, as opposed to the Anglo-Saxon inquisitorial approach, to both arbitration and litigation. This makes that the individual right and ability to present one's own case form an essential element of the way in which the proceeding is to be conducted.

5 PRESENTATION OF EXISTING COLLECTIVE REDRESS TOOLS IN SELECTED EU JURISDICTIONS

A. The Netherlands

In 1994, a collective interest action article was introduced into the Dutch Civil Code (Article 3:305a) under which an interest organization can, in certain circumstances, initiate a collective action for the benefit of the individuals whose interests it protects. However, the wording of this article suggests that a collective action for damages would not be allowed.

There is however another way in which Dutch legislation may be of particular interest in relation to class arbitrations. As mentioned before, US class arbitration tends to deliver settlements. In 2005, the Netherlands incorporated the Dutch Act on collective redress of mass damages ("*Wet collectieve afwikkeling massaschade*" or "WCAM"), which adds to Article 3:305a of the Dutch Civil Code, by enabling the Court of Appeal in Amsterdam to declare an agreement on mass claims binding, regardless of it being an agreement obtained through litigation on the one hand or arbitration, mediation or negotiation on the other.

So far, six high profile cases have been treated under the 2005 Dutch Act on collective redress of mass damages. The most recent decision of the Amsterdam Court of Appeal in *Converium* appears to have had an impact on global securities class actions. The court ruled that it had international jurisdiction to approve the settlement for non-US class members, even though the class mainly consisted of non-Dutch class members. In its final decision of January 2012, the court declared the settlement binding on all class members. After the US Supreme Court's decision in *Morrison v National Australia Bank, Ltd.*[16] invalidating class actions brought in the US on behalf of foreign class members, Amsterdam may be poised to become increasingly involved in claims involving non-US mass damages.

To date, the only corollary of arbitration under the WCAM is that certain agreements (e.g. certain settlement agreements obtained during arbitral proceedings) may be given class-wide effects by the dedicated judge. The consequences may be far-reaching, as a US class settlement may be converted into a Dutch Judgement, which in turn may be enforceable across the EU on the basis of the Brussels I bis Regulation.[17]

The above demonstrates that the Netherlands may serve as an 'entrance gate' to the EU, through which US class settlements may be converted into a judgement that could in turn be executed throughout the EU.[18]

Besides this, it is worth making reference to Dutch case law demonstrating a thin line between the question of whether the Netherlands allows group arbitration or collective interest arbitration: The Supreme Court (*'Hoge Raad'*) of the Netherlands ruled already in 1993 that an association which represents the interests of its members can participate in an arbitration procedure by invoking an arbitration clause that was previously entered into between its members and a third party, if there are certain circumstances that demonstrate a special relation between the association and its members that allow to assume that the arbitration clause should (also) be binding upon the association.[19] One could conclude that this finding amounts to a representative action within the Dutch arbitration forum. The case concerned an association that grouped members in the agricultural sector who used gas to grow crops. A special relationship existed between the association and its members, as it was the association that conducted negotiations with the concerned gas supplier to set out the terms and conditions for gas supply between the supplier and the members of the association. The arbitration clause was contained on those terms and conditions. The Supreme Court clarified that an arbitration clause only binds the party to it and that its ruling does not amount to giving binding effects of the clause towards third parties. The Supreme Court found that the association itself should in this particular case not be considered a 'third party' towards its members, provided the special relationship with its members and the fact that it acted merely in the interest of its members. This ruling may create a rather strange interface between the concept of being a 'party to the arbitration clause' and the concept of being a 'party to the arbitration'. Indeed, in the present case the interest association was found to be a party to the arbitration clause, while its members were not themselves individually party to the arbitration proceedings. Consequently, it can be said that, although the Dutch Arbitration Act provides no explicit basis for a representative action within arbitration, such action can be allowed under certain circumstances.

B. Czech Republic

The protection by courts under Czech law is characterized by individualism, as Czech courts decide only on individual rights and obligations of specific individual persons.

Collective redress in the Czech Republic reflects this approach by providing for particular forms of group actions, in which all persons involved are regarded as individual parties to the proceedings, with a full set of rights afforded to such parties:

- Section 91 of the Czech Code of Civil Procedure provides for instance that if there is more than one claimant or respondent in the same matter, then each of them acts on their own behalf in proceedings. However, where the case concerns common rights or obligations of the kind that necessarily entail that the judgment will refer to all parties on one side of the dispute, then acts of any of them also extend to the others. However, modifying or withdrawing motions, recognizing claims, or entering into settlements all require the consent of all parties on one side of the dispute.
- Section 112 of the Czech Code of Civil Procedure provides that in the interest of efficiency, the court may merge several matters initiated before it to hear them in joint proceedings, provided that they concern the same facts or events, or the same parties. If the motion for the initiation of proceedings refers to matters that are unfit for a merger of proceedings, or if the grounds for which certain matters were merged by the court no longer apply, the court may decide to set aside a given matter for separate hearings.

- Consumer rights organizations may only bring actions for injunction, but not for damages. In other words, the right to seek a ruling of compensation is exclusively allocated to individual consumers.

Czech procedural law offsets the consequences of its individualistic approach by providing for a particular application of the principles of *litispendence* and *res judicata*, amounting to a truly unique form of collective redress.

Indeed, section 83(2)(a) and (b) of the Code of Civil Procedure was described by Alexander J. BELOHLAVEK to have an effect that

> the initiation of proceedings for an injunction or remedy in matters of the protection of rights infringed upon or endangered by unfair competition, or the initiation of proceedings for an injunction in matters of the protection of consumer rights, precludes other litigation against the same respondent in matters of action filed by other claimants who raise the same claims on grounds of the same kind of conduct or the same state of affairs.[20]

In other words, in such cases, an obstacle of (enhanced) *litispendence* has been created in which the (same or different) identity of the claimants will have little relevance.

In addition hereto, section 159a (2) stipulates that the operative part of a non-appealable judgment on the kind of matters referenced in section 83(2) is binding not only upon the parties to the proceedings, but also upon other persons who are entitled persons or beneficiaries vis-à-vis the respondent on the grounds of the same claims (brought about by the same conduct of the respondent, or the same state of affairs). In other words, in addition to the forementioned enhanced *litispendence* principle, there is also an enhanced *res judicata* obstacle, precluding that a similar action against the respondent for the same claims brought about by the same conduct or state of affairs would be filed. This means that rulings in the Czech Republic can bind third parties that are in the same position of an entitled person towards the respondent on grounds of the same claims that have arisen from the same conduct or state of affairs.

The later claimant can enter into the earlier procedure (if still pending) as a secondary party (acceding to the claimant's action) or as an additional party (with all procedural rights, e.g. to file any kind of remedy). Becoming an additional party is however only possible upon request from the original claimant. Moreover, the general public will not be informed of the initiation of proceedings nor of the results of a dispute. On top of this, procedural objections in relation to *litispendence* and *res judicata* may even be invoked *ex officio* by the Czech judge. This all suggests the importance of the first claimant being able to present and defend its claim in a proper way.

Upon service, rulings issued within the arbitration forum have the same effects as court decisions. Arbitration awards therefore also represent the aforementioned obstacles of *res judicata*. However, arbitrators are in no position to decide on the validity of contracts between certain parties unless each of them is also party to the arbitration procedure.[21] Additionally, Czech consumer claim arbitration requires a separate deed, apart from the document that governs other rights and obligations of the parties.

For these reasons, taking into account the individualistic approach and the *de facto* limited application of said principles in arbitration, one can conclude that there is only very little room for collective redress through arbitration in the Czech Republic.

C. Denmark

Denmark is one of the exceptions among European jurisdictions that, above an ordinary joinder of claims, also provides for a law on class actions. This Act is embedded within the Danish Administration of Justice Act — hereafter "AJA" and is in force since 1 January 2008. The AJA sets the principle of an opt-in mechanism for class determination, with the possibility for the court to decide that the class action includes all class members not opting out.

However, the Danish Arbitration Act (hereafter "AA") does not include any provision on class arbitration and therefore does not offer any required basis for class arbitration. An arbitration agreement between one or more potential class members and the opposing party may even prevent that the member(s) concerned could opt in to the class action.

The AA does not even include any provision on consolidation of disputes. Consequently, a third party can only be included in the arbitration following cumulative consent from 1) such third party, 2) the parties to the pending arbitration and 3) the arbitral tribunal. The underlying reason for this refers to the consensual nature of arbitration and the legitimate interest of the claimant or respondent, as the case may be, in avoiding a delay or an increase in costs.[22]

Moreover, no Danish arbitration institute has adopted procedural rules on class arbitration and it seems that the introduction of class arbitration in Denmark has been given little or no discussion among practitioners, academics and politicians. The reasons likely refer to 1) the consensual nature of arbitration, 2) the fact that class litigation is found more efficient as it also allows addressing tortious acts and 3) the fact that, in line with other European Jurisdictions, consumer arbitration requires the arbitration agreement to be entered into after the dispute has already arisen.

The Danish example demonstrates that collective redress in the form of class action may be reserved to the litigation forum, whereas the parallel arbitration forum only applies a strict individualistic approach.

D. Hungary

The Hungarian legislator takes the view that plaintiffs can share costs of litigation by suing jointly, making it affordable for them to litigate small claims of which the enforcement would otherwise be too burdensome in comparison to the achievable gain.

Instead of introducing class actions, the Hungarian legislator addressed this issue by introducing the so-called *actio popularis* model. This means that a third party (typically state organs and/or civil organizations) are authorized in legislative acts to initiate legal actions on behalf of a group of persons. Different sets of rules exist in relation to the *actiones popularis*, depending on the type of claims and sectors. The representing entities have discretionary powers as to whether they initiate a lawsuit and the beneficiary (usually consumers) will automatically enjoy the benefits.

If an affected consumer decides to pursue a claim individually (either parallel or subsequently), the claim will not be dismissed, as the conditions for *res judicata* have not been fulfilled, due to the different identity of parties. Indeed, public actions are therefore without prejudice to the individual actions. This approach is based on the Hungarian understanding of procedural fairness.

Leading authors believe that representing entities can use alternative dispute resolution methods, such as arbitration, in public actions.[23] There are indeed no grounds for establishing the exclusive jurisdiction of state courts to adjudicate public actions. However, an arbitration clause is required to enable public actions through arbitration.

Regarding arbitration, it must be noted that the Hungarian Arbitration Act grants exclusive jurisdiction to the Arbitration Court attached to the Hungarian Chamber of Commerce and Industry in international matters. Moreover, the Arbitration Act is silent on the issue of class arbitration and no Hungarian arbitration institute provides rules on class arbitration.

Leading authors agree that self-regulated class actions are conceivable in Hungary but the procedural right of individuals to be heard constitutes a serious obstacle to the simplification of the procedure.[24]

E. Sweden

Sweden has a Group Proceedings Act (2002:599) since January 2003, making Sweden the first country in the world, outside the common law states, which provided the right to initiate (enhanced) group actions within a court system.

In the Swedish group action the claimant represents a group of individuals and/or legal entities that are not themselves parties to the proceedings, against one or more defendants. Since the group members are not parties to the proceedings, they do not have to appear during the trial. The claims are presented individually, which makes that the representing body may claim differing damages for different members. A ruling on a claim within the group does not automatically create a precedent for the other claims within that group. The judge will therefore render a specific ruling in relation to each group member's claim. The subsequent court rulings bind the group and group members have the right to appeal. Group procedures are governed by the same procedural rules as conventional legal proceedings.

The Groups Proceedings Act provides conditions regarding the identity of the representing body and does not apply to labour law nor to marketing law, which tend to be important affected sectors in US class actions. The Act may nevertheless be applied for consumer disputes, product liability disputes, insurance disputes, damages for disasters, environmental disputes, etc.

On the subject of arbitration, Swedish courts tend to dismiss an arbitration clause if one of the parties is considered weaker than the other, e.g. in employment disputes. Indeed, the Swedish Supreme Court has ruled that such fairness test is to be applied.[25] Moreover, under Swedish law parties cannot validly enter into an arbitration clause prior to the time the dispute has arisen in consumer claims, labour disputes, disputes involving sex discrimination, right of assembly or ethnic discrimination. In addition, disputes regarding the validity of collective agreements or exemptions from such agreements cannot be settled by arbitrators. This leaves very little scope for class arbitration in Sweden within the current state of law.

F. England

Collective redress in English law and practice can be referred to as representative actions and group actions.

The tradition of representative actions goes back at least as far as the middle of the 18th Century, when the Court of Chancery required the presence of all parties interested in the matter to select a few individuals to represent the rest, so that the right might be fairly decided between all parties in a suit so constituted.

The same principle can be found today in CRP rule 19.6. Tellingly, the rule sets out that the representing parties and those persons represented must have the same interests. The representative proceeding involves a single action, making it unnecessary to assess particular represented persons or their claims. The subsequent decision will apply to all parties and to all represented persons, which poses an exception to the characteristics of a traditional representative action.

Regarding the group action on the other hand, the applicable rules can be found in CPR rules 19.10 — 19.15, requiring a so-called group litigation order (GLO), which comes down to a case management decision enabling the court to manage various separate actions that have already been commenced or are about to be commenced and that raise or are likely to raise the same or similar issues of fact and law.

Regarding arbitration, leading authors believe that there can be no consolidation of arbitrations without the consent of the parties, as the arbitral tribunal in itself has no powers to consolidate arbitrations.[26] Further obstacles to class arbitration in England relate to concerns vis-à-vis the right of each party to have a reasonable opportunity to defend party autonomy and confidentiality. England takes a fundamental view on arbitration as naturally based on consent rather than coercion. These observations urge to conclude that, without legislative change, there is stony ground for the development of class arbitration in England.

Leading authors have stated that

> were a tribunal having its seat in England to attempt to certify a class and seek to permit class arbitration along the lines of the AAA supplementary rules or the JAMS procedures, it could in our view be successfully challenged under sections 67, 68 and possibly 69 of the Act (appeals on a point of English law, which are allowed in the absence of a waiver against any such appeals). The only difficulty about doing so is that each of these sections refers to a challenge being made (or in the case of section 69 an appeal being made) by a 'party to arbitral proceedings', and of course the challenge or appeal would be made by a person whose case is that he is not a party to any of the arbitral proceedings. But that is addressed by section 72 of the Act, which provides that a person alleged to be a party to arbitral proceedings but who takes no part in the proceedings is fully entitled to challenge any award made against them on the grounds of lack of jurisdiction or serious irregularity, or indeed to question whether there is a valid arbitration agreement which binds them"[27] and that "it would be difficult to conceive of

any greater threat to the success of English arbitration than the removal of the general principles of confidentiality and privacy.[28]

What is more, the Unfair Terms in Consumer Contracts Regulations 1999 read together with section 91(1) of the Arbitration Act, makes that an arbitration clause in a consumer contract is considered unfair if the claim is for a modest amount (currently 5000 GBP or less).

During the last decade there has been a lively debate in the UK as to the adequacy of existing collective redress mechanisms. The debate has however been almost entirely focused on judicial remedies and extra-judicial dispute resolution mechanisms such as mediation and conciliation. In proportion hereto, only little reference was made to mass claims in arbitration.

G. France

Recent evolutions in France demonstrate that the introduction of an EU type of class actions is possible even when US-style class actions seem not in line with fundamental principles of law in the jurisdiction concerned. To visualize this, a distinction will be made for France between on the one hand, the perspective on class actions prior to the 2014 French class action law, and on the other hand the perspective applied since the implementation of such law.

The French Perspective on Class Actions Prior to the French 2014 Class Action Law

US-style class actions are fundamentally contrary to basic principles of French procedural law as 1) a member would in principle be considered a party to the procedure unless he or she opts out, and 2) all members of the class would be bound by the class judgment even if they did not receive notice and consequently were not even aware of the pending lawsuit. Indeed, these findings are not in conformity with the principle '*Nul ne plaide par procureur*' laid down in article 31 of the French Code of Civil Procedure. Other obstacles that have prevented the existence of class arbitration in France are the main requirements set for arbitration proceedings, such as the principle of confidentiality,[29] consent to arbitration,[30] different regimes applied to domestic and international arbitration,[31] etc.

Consequently, French collective redress tools do not include class actions but rather take the form of 'enhanced' group actions. These enhanced group actions are limited to very specific sectors.

In relation to employment matters, articles L1247-1 and L1251-59 of the French *Code du Travail* enables workforce representatives to bring certain actions without the need to be empowered by a designated plaintiff. The employee(s) will be informed and may file his or her objection to Court within a set deadline. Every employee concerned therefore keeps control over the procedure and may personally intervene, while maintaining the power to put an end to the procedure.

In relation to consumer matters, articles L422-1 and L422-3 of the French Consumer Code enable the so-called '*action en representation conjointe*'. This action enables associations duly authorized by at least two consumers to start legal proceedings in order to obtain damages on behalf of those consumers. As opposed to US class actions, each consumer's mandate must be given in writing and the association is not allowed to solicit mandates.[32]

French procedural law distinguishes between domestic arbitration and international arbitration. Rules on domestic arbitration are stricter than rules applicable to international arbitration and are subject to greater court review from French courts.[33]

In relation to domestic arbitration it must be understood that some matters typically trialled in US class arbitration, such as employment matters and consumer matters, are explicitly excluded from the French arbitration forum.

Regarding disputes between employees and employers, article L1411-4 of the French Code du Travail allocates exclusive competence to the French labour Court (*Conseil des Prud'hommes*). In case of doubt as to the contract's characterization, the arbitrator does not even have jurisdiction to determine whether the contract is a labour contract or not, and is therefore deprived from the competence-competence principle.[34]

On consumer disputes, article 2061 of the French Civil Code excludes these from the arbitration forum by stipulating that an arbitration clause is only valid in contracts entered into in relation to a professional activity pursued by both parties. The underlying idea is that arbitration clauses in consumer contracts would have an abusive character. This article of the Civil Code tends therefore not to be interpreted in favour of arbitration.[35] It is of course not forbidden to enter into an arbitration agreement with a consumer after the occurrence of the dispute.[36]

Moreover, it is clear that domestic class arbitration awards would be considered null and void in general, for various reasons:

First of all, the defendant would be deprived of the possibility to appoint his or her arbitrator for each individual dispute with each class member.[37] Moreover, some class members may not be able to participate in the arbitrator's appointment. This would violate a fundamental procedural principle regarding the equality of each party in the appointment of the arbitrator.[38] Such principle of equality amounts to French public policy.

Secondly, the principle of an adversarial process is a basic principle of French due process.[39] This requires the procedure to be organized in such way as to ensure that all class members can participate in the adversarial process.

Thirdly, the principle *'nul ne plaide par procureur'*, although not explicitly characterized as part of French public policy, is included in French constitutional rights.[40]

As regards international arbitration, a further distinction must be made between the enforcement in France of a class arbitration award rendered abroad (that is addressed in a separate title of this article) and the possibility of organizing a class arbitration in France in an international case. Concerning the latter point, although parties enjoy a large freedom in the choice of the rules or the law applicable to the proceedings and in spite of a relaxation of the principles of arbitrability on matters not governed by French law, the absence of consent of some class members to arbitration and their resulting non-participation in the proceedings pose hurdles that cannot be overcome.[41] Indeed, even the parties' right to waive the right to annul the award does not provide a solution, as the execution of such right requires a special agreement from the parties and implies their acceptance of the arbitration.

The 2014 French Law on Class Actions

On 18 March 2014 the French law on class actions was adopted following extensive debate within political and academic circles.[42]

The law emphasizes on settling mass claims and applies an opt-in mechanism (enabling to opt in only after the liability of the professional has been established) to determine the class members. It further reflects the fore-mentioned concerns through the following restrictions:

- Only consumer associations authorized pursuant to Article L 411-1 of the French Consumer Code may file class actions on behalf of individual consumers;
- Only individual consumers can file damages claims from anti-competitive practices or any breach of contractual or statutory duties against professionals;
- The potential class action claims are limited to remedies for material loss suffered and cannot be used to obtain damages for physical and/or moral loss;
- The *Tribunal de Grande Instance* has exclusive jurisdiction to hear French class actions.

The French law on class actions may only constitute a form of (enhanced) group action. Practice will demonstrate to what extent the law actually introduces class actions (procedural joinders) in the French jurisdiction.

It seems that the French legislator was open to include only certain types of ADR, such as mediation, and did not involve arbitration.

In light of the above, there is today still no explicit legal basis for class arbitration in France.

6 CLASS ARBITRATION REQUIRES A PROCEDURAL RULE ENABLING PROCEDURAL JOINDERS IN ARBITRATION

The European arbitration practice is nowadays characterized by flexibility and a pro-arbitration stance. Liberal decisions exist in relation to the identification of parties to an arbitration clause allowing a broad and more pragmatic identification of parties through analysis of third-party beneficiaries, incorporation by reference, the existence of a community of rights and interests and theories of implied consent. There is also an evolution taking place on the extension to non-signatories within a group of companies, e.g., towards a parent company, another company of the group, a sister corporation, an employee or even a director or general manager.[43] Moreover, doctrines have been developed such as 'the group of contracts doctrine' concerning multiple related contracts that are not linked to the same arbitration agreement and which are entered into by the same parties.[44] In addition, several arbitrators have demonstrated to be in favour of the consolidation of parallel proceedings, e.g. in order to consolidate parties who have participated in the performance of one economic transaction through interrelated contracts.[45]

Nevertheless, class arbitration requires more and cannot be obtained by mere liberal doctrines. Indeed, a class action requires a procedural joinder embedded within a procedural rule. The introduction of class arbitration therefore requires explicit legislative intervention providing for a procedural joinder within the arbitration forum.

7 THE ROLE OF THE EU COMMISSION

On 11 June 2013, the European Commission made a recommendation to the EU Member States to adopt a horizontal collective redress mechanism in order for citizens and companies to be able to enforce their rights under EU law.[46] The main motivation grounds would consist in saving litigation costs for citizens and businesses, and time by reducing various individual claims to one single proceeding.

The European Commission suggested in its recommendation a number of procedural rules to which the Member States should adhere and which would include: 1) Introducing an opt-in system in contrast to the US opt-out system with only those claimants participating in the proceeding who actively decided in favour of it; 2) Making the collective redress mechanism available on a horizontal level for different areas of law, such as consumer protection, data protection, competition, etc.; and 3) Excluding contingency fees and punitive damages, usual for the US litigation system.

When these rules would be followed, the European Commission believes that the collective redress mechanism would not violate main legal principles within the EU Member States.

8 RECOGNITION AND ENFORCEMENT OF FOREIGN CLASS ARBITRATION AWARDS

The fact that EU jurisdictions do not, at present, provide for a procedural joinder, enabling class arbitration to take place, does not *per se* prevent foreign class arbitration awards from being recognized and enforced in European jurisdictions.

Unfortunately, very little case law exists on the recognition and enforcement of foreign class arbitration awards in European jurisdictions.

It is worth mentioning the *Vivendi* case.[47] In this case, French shareholders of Vivendi Universal SA, the US Claimants, requested before US Courts certification of a class consisting of *"all persons, foreign and domestic, who purchased or otherwise acquired ordinary shares or American Depositary Shares (ADS) of Vivendi Universal, S.A"*. This means that any purchaser of Vivendi stock, including French purchasers, would become a member of the US class action, unless he or she expressly notified a decision to opt out. The New York Southern District Court interpreted French law and ruled on 22 March 2007 that only those French shareholders who had bought shares on the New York stock exchange as well as on the Paris stock exchange, are admitted to the class. [48]

In this case the defendants had argued that the opt-out system is contrary to the doctrine '*nul ne plaide par procureur*', to due process under French law (which requires that one cannot be a claimant without one's knowledge) and to the principle of an adversarial procedure. They also suggested that the prohibition of contingency fees for lawyers in France is incompatible with class actions.[49]

The US Court considered that international public policy was the most problematic issue, since France does not allow opt-out class actions. *A contrario* it seems that the application of an opt-in mechanism for the constitution of the class enables to conclude that international public policy would not have been affected.

It is unfortunate that this question on French international public order was only answered by the US Court, especially considering that the Paris Court of Appeal was also seized in this case (in 2010) but dismissed the claim by deciding that it had no jurisdiction to rule upon these issues or evaluate the scope of a US class action decision in France.[50] The latter finding may suggest that class actions involving French citizens and providing for an opt-out mechanism would actually not be in violation with French international public policy as the French judge seems to have left freeway to his US colleagues to rule.

In order to determine the potential effects of class arbitration awards in Europe, one should take into account Article V of the New York Convention, which offers exhaustive means to challenge the recognition and enforcement of an award. The main grounds refer to (1) due process (Article V(1)(b)) and (2) public policy (Article V(2)(b)) concerns. The basis for objection found in article V(1)(b) can only be raised by the parties whereas the basis for objection in article V(2)(b) can be raised by the parties or by the court *ex officio*.[51]

Both grounds *"must be construed narrowly, they are exceptions to the general rule that foreign awards must be recognized and enforced"*[52] and *"none of the existing objections to enforcement can be interpreted in such a way as to allow opponents to international class arbitration to overcome the New York Convention's presumption in favor of enforcement"*.[53]

However, different EU jurisdictions may have differing perspectives on due process and public policy. Civil law jurisdictions, as opposed to common law jurisdictions, tend to emphasize the individual nature of legal claims, a reason why in several EU jurisdictions an aversion may exist towards a representative mechanism that 'disposes' of the rights of absent class members. This may explain why some courts routinely refuse to enforce US rulings, particularly those arising from class actions.[54]

Civil law jurisdictions tend to take the view that claimants should have the right to choose the time and manner of bringing a cause of action, while defendants should have the right to mount a full, individualized defense of all legal and factual claims brought against them.[55] Hereby it is often found that absent class members are not considered to have effectively chosen to exercise their right to a cause of action, even if they could have opted out of the proceedings. Moreover, defendants are often considered to be unable to defend themselves adequately against the generalized claims of absent class members.[56]

Civil law traditions also tend to emphasize arbitration being a contractual construction and therefore argue that if the parties to the arbitration did not explicitly agree to be subject to class treatment, it would be improper to proceed as such.[57]

Nevertheless, in light of an ongoing pro-arbitration stance, the aforementioned concerns about public policy and due process should not overcome the pro-enforcement presumption of the New York Convention. In this regard the enforcement of class arbitration should be treated in the same way as if the award resulted from a bilateral arbitration, permitted on the basis of the special nature of class arbitration.[58] This makes that even states that oppose representative actions should still enforce class arbitration awards, as arbitration welcomes flexibility, informality and innovation.[59]

Consequently, absent class members should be considered as having chosen to exercise their individual rights at such moment and in such manner. This view is in line with the fact that the initial agreement to arbitrate binds the parties to whatever procedure the arbitrator deems proper in his or her discretion, subject only to the parties' explicit instructions and the application of relevant arbitration rules.

This suggested perspective complies with due process, however admitting that the requirements of due process may not be uniform.[60] Indeed, at a minimum,[61] due process would require that parties be provided with a reasonable notice and an opportunity to be heard. Both conditions can certainly be met within class arbitration.

This suggested perspective also complies with public policy, as the underlying rationale to public policy is the right of a State and its courts to exercise ultimate control over the arbitration process,[62] reason why public policy is a fluid concept changing according to the needs of society.[63] It was therefore described as *"violations of basic notions of morality and justice"*[64] and as the *"fundamental economic, legal, moral, political, religious, and social standards of every state or extra-national community"*.[65] Class arbitration as such does not constitute a violation of public policy.[66]

9 CONCLUSIONS

EU policymakers currently do not attribute a significant role to class actions and do not look at the arbitration forum for the resolution of mass claims, even when the claim is a contractual one involving claims under a series of similar contracts raising similar issues, each containing an enforceable arbitration agreement.

Instead, as demonstrated by a paper published in 2010, entitled *"Collective Redress in Europe: The New Model"*,[67] Professor Christopher Hodges has pointed out the rejection of the US model of class action and the gradual development in European jurisdictions of a new model. Such a new model would involve collective ADR with focus on a negotiated voluntary settlement, backed up by the involvement of public enforcement authorities, which can play a significant role in facilitating or delivering collective redress. This latter element was described by him as a "regulatory oversight".

The US class arbitration practice demonstrates high settlement rates, suggesting that arbitration can certainly fulfil a useful role in guiding mass claims to negotiated voluntary settlements. The US practice also validates the importance of arbitration institutes setting out rules on class arbitration, which currently does not exist in Europe.

Class arbitration will not, however, develop merely through practice as it requires a legal basis through legislative intervention explicitly providing for a procedural joinder within the arbitration forum. Currently such a basis does not exist anywhere in Europe.

Moreover, the pro arbitration stance and the flexible characteristics and doctrines in relation to arbitration do not suffice to enable first class arbitrations taking place in Europe, not even through an opt-in mechanism. It is also uncertain to what extent a valid class arbitration could take place in Europe if merely based on the procedural rules agreed upon by the parties, as such 'consensus' may be questionable in relation to non-participating class members.

NOTES

1 For a detailed analysis, see P. Billiet, Y. Derains, B. M. Cremades, G. Crespi Reghizzi, I. Hunter, L. Flannery, J-M Judice, L. Kecskes, H. Bagner, A. J. Belohlavek, S. Ribbeklint, P. Ewerlöf, J. Skadhauge, L. Wallacher, R. Cortes, A. P.P. Monteiro, A. Descombes & M. Dragoni in *Class arbitration in the European Union*, Philippe Billiet (editor) & Association for International Arbitration IVZW (co-editor), 2013, Maklu, 241 p.

2 Thomas D. Rowe, Jr., *A Distant Mirror: The Bill of Peace in Early American Mass Torts and Its Implications for Modern Class Action*s, Arizona Law Review, Vol. 39:711, at p. 711 and subseq.; Zechariah Chafee, Jr., *Bills of Peace with Multiple Parties*, 45 Harv. L. Rev. 1297 (1932) and others.

3 *Keating v Superior Ct.,* 645 P.2d 1192, 1209-10 (Cal. 1982), *Southland Corp. v Keating*, 465 USUS 1 (1984): this was one of the first class arbitration cases in the USUS history.

4 *Abaclat and Others v Argentine Republic*, ICSID case, No. ARB/07/5: claim filed by around 200,000 Italian claimants against the Republic of Argentina; *Yukos Universal Limited (Isle of Man) v The Russian Federation*, PCA case No. AA 227: claim filed by shareholders of the Yukos oil company against the Russian Federation.

5 Strong, SI, *From Class to Collective: The De-Americanization of Class Arbitration*, LCIA, *Arbitration International*, Vol. 26, Is. 4, p. 494-495; Renate Dendorfer, *ADR and Arbitration Compromise or Development in Corporate Disputes*, CILS Symposium on Arbitration, Mediation and ADR (June 2010, Austria), at p. 10.

6 Gary B. Born, *International Commercial Arbitration* (2009), p. 1231-1232; Jeffrey S. Leon et al., *Class Arbitrations in Canada: the Business Case (2010) Canadian Class Action Review*, vol. 6; Strong, SI, *Class Arbitration Outside the United States: Reading the Tea Leaves*' in Bernard Hanotiau and Eric A. Schwartz (eds.), *Dossier VII: Arbitration and Multiparty Contracts* (2010) and other authors.

7 Linklaters, *Collective actions across the globe — a review*, 2011, available at: http://www.linklaters.com/pdfs/mkt/london/1103_Collective_actions.pdf

8 W. Mark C. Xeidemaier, *Arbitration and the Individuation Critique,* 49 Ariz. L. Rev. 69, 70 (2007).

9 See the extended AAA's class arbitration case docket on: https://www.adr.org/aaa/faces/services/disputeresolutionservices/casedocket;jsessionid=ja9wuvhZoHIQ1uXA-ChOVlxi-bDpsft9jsr7u9lg2TKZSHTTLEHY!1081756379?_afrLoop=755508557901180&_afrWindowMode=0&_afrWindowId=null#%40%3F_afrWindowId%3Dnull%26_afrLoop%3D755508557901180%26_afrWindowMode%3D0%26_adf.ctrl-state%3Ddj902fi22_4

10 Once the arbitrator decides whether the arbitration should proceed as a class, he issues the class determination award, which is a reasoned partial award. If class arbitration is to proceed, this award shall define the class, identify the class representative(s) and counsel, describe the mode of delivery to class members, describe when and how members of the class may be excluded and shall set forth the class claims, issues, or defenses.

11 *Connecticut General Life Insurance Co. v Sun Life Assurance Co. Of Canada* a.o., 2010 F. 3d 771, NOS.99-4085, 99-4106 (7th Cir. 2000); *Dickler v Shearson Lehman Hutton Inc.*, 596 A. 2d 860 (Pa. Super. 1991).

12 JAMS class certification requires satisfaction of rules that, like the AAA's Rules, are based on Rule 23 of the Federal Rules of Civil Procedure.

13 EU's Consultation Paper "Towards a Coherent European Approach to Collective Redress" :http://ec.europa.eu/dgs/health_consumer/dgs_consultations/ca/collective_redress_consultation_en.htm

14 Directive 2013/11/EU of the European parliament and of the Council of 21 May 2013 on alternative dispute resolution for consumer disputes and amending Regulation (EC) No 2006/2004 and Directive 2009/22/EC (Directive on consumer ADR) and Regulation (EU) No 524/2013 of the European Parliament and of the Council of 21 May 2013 on online dispute resolution for consumer disputes and amending Regulation (EC) No 2006/2004 and Directive 2009/22/EC (Regulation on consumer ODR). See also: C. Hodges, I. Benöhr and N. Creutzfeld-Banda, *Consumer ADR in Europe: Civil Justice Systems* (2012), C.H. Beck-Hart-Nomos, First edition.

15 Case C-168/05, *Elisa Maria Mostaza Claro v Centro Movil Milenium SL*.

16 *Morrison v National Australia Bank*, 561 USUS 247 (2010)

17 Council Regulation (EC) No. 1215/2012 of 12 December 2012 on jurisdiction and the recognition and enforcement of judgments in civil and commercial matters (recast).

18 Philippe Billiet and Laura Lozano, *Class Actions and Arbitration in Belgium and The Netherlands,* in P. Billiet, Y. Derains, B. M. Cremades, G. Crespi Reghizzi, I. Hunter, L. Flannery, J-M Judice, L. Kecskes, H. Bagner, A. J. Belohlavek, S. Ribbeklint, P. Ewerlöf, J. Skadhauge, L. Wallacher, R. Cortes, A. P.P. Monteiro, A. Descombes & M. Dragoni in *Class arbitration in the European Union*, Philippe Billiet (editor) & Association for International Arbitration (AIA) (co-editor), 2013, Maklu, 241 p., pp. 223-233.

19 Hoge Raad, 1 July 1993, nr. 15016, LJN : ZC1028.

20 Alexander J. Belohlavek, *Class Actions and Arbitration Procedures — Czech Republic,* in P. Billiet, Y. Derains, B. M. Cremades, G. Crespi Reghizzi, I. Hunter, L. Flannery, J-M Judice, L. Kecskes, H. Bagner, A. J. Belohlavek, S. Ribbeklint, P. Ewerlöf, J. Skadhauge, L. Wallacher, R. Cortes, A. P.P. Monteiro, A. Descombes & M. Dragoni in *Class arbitration in the European Union*, Philippe Billiet (editor) & Association for International Arbitration (AIA) (co-editor), 2013, Maklu, 241 p., pp. 49-70.

21 See, for instance, interim arbitral award Rsp 981/11 handed down in an arbitration procedure before the Arbitration Court attached to the Economic Chamber of the Czech Republic and the Agricultural Chamber of the Czech Republic. Annotated by: RŮŽIČKA, Květoslav, in: BĚLOHLÁVEK, Alexander and ROZEHNALOVÁ, Naděžda, CYArb — Czech (& Central European) Yearbook of Arbitration. Huntington (New York): JurisNet, 2012, Vol. II. The said decision, *e.g.* states, inter alia (citing from the abovementioned annotation): "*A final (non-appealable) arbitral award has the same effects as a non-appealable judgment by a [general] court. However, with a few specific exceptions [that need not*

interest us in the present case], an arbitral award is a decision whose effects are limited to the parties (inter partes effects). [...] The arbitrators are not in a position to pass any decision that affects the rights and obligations of a third party" .

22 Jakob Juul and Peter Faurholdt Thommesen Voldgiftsret p 225 (2nd edition) (2008) Thomson and Håkun Djurhuus, Christian Lundblad, Steffen Pihlblad and Claus Søgaard-Christensen Praktisk voldgiftsret p 46 (2011) DJØF.

23 Laszlo KECSKES and Lajos WALLACHER, *Class Actions and Arbitration Procedures — Hungary,* in Y. Derains, B. M. Cremades, G. Crespi Reghizzi, I. Hunter, L. Flannery, J-M Judice, L. Kecskes, H. Bagner, A. J. Belohlavek, S. Ribbeklint, P. Ewerlöf, J. Skadhauge, L. Wallacher, R. Cortes, A. P.P. Monteiro, A. Descombes & M. Dragoni in *Class arbitration in the European Union*, Philippe Billiet (editor) & Association for International Arbitration (AIA) (co-editor), 2013, Maklu, 241 p., pp. 87-113.

24 Laszlo KECSKES and Lajos WALLACHER, *Class Actions and Arbitration Procedures — Hungary,* in Y. Derains, B. M. Cremades, G. Crespi Reghizzi, I. Hunter, L. Flannery, J-M Judice, L. Kecskes, H. Bagner, A. J. Belohlavek, S. Ribbeklint, P. Ewerlöf, J. Skadhauge, L. Wallacher, R. Cortes, A. P.P. Monteiro, A. Descombes & M. Dragoni in *Class arbitration in the European Union*, Philippe Billiet (editor) & Association for International Arbitration (AIA) (co-editor), 2013, Maklu, 241 p., pp. 87-113.

25 Judgment June 12, 1981, Supreme Court, case No Ö 1106/79 (NJA 1981 p. 711) and Judgment June 28, 1983, Supreme Court, case No Ö 375/82 (NJA 1983 p. 510).

26 Ian HUNTER and Louis FLANNERY, *Class Action and Arbitration Procedures — United Kingdom,* in P. Billiet, Y. Derains, B. M. Cremades, G. Crespi Reghizzi, I. Hunter, L. Flannery, J-M Judice, L. Kecskes, H. Bagner, A. J. Belohlavek, S. Ribbeklint, P. Ewerlöf, J. Skadhauge, L. Wallacher, R. Cortes, A. P.P. Monteiro, A. Descombes & M. Dragoni in *Class arbitration in the European Union*, Philippe Billiet (editor) & Association for International Arbitration (AIA) (co-editor), 2013, Maklu, 241 p., pp. 185-221.

27 Ian HUNTER and Louis FLANNERY, *Class Action and Arbitration Procedures — United Kingdom,* in P. Billiet, Y. Derains, B. M. Cremades, G. Crespi Reghizzi, I. Hunter, L. Flannery, J-M Judice, L. Kecskes, H. Bagner, A. J. Belohlavek, S. Ribbeklint, P. Ewerlöf, J. Skadhauge, L. Wallacher, R. Cortes, A. P.P. Monteiro, A. Descombes & M. Dragoni in *Class arbitration in the European Union*, Philippe Billiet (editor) & Association for International Arbitration (AIA) (co-editor), 2013, Maklu, 241 p., pp. 185-221.

28 Ian HUNTER and Louis FLANNERY, *Class Action and Arbitration Procedures — United Kingdom,* in P. Billiet, Y. Derains, B. M. Cremades, G. Crespi Reghizzi, I. Hunter, L. Flannery, J-M Judice, L. Kecskes, H. Bagner, A. J. Belohlavek, S. Ribbeklint, P. Ewerlöf, J. Skadhauge, L. Wallacher, R. Cortes, A. P.P. Monteiro, A. Descombes & M. Dragoni in *Class arbitration in the European Union*, Philippe Billiet (editor) & Association for International Arbitration (AIA) (co-editor), 2013, Maklu, 241 p., pp. 185-221.

29 Art. 1464 of the CPC: confidentiality of an arbitration proceeding is one of the main features of arbitration and the reason why parties choose it over other means of dispute resolution. In contrast to a confidential arbitration proceeding, a class action would have to be made public, as it involves *per se* interests of a certain class of claimants, which would in the end contradict the principle of confidentiality.

30 It is hard to establish unilateral consent of a certain class of claimants to arbitration, as they are usually parties to different contracts with different arbitration clauses or are not even aware of a class arbitration proceeding taking place.

31 Guido Carducci, *The Arbitration Reform in France: Domestic and International Arbitration Law, Arbitration International,* Kluwer Law International 2012, Vol. 28, Issue 1, at p. 147: The difference between domestic and international arbitration means that domestic arbitral awards would be much more controlled by French courts rather than international ones. However, both kinds of arbitration would still have to comply with conditions of French procedural law, set out for arbitral proceedings. Thus, class action would likewise be unacceptable for international arbitration.

32 Cass. Civ. 1re 26 mai 2011, n°10-15-676, *Assoc. Union fédérale des consommateurs- Que choisir v SA société Bouygues Telecom*, commentary by Anne Debet, « Interdiction pour une association de consommateurs de solliciter un mandat pour agir en justice par le biais d'un site Internet », Communication Commerce électronique n°9, Sept. 2011, comm. 77. See also: Cass. Civ 1re, September 30, 2008, Pourvoi n°06-21.400, Decision n°909, *Société Class action. fr.*

33 Guido Carducci, *"The Arbitration Reform in France: Domestic and International Arbitration Law, Arbitration International"*, Kluwer Law International 2012 Volume 28 Issue 1, p.147.

34 Cass Soc, November 30, 2011, claim n°11-12905. See also: Eric Borysewicz et Gilles Jolivet, „*Arbitrage et droit du travail : le principe compétence-compétence n'est pas applicable en matière prud'homale*", Alerte Jurisprudence, 13.12.2011.

35 Cass. Civ. 1re, February 29, 2012, claim n°11-12782, commentary by Joël Monéger, Activité professionnelle des parties et clause compromissoire, La semaine Juridique Entreprise et Affaires n°19, May 11, 2012, 1314.

36 Cass. 1re civ., February 25, 2010, claim n°09-12126, commentary by Anne Pélissier, „ *Le compromis d'arbitrage n'est pas une clause abusive* «, La semaine Juridique Edition Générale n°24, June 14, 2010, 659 .

37 Gabrielle Nater-Bass, "*Class Action Arbitration: A New Challenge?*" ASA Bulletin, 2009, Vol.27/4, p.684.

38 Cour de Cassation, Judgment of January 7, 1992, Rev. arb. 1992, p. 470 and English translation is available in 18.Y.B. Com. Arb. 140 (1993). See also: Ricardo Ugarte & Thomas Bevilacqua, "*Ensuring Party Equality in the Process of Designating Arbitrators in Multiparty Arbitration : An Update on the Governing Provisions*", Journal of International Arbitration 27 (1), 2010, p.11.

39 Yves Derains and Aurore Descombes, *Class Action and Arbitration inthe European Union — France,* in P. Billiet, Y. Derains, B. M. Cremades, G. Crespi Reghizzi, I. Hunter, L. Flannery, J-M Judice, L. Kecskes, H. Bagner, A. J. Belohlavek, S. Ribbeklint, P. Ewerlöf, J. Skadhauge, L. Wallacher, R. Cortes, A. P.P. Monteiro, A. Descombes & M. Dragoni in *Class arbitration in the European Union*, Philippe Billiet (editor) & Association for International Arbitration (AIA) (co-editor), 2013, Maklu, 241 p., pp. 29-47.

40 Conseil Constitutionnel, July 25, 1989, decision n°89-257 DC. See also : Agnès Viottolo, Margaux Nectoux, *«Actions collectives : quel avenir pour les « class actions » ?»*, Les cahiers Lamy du CE- 2011100 ; Jacques Lemontey, *"Les "class actions" américaines et leur éventuelle reconnaissance en France «,* JDI N°2/2009, p.553.

41 Yves Derains and Aurore Descombes, *Class Action and Arbitration inthe European Union — France,* in P. Billiet, Y. Derains, B. M. Cremades, G. Crespi

Reghizzi, I. Hunter, L. Flannery, J-M Judice, L. Kecskes, H. Bagner, A. J. Belohlavek, S. Ribbeklint, P. Ewerlöf, J. Skadhauge, L. Wallacher, R. Cortes, A. P.P. Monteiro, A. Descombes & M. Dragoni in *Class arbitration in the European Union*, Philippe Billiet (editor) & Association for International Arbitration (AIA) (co-editor), 2013, Maklu, 241 p., pp. 29-47.

42 Loi du 17 mars 2014 relative à la consommation (Loi Hamon).

43 B. Hanotiau *Problems Raised by Complex Arbitrations Involving Multiple Contracts-Parties-Issues,* Kluwer Law International, Journal of International Arbitration 18 (3); 251-360, 2001.

44 These contracts are entered into by the same parties, as opposed to class arbitration where different parties entered into the multitude of independent contracts without there being any economical and/or operational link existing between the members. The members of a class generally do not even know each other. See: Fernando Mantilla-Serrano, "*Multiple parties and multiple contracts : divergent or compatible issues?*", in *Multiparty Arbitration*, edited by Bernard Hanotiau and Eric A. Schwartz, Dossiers VII ICC Institute of World Business Law, 2010, p. 13.

45 B. Hanotiau *Problems Raised by Complex Arbitrations Involving Multiple Contracts-Parties-Issues,* Kluwer Law International, Journal of International Arbitration 18 (3); 251-360, 2001.

46 Available at: **http://europa.eu/rapid/press-release_MEMO-13-530_fr.htm** and **http://europa.eu/rapid/press-release_IP-13-525_en.htm.**

47 J.F. Dubos, F. Crépin, „*Affaire Vivendi.- Quand le juge américain s'érige en défenseur de la souveraineté judiciaire française*", La semaine Juridique Edition Générale n°36, 5/09/2011, 944 ; J.P. Grandjean, „*Class Actions américaines et ordre public français*", Les Echos n°20613 du 11 février 2010, p.13 ; Blake Redding, "*If Class Actions Do Not Come To The French, The French Can Go to Class Action*", RDAI/IBJL, N°3, 2007, pp.351 s.

48 Trib. Fed. New York Southern District, Decision March 22, 2007, Vivendi Universal, S.A. Sec. Litig., 242 FRD 76.

49 Pursuant to article 10 of the law dated July 10, 1991 and to article 11.3 and 21.3.3 of the RIN, the "*pacte de quota litis*" is prohibited. The fees shall partially be determined depending on the result, and any agreement settling success fees only, would be null and void. However, such prohibition seems not to apply to foreign lawyers (CA Paris, June 25, 1981, Gaz. Pal 1982, 1, somm. 9.) and not to be contrary to international public policy (Civ. 1er, February 28, 1984, Rev. crit. DIP 1958, 131, commentary by E. Mezger.) to the extent that such remuneration is not abusive (CA Paris, July 10, 1992, D. 1992, 459, commentary by Jarrosson). See also: Henri Ader/ André Damien, Règles de la Profession d'Avocats, Dalloz Action, 2008-2009, paragraph 46.27, pp. 423-424.

50 CA Paris, April 28th, 2010, Rôle: 10/01643.

51 Troy L. Harris, *The "Public Policy" Exception to Enforcement of International Arbitration Awards Under the New York Convention: With Particular Reference to Construction Disputes*, 24 J. INT'L ARB. 10 (2007).

52 Alan Redfern and Martin Hunter, *Law and Practice of International Commercial Arbitration,* paras. 10-33 to 10-34 (4th ed. 2004), noting that the grounds for objections to enforcement set out in article V of the New York Convention are "exhaustive". See also: D.M. Julian. Lew et al., *Comparative International Commercial Arbitration,* para. 26-66 (2003).

53 Strong, SI, *Enforcing Class Arbitration in the International Sphere: Due Process and Public Policy Concerns* (2008). University of Pennsylvania Journal of

International Law, Vol. 30, No. 1, 2008; University of Missouri School of Law Legal Studies Research Paper No. 2009-01. Available at SSRN: **http://ssrn.com/abstract=1330611** (p. 55).

54 Ilana T. Buschkin, Note, *The Viability of Class Action Lawsuits in a Globalized Economy–Permitting Foreign Claimants to Be Members of Class Action Lawsuits in the USUS Federal Courts*, 90 CORNELL L. REV. 1563, 1566 (2005); Richard H. Dreyfuss, *Class Action Judgment Enforcement in Italy: Procedural "Due Process" Requirements*, 10 TUL. J. INT'L & COMP. L. 5, 6-7 (2002) (discussing Italian courts' close scrutiny of American class action judgments); Michele Taruffo, *Some Remarks on Group Litigation in Comparative Perspective*, 11 DUKE J. COMP. & INT'L L. 405, 415–17 (2001) (outlining grounds for European resistance to American-style class actions). See also: 519 F.2d 974, 996–97 (2d Cir. 1975) (admitting affidavits from practitioners from the United Kingdom, the Federal Republic of Germany, Switzerland, Italy, and France stating that courts in those jurisdictions would not enforce judgments resulting from American class actions).

55 Strong, SI, *Enforcing Class Arbitration in the International Sphere: Due Process and Public Policy Concerns* (2008). University of Pennsylvania Journal of International Law, Vol. 30, No. 1, 2008; University of Missouri School of Law Legal Studies Research Paper No. 2009-01. Available at SSRN: **http://ssrn.com/abstract=1330611** (p. 9).

56 Richard H. Dreyfuss, *Class Action Judgment Enforcement in Italy: Procedural "Due Process" Requirements*, 10 TUL. J. INT'L & COMP. L. 5, 14 (2002) (discussing Italian courts' close scrutiny of American class action judgments) and Michele Taruffo, *Some Remarks on Group Litigation in Comparative Perspective*, 11 DUKE J. COMP. & INT'L L. 405, 415–17 (2001) (outlining grounds for European resistance to American-style class actions).

57 W. Laurence Craig, *Some Trends and Developments in the Laws and Practice of International Commercial Arbitration*, 30 TEX. INT'L L. J. 1, 8 (1995) (stating "*designed as a system of private justice, arbitration is a creation of contract*"); Thomas J. Stipanowich, *Arbitration and the Multiparty Dispute: The Search for Workable Solutions*, 72 IOWA L. REV. 473, 476 (1987) (noting "*arbitration is . . . a creature of contract*").

58 Strong, SI, *Enforcing Class Arbitration in the International Sphere: Due Process and Public Policy Concerns* (2008). University of Pennsylvania Journal of International Law, Vol. 30, No. 1, 2008; University of Missouri School of Law Legal Studies Research Paper No. 2009-01. Available at SSRN: **http://ssrn.com/abstract=1330611.** See also: D.M. Julian Lew et al., *Comparative International Commercial Arbitration* para. 16-1 (2003) ("*There is a general tendency to presume that arbitration involves only two parties*.")

59 Strong, SI, *Enforcing Class Arbitration in the International Sphere: Due Process and Public Policy Concerns* (2008). University of Pennsylvania Journal of International Law, Vol. 30, No. 1, 2008; University of Missouri School of Law Legal Studies Research Paper No. 2009-01. Available at SSRN: **http://ssrn.com/abstract=1330611,** P. 64.

60 Judith O'Hare, *The Denial of Due Process and the Enforceability of CIETAC Awards Under the New York Convention: the Hong Kong Experience*, 13 J. INT'L ARB. 179, 184 (1996) (discussing the waiver of due process rights in Hong Kong); Troy L. Harris, *The "Public Policy" Exception to Enforcement of International Arbitration Awards Under the New York Convention: With Particular Reference to Construction Disputes*, 24 J. INT'L ARB. 9, 11, 16 (2007) (noting that public policy arguments can vary depending on the basic notions of

morality and justice in forum states); Gabrielle Kaufmann-Kohler, *Globalization of Arbitral Procedure*, 36 VAND. J. TRANSNAT'L L. 1313, 1321–1322 (2003) (noting the harmonization of due process "across national arbitration regimes").

61 Maureen A. Weston, *Universes Colliding: The Constitutional Implications of Arbitral Class Actions*, 47 WM. & MARY L. REV. 1770 (2005–2006) and *Mullane v Cent. Hanover Bank & Trust Co.,* 339 USUS 306, 314 (1950) (stating that notice reasonably calculated to inform parties of pendency of action is fundamental to due process).

62 D.M. Julian Lew et al., *Comparative International Commercial Arbitration,* para. 26-114 (2003).

63 D.M. Julian Lew et al., *Comparative International Commercial Arbitration,* para. 24-114 (2003) and Karl-Heinz Böckstiegel, *Public Policy and Arbitrability*, in *Comparative Arbitration Practice and Public Policy in Arbitration* 177, 179 (Pieter Sanders ed., 1986).

64 International Law Association, *Final report on public policy as a bar to enforcement of international arbitral awards* (2002).

65 P.B. Carter, *The Role of Public Policy in English Private International Law*, 42 INT'L & OMP. L.Q. 1, 7 (1993). See also: *Deutsche Schachtbau-und Tiefbohrgesellschaft m.b.H. v Ras Al Khaimah Nat'l Oil Co.* [1987] 2 Lloyd's Rep. 246, 254.

66 Strong, SI, *Enforcing Class Arbitration in the International Sphere: Due Process and Public Policy Concerns* (2008). University of Pennsylvania Journal of International Law, Vol. 30, No. 1, 2008; University of Missouri School of Law Legal Studies Research Paper No. 2009-01. Available at SSRN: **http://ssrn.com/abstract=1330611.**

67 **(2010) 7 Civil Justice Quarterly 370**.

Chapter 6

Collective Arbitration: The European experience

Germany and the DIS Supplementary Rules for Corporate Law Disputes (DIS-SRCoLD)

Christian Borris*

1 CLASS & GROUP ACTIONS IN GERMANY

The concept of class and group actions is essentially unknown and non-existent in both the German law of civil procedure applicable before German state courts, as well as in the law applicable to arbitrations seated in Germany. Concerns deeply rooted in the fundamental principles of civil procedure have so far been considered incompatible with that concept. Such concerns relate, in particular, to the right to be heard and to the scope of the *res iudicata* effect of a decision on parties not involved in the proceedings. Moreover, the phenomenon of "mass claims", i.e. claims of a large number of claimants substantially based on the same or similar facts raising the same legal issues, has not been prevalent in German civil litigation practice historically, perhaps because of the absence of a type of proceeding allowing for the economic and efficient pursuit of multiple small claims. It appears though that this is changing. Inspired by US-type class actions, certain law firms in Germany have meanwhile specialized in organizing and bringing mass claims in the state courts, e.g. claims of shareholders against listed stock corporations, investors against banks, customers against insurance companies and more recently cartel damages claims. The German court system and German procedural law is not really suited to adequately deal with the challenges such mass individual claims create. I believe, therefore, that the time has now come for the German legislature to consider options for handling such cases in a fair and efficient manner, including introducing class action type procedures in German civil procedure before the German state courts. The proposals discussed and — in part — brought under way so far, however, do not seem to go further than 'model' proceedings designed to clarify certain issues common to mass claims, while the individual claims are suspended pending a decision in the 'model' case, rather than integrated class action type proceedings.[1]

Class actions in arbitration clearly are not on the agenda in German arbitration practice today. But there is a niche of particular disputes. The German Federal Supreme Court in its landmark 2009 decision Arbitrability II,[2] paved the way for the concept of 'group' or 'collective' arbitration in certain type of shareholder disputes subject to certain conditions. The German Arbitration Institution (*DIS*) in an effort to help implementing that concept developed a special set of arbitration rules: the DIS Supplementary

* Partner, Borris Hennecke Kneisel, Germany

Rules for Corporate Law Disputes (*DIS-SRCoLD*) promulgated in 2009 (herein referred to as *DIS Supplementary Rules*).[3]

S.I. Strong in 2011 published an article entitled *"Germany's Answer to Class Action: Collective Arbitration under the DIS Supplementary Rules for Corporate Law Disputes"*.[4] As a member of the DIS' drafting committee developing these rules, I frankly admit that it had not been our ambition, nor had it even crossed our minds at the time that these rules might be seen as a revolutionary step to introducing the concept of class arbitration in Germany. All we had in mind was to find a solution for a problem in arbitrating a particular type of shareholder dispute under German corporate law, certainly a niche type of dispute though practically quite relevant and important in view of the preference of shareholders in closely held companies in Germany to settle shareholder disputes confidentially and expeditiously by arbitration. So, at first, I was stunned that this project raised attention even on the other side of the ocean and even more by Ms Strong's proposition. After having read her article more carefully (and others written by her on the subject[5]), I realized that while the title of her article may have been somewhat pointed, conceptually Ms Strong's proposition is not too farfetched.

2 THE DIS SUPPLEMENTARY RULES

The DIS Supplementary Rules have been conceived for a specific and relatively narrow purpose, namely the arbitration of disputes among shareholders of closely held limited liability companies (GmbH) over the validity of shareholder resolutions.[6] The GmbH is the most popular legal form of a limited liability company in Germany. Almost a million of them are registered in Germany. Typically, they have between one and perhaps 10 shareholders. In contrast, the legal form of an "AG" (stock corporation) is better suited for and often chosen by companies with a larger number of shareholders and the legal form required for companies listed on a stock exchange in Germany.

In order to understand the nature of shareholder disputes as discussed here, it is necessary to explain briefly certain elements of German law governing GmbHs. Typically, a GmbH is governed by two bodies ('organs'): the Management Board and the Assembly of Shareholders. The Assembly of Shareholders in a GmbH, in contrast to an AG, has an almost all-encompassing competence with regard to intra-corporation matters, including, e.g., taking decisions on the appointment or removal of managing directors, approval of important business transactions proposed by the Management Board, expulsion of shareholders, etc. The *Management Board* is responsible for the day-to-day management and generally the representation of the company vis-à-vis third parties. It is bound to follow instructions from the Assembly of Shareholders.

The Assembly of Shareholders takes decisions by way of shareholder resolutions. Normally, shareholders pass their resolutions by majority vote. The articles of association and/or statutory law may contain provisions protecting minority shareholders, imposing restrictions on exercising voting rights (e.g. in case of conflicts of interest) and establishing the formalities of passing shareholder resolutions (such as minimum invitation periods, formal requirements for proposing the agenda for shareholder assemblies, etc.).

Shareholder resolutions are the key instrument in the corporate governance of a GmbH. Shareholder resolutions passed in violation of statutory provisions or provisions in the articles of association may be null and void or voidable (depending on the gravity of the violation).

Where shareholders have diverging interests and the atmosphere between them is not harmonious (not so rare), quite often outvoted minority shareholders challenge the validity of shareholder resolutions. An example: Majority shareholders A and B claim that minority shareholder C is engaging in competing activities in violation of his duties as a shareholder. They call an Assembly of Shareholders with the agenda point: "Expulsion of C as a shareholder". C was invited to attend the Assembly of Shareholders, but did not attend. Nevertheless, A and B by majority vote pass a resolution by which shareholder C is expelled from the company for "important reasons". C denies that he is engaging in competing activities and also invokes that the minimum invitation period for the Assembly of Shareholders had not been observed. A and B instruct the Management Board to strike C from the list of shareholders filed with the court registry.

C has the right to challenge the validity of the shareholder resolution by filing legal action — and that is perhaps a particularity of German law — against the company, not against the other shareholders (who have no legal standing in regard to this kind of action). The court will then decide in the proceedings between C and the company on the validity of the shareholder resolution. The court's decision has *res iudicata* effect on all shareholders (erga omnes)[7], because it is inconceivable that the same shareholder resolution is regarded invalid only vis-à-vis the claimant shareholder and valid vis-à-vis others. All shareholders are *notwendige Streitgenossen*, a concept perhaps similar to 'compulsory joinder' in US civil procedure. Therefore, in proceedings before the state courts all shareholders will be invited to join the proceedings as 'intervenors' (*Nebenintervenient*) on either the claimant or respondent side. They are bound by the court judgement regardless of whether they opt to join the proceedings as an intervenor or not.

Unfortunately, arbitrating this type of dispute raises a problem: the incongruence between the parties to the dispute (the claimant shareholder and the respondent company) and the compulsory *res judicata* effect of the arbitral award on all shareholders (*erga omnes*), i.e. also those who are not a party to, and accordingly have not participated in, the arbitration). This incongruence was considered by a number of courts and legal writers to be impossible to overcome, so that shareholder disputes over the validity of shareholder resolutions were regarded to be non-arbitrable.[8]

Only in its landmark decision Arbitrability II rendered in 2009,[9] the German Federal Supreme Court held that shareholder disputes over the validity of shareholder resolutions are arbitrable provided that four prerequisites are fulfilled:

- All shareholders are bound by an arbitration agreement (usually contained in the articles of association).
- All shareholders must have been invited to participate in the arbitral proceedings, i.e. to join either the claimant or the respondent.

- All shareholders must have had an opportunity to participate in the constitution of the arbitral tribunal.
- All disputes regarding one and the same shareholder resolution (that is conceivable where different shareholders seek to challenge the same shareholder resolution by instituting separate legal actions against the company) must be concentrated in one arbitral proceeding in order to avoid conceivably inconsistent decisions in parallel arbitral proceedings.

The truly innovative effect of the Arbitrability II decision rendered by the Federal Supreme Court, unprecedented in German arbitration law, is that the award rendered by an arbitral tribunal in arbitral proceedings, where all these requirements have been met, has binding effect on all shareholders regardless of whether they have opted to become a party to the arbitral proceedings. Thus, for purposes of this type of dispute, all shareholders of a GmbH are regarded to form a 'group' that is collectively bound by the outcome of the arbitration, regardless of whether they have chosen to participate in the proceedings. This indeed appears to be a characteristic feature of a 'class', 'group' or 'collective' arbitration, however one wants to call it.

While prior to Arbitrability II the view had been taken that a statutory basis is required to allow for arbitrating this type of dispute,[10] the Federal Supreme Court held that the four requirements set out above can and must be addressed by appropriate provisions in the arbitration agreement. Unfortunately, drafting an arbitration agreement ensuring that these requirements are fulfilled is not at all simple. When I once made an effort drafting such a clause in the context of a mandate, I ended up with a monstrous arbitration clause extending over eight contract pages. Neither my client nor opposing counsel liked it. That triggered the idea to outsource all the indispensable complex technical provisions in a set of DIS Supplementary Rules to the standard DIS Arbitration Rules which could simply be referred to in the articles of association. So the monster was caged and placed in another room where one could not see it (unless and until necessary). It seems that the DIS Supplementary Rules become more and more accepted in corporate practice, as we see an increasing number of cases filed with the DIS under these rules.

In a nutshell, the characteristic features of the DIS Supplementary Rules are the following:

- All shareholders (other than the claimant shareholder) (in the DIS Supplementary Rules called "Concerned Others") are to be invited to join the arbitral proceeding as a party or an intervenor.
- Concerned Others so invited have the right and may choose whether to join the arbitral proceedings and, if so, on which side, within fixed time limits.
- If a Concerned Other chooses not to join, he or she remains entitled to be informed of the course of the proceedings and may still join the proceedings at a later stage, provided, however, that he or she does not object to the constitution of the arbitral tribunal and accepts the proceedings in the state they are in at the time of joinder.
- If a Concerned Other chooses to join, he or she is entitled to participate in the proceedings as a party or intervenor.

- Once it is established who the parties are on the claimant's side and on the respondent's side, both sides shall appoint an arbitrator each and the two party appointed arbitrators will appoint the president. If no such agreement can be reached on either side, all three arbitrators, or the sole arbitrator, as the case may be, will be appointed by the DIS.
- Parallel proceedings initiated with the same subject matter (e.g. the same shareholder resolution) will be joined with the proceeding instituted first (in the following referred to as the "First Arbitration"). In such case, the parties to the second arbitration will have the same rights as the parties to the First Arbitration, including in regard to participating in the process of appointing the arbitrators.
- Concerned Others are bound by the arbitral award regardless of whether they have participated in the proceedings.
- The arbitral award has binding effect on all shareholders.

The ultimate purpose of the mechanism established by the DIS Supplementary Rules is to force shareholders to either join the arbitral proceedings as a party (or intervenor) or else accept to be bound by their outcome, i.e. an extension of the *res judicata* effect of an arbitral award to non-parties to the arbitration. If more than two parties participate in the arbitral proceedings, they will have to be conducted substantially like a multi-party arbitration.

As is probably true for any multi-party arbitration, it may become procedurally and technically unmanageable if the number of parties (or Concerned Others within the meaning of the DIS Supplementary Rules) is too large. It seems to me that generally conducting arbitral proceedings under the DIS Supplementary Rules with more than 15 to 20 parties will become very difficult, if not impossible. Therefore, they would probably not work for shareholder disputes in listed stock corporations with a large number of shareholders, unless additional class action-like organizational structures were to be integrated into the process. Moreover, the traditional view in Germany has been that disputes in stock corporations (AG) are not arbitrable, at all, due to statutory restrictions. That view, however, has received more criticism recently and after Arbitrability II may no longer accurately reflect the position of the German courts.[11] Theoretically, then collective arbitration under the DIS Supplementary Rules (conceivably combined with class action type organizational structures) could work in large stock corporations, as well. But that is science fiction, for the time being. I do not see that in Germany an urgent need is perceived for implementing class action type arbitral proceedings in listed or other large stock corporations. Shareholders in closely held stock corporations, however, may prefer to settle shareholder disputes by way of arbitration using the DIS Supplementary Rules.

3 THE DIS SUPPLEMENTARY RULES IN THE SPECTRUM OF CLASS & GROUP ARBITRATION

Where are the DIS Supplementary Rules to be located in the spectrum of class & group actions discussed here?

Common features are:

- Arbitrations under the DIS Supplementary Rules are a form of collective or group arbitration, though not a 'class' arbitration in the ordinary sense.
- An arbitral award rendered under the DIS Supplementary Rules may have *res iudicata* effect upon third parties (Concerned Others) who have not become a party to the arbitral proceedings.
- Third parties (Concerned Others) have a right, but not an obligation to join the arbitral proceedings as a party ('opt-in').

Distinguishing features are:

- No opt-out as regards the binding effect of the arbitral award on Concerned Others.
- Apart from the concept of extending the binding effect of an arbitral award to non-parties to the arbitral proceedings, arbitrations conducted under the DIS Supplementary Rules with more than two parties are essentially multi-party arbitrations with their inherent procedural and organizational challenges.
- Because substantially in the nature of traditional multi-party arbitration, arbitrations under the DIS Supplementary Rules are not designed and not suited to resolve the procedural and organizational challenges of arbitrating mass claims.

Could the concept underlying the DIS Supplementary Rules inspire solutions beyond the very narrow purpose for which they have been designed? Perhaps. The problem the DIS Supplementary Rules seek to resolve is one arising in a procedural situation where a decision by nature inevitably has effect on a defined group of individuals. I understand that situation is addressed, e.g., in the US Federal Rules of Civil Procedure by the concept of 'compulsory joinder of parties'.[12] Of course, conceivably that problem could be resolved by forcing a claimant to institute arbitral proceedings against all parties to be compulsorily joined. But as the shareholder situation in Germany demonstrates, that may not necessarily be appropriate, first because third parties may not be interested in participating in costly arbitral proceedings because they are indifferent as regards the outcome, and second because they may not wish to be forced into a respondent position when they in fact favor the claimant's position. In German (GmbH) shareholder disputes, other shareholders would even lack standing to be sued (as the suit is to be brought against the company).

A situation that comes to my mind in this context is one rather frequently encountered, in particular in construction disputes, and difficult to deal with in consent-based arbitration: How can the result of an arbitration between the owner and the general contractor be made binding on a follow-up dispute between the general contractor and the sub-contractor? It seems to me that the mechanism established under the DIS Supplementary Rules, or at least elements of it, could be used to invite the sub-contractor to join the arbitration between the owner and the general contractor, or else accept to be bound by the outcome of that arbitration in the relationship between the general contractor and the subcontractor (*Streitverkündung*). But that is not really part of this seminar's topic.

NOTES

1 Cf. Wolf & Lange, „Wie neu ist das neue Kapitalanleger-Musterverfahrens-gesetz?", 2012 NJW 3751; Axel Halfmeier, „Zur Neufassung des KapMuG und zur Verjährungshemmung bei Prospekthaftungsansprüchen", 2012 DB 2145.

2 German Federal Court of Justice (BGH), judgment of 6 April 2009, II ZR 255/08, BGHZ 180, 221.

3 See Annex I.

4 S.I. Strong, "Germany's Answer to Class Arbitration: Collective Arbitration under the DIS Supplementary Rules for Corporate Law Disputes", TDM 2011, Vol. 8, issue 2.

5 S.I. Strong, „Arbitration of Trust Disputes: Two Bodies Collide", 45 Vand. J. Transnat'l L. 1157; S.I. Strong, "Mandatory Arbitration of Internal Trust Disputes: Improving Arbitrability and Enforceability Through Proper Procedural Choices", 28 Arb Int'l 591 (2012); S.I. Strong, "Empowering Settlors: How Proper Language Can Increase the Enforceability of a Mandatory Arbitration Provision in a Trust", 47 Real Prop. Tr. & Est. L. J. 275, (2012).

6 Christian Borris, "Arbitrability of Corporate Law Disputes in Germany", 5 Int. A.L.R. 2012, 161 *et seqq*; Christian Borris, „Die Schiedsfähigkeit gesellschafts-rechtlicher Streitigkeiten in der Aktiengesellschaft", 2010 NZG 481; Christian Borris, "Die „Ergänzenden Regeln für gesellschaftsrechtliche Streitigkeiten" der DIS („DIS-ERGeS")", 2009 SchiedsVZ 299.

7 Christian Borris, "Arbitrability of Corporate Law Disputes in Germany", in C.J.M. Klaassen et. al., "Onderneming en ADR", Kluwer 2011, 55 *et seqq*.

8 Christian Borris, "Arbitrability of Corporate Law Disputes in Germany", in C.J.M. Klaassen et. al., "Onderneming en ADR", Kluwer 2011, 55 *et seqq*; BGH, 1996 NJW 1753 (1755); BGH, 1979 NJW 2567 (2569); Henze, 1988 ZGR 542 *et seqq*.

9 BGH, *supra* note 1.

10 BGH, 1996 NJW 1753; Schwedt/Lilja/Schaper, „Schiedsfähigkeit von Beschlussmängelstreitigkeiten: Die neuen Ergänzenden Regeln für gesellschafts-rechtliche Streitigkeiten der DIS", 2009 NZG 1281 (1282).

11 Christian Borris, „Die Schiedsfähigkeit gesellschaftsrechtlicher Streitigkeiten in der Aktiengesellschaft", 2010 NZG 481 (482 *et seq*).

12 US Federal Rules of Civil Procedure, Title IV, Rule 19: Required Joinder of Parties

(a) Persons Required to Be Joined if Feasible.

(1) Required Party. A person who is subject to service of process and whose joinder will not deprive the court of subject-matter jurisdiction must be joined as a party if:

(A) in that person's absence, the court cannot accord complete relief among existing parties; or

(B) that person claims an interest relating to the subject of the action and is so situated that disposing of the action in the person's absence may:

(i) as a practical matter impair or impede the person's ability to protect the interest; or

(ii) leave an existing party subject to a substantial risk of incurring double, multiple, or otherwise inconsistent obligations because of the interest.

(2) Joinder by Court Order. If a person has not been joined as required, the court must order that the person be made a party. A person who refuses to join as a plaintiff may be made either a defendant or, in a proper case, an involuntary plaintiff.

(3) Venue. If a joined party objects to venue and the joinder would make venue improper, the court must dismiss that party.

(b) When Joinder Is Not Feasible. If a person who is required to be joined if feasible cannot be joined, the court must determine whether, in equity and good conscience, the action should proceed among the existing parties or should be dismissed. The factors for the court to consider include:

(1) the extent to which a judgment rendered in the person's absence might prejudice that person or the existing parties;

(2) the extent to which any prejudice could be lessened or avoided by:

(A) protective provisions in the judgment;

(B) shaping the relief; or

(C) other measures;

(3) whether a judgment rendered in the person's absence would be adequate; and

(4) whether the plaintiff would have an adequate remedy if the action were dismissed for nonjoinder.

(c) Pleading the Reasons for Nonjoinder. When asserting a claim for relief, a party must state:

(1) the name, if known, of any person who is required to be joined if feasible but is not joined; and

(2) the reasons for not joining that person.

(d) Exception for Class Actions. This rule is subject to Rule 23.

Chapter 7

Collective Consumer Arbitration in Spain

What's in a Name?

Laura Carballo Piñeiro*

1 INTRODUCTION

Collective actions have been part of the Spanish justice system since 1984,[1] but they still raise many doubts as to how they should be approached in both constitutional and procedural terms.[2] Despite these issues, an attempt has been made to transplant this model into the Spanish Consumer Arbitration System (hereafter, CAS) and 'collective consumer arbitration' was established by Royal Decree 231/2008 of 15 February.[3] This piece of legislation stems from Spanish Law on Consumer Protection and is in line with Law 60/2003 of 23 December on Arbitration. The former conceives CAS as a means to satisfy the constitutional principle of consumer protection that should pervade the Spanish legal system, including the legal conception and practice of consumer arbitration.[4] The latter — which was drafted following the UNCITRAL Model Law on International Commercial Arbitration[5] — provides the legal framework for arbitration matters, and its principles also embrace CAS.[6] However, the Spanish Law on Arbitration does not stipulate any form of collective arbitration and the model for drafting the consumer version is to be found in the Spanish Civil Procedure Act or *Ley de Enjuiciamiento Civil* (hereafter, LEC).[7]

Against this background, and unlike US class arbitration,[8] collective consumer arbitration in Spain is not a by-product of the interaction between arbitration and collective actions, but a legislative product that aims to enhance consumer protection.[9] However, collective consumer arbitration apparently aims to mirror collective actions in Spain, as does class arbitration.[10] It should be noted that collective action provisions in Spain distinguish between diffuse and collective interests — where the former concerns an undetermined number of people and the latter a determined or determinable number — that give rise to different collective actions.[11] As the second part of this chapter shows, collective consumer arbitration focuses on collective interests and excludes diffuse interests from its scope. However, Royal Decree 231/2008 fails to address some key issues for making arbitration work as a representative device, i.e. one that is capable of deciding on the affairs of absent group members. In the light of this, it has to be concluded that it is a procedural joinder but not a truly collective arbitration. The third part of this chapter elaborates on this point by examining the provisions devoted to dealing with this type of arbitration in Royal Decree 231/2008. The fourth part addresses some recognition and enforcement issues of arbitral awards rendered in this type of proceedings and the chapter finally concludes with some brief remarks on future legislative action.

* Associate Professor of Private International Law, University of Santiago de Compostela, Spain

2 HOW 'COLLECTIVE' IS SPANISH COLLECTIVE CONSUMER ARBITRATION?

The consumer arbitration administrative system was set up on the basis of the 1984 Law on Consumer Protection,[12] although it was not legally established until 1993.[13] In 2008, CAS was rearranged as a consequence of Law 60/2003, which abrogated the 1988 Law on Arbitration,[14] with a view to filling in the gaps and shortfalls in the former system, such as the lack of collective arbitral proceedings.[15] CAS only applies to disputes over consumer matters between consumers and professionals or businesses and does not cover cases involving poisoning, injury and death, or that show reasonable signs of a criminal offence.[16] As said above, the system is pervaded by the principle of consumer protection, and that is why it is only consumers that are entitled to claim their legal and contractual rights before an arbitral tribunal, i.e. professionals and businesses cannot initiate this type of arbitration.[17] CAS is in line with Directive 93/13/ECC of 5 April 1993 on unfair terms in consumer contracts,[18] according to which consumer arbitration is only feasible and any arbitral awards are only enforceable in Spain when the arbitration agreement either submits the dispute to a system established by law or was concluded after the dispute arose.[19]

CAS is structurally conceived as a free administrative service to resolve consumer matters, using a device that in principle sets formalities aside.[20] As a result of the 2008 reform the system is now made up of several bodies, namely, Consumer Arbitration boards, the Commission of Consumer Arbitration boards and the General Council, which are administrative bodies, on the one hand, and arbitration tribunals on the other. The main administrative bodies are the Consumer Arbitration boards, which are responsible for managing the system and providing administrative and technical services to arbitrators and parties to arbitration; in addition to the National Consumer Arbitration board, local boards can be established under the authority of the respective public administration. As mentioned previously, only the consumers are entitled to request arbitration before the board chosen by both parties to the arbitration; if no board is chosen, the local board nearest to the consumer's domicile is competent to administer the arbitration.[21] Should a request (not) be admitted for arbitration, this decision can be challenged before the Commission of Consumer Arbitration boards.[22] The Commission is also in charge of issuing guidelines and reports, with the aim of coordinating arbitrators and avoiding contradictions.[23] However, it must be highlighted that as arbitrators' actions are governed by the principles of independence and impartiality, they are not obliged to apply these guidelines as long as they give their reasons. In general, arbitrators have to comply with specific requirements and show their qualifications as requested by the General Council.[24]

The debate as to whether arbitration can be conducted on a collective basis has not been settled in Spain.[25] However, it has been concluded that arbitration is suitable for pursuing collective but not diffuse interests, inasmuch as they are neither legal nor contractual rights,[26] while the fact of arbitration's voluntary nature seems to be in contradiction with interests that concern an undetermined number of people.[27] Accordingly, collective consumer arbitration aims at 'the resolution in a single consumer arbitration of conflicts that, based on the same factual presumptions, would have the power to injure the collective interests of consumers and users and that affect a determined or determinable number of such persons'.[28] Remarkably, the language of this provision closely follows Article 11(2) LEC, which deals with the issue of who has standing to bring collective interests before the courts.[29] But there is one key issue that makes all the difference between both pieces of legislations, i.e. Royal Decree 231/2008 does not address the question of who has standing to bring collective interests before arbitral tribunals.

It is well-known that European legal systems have been highly reluctant to admit the introduction of collective actions, due to their apparent failure to guarantee the right to present one's case.[30] The benefits of collective actions lie in the fact that they provide access to justice and procedural economy, and for this reason the trend is slowly undergoing a change and civil law countries are also establishing collective actions in their systems.[31] Standing has been a key issue on the path to setting these up. Civil law systems construe the civil procedure on a bilateral basis, meaning that litigation is for those claiming a contractual or legal right. This is not the case of collective actions, in which the representative claimant litigates on behalf of absent group members. The shortcomings of traditional legal theory's approach to civil procedure have meant that civil law systems have evolved and new concepts have emerged to cover disputes involving a determined, determinable or even undetermined number of persons;[32] in other words, along with subjective rights, 'collective and diffuse interests', and even 'homogeneous individual rights' have now been identified.[33] The next step was the legal designation of the person or body who had the standing to bring such interests before the courts.

Spain is no exception to this trend.[34] Spanish collective actions are not trans-substantive but are basically related to employment and consumer matters. More specifically, collective consumer actions are characterized by their typicality, which means that there are a significant number of consumer laws, and almost all contain a rule about what type of collective actions are available to pursue the collective and diffuse consumer interests enshrined therein, and indicating who is entitled to bring such actions before the courts.[35] While these rules are scattered among several laws,[36] further specifications about collective proceedings are to be found in LEC. In particular, Article 222(3) LEC makes an exception to the general rule that the final judgment is only binding on the parties to the proceedings and their successors, i.e. it will also be binding on non-parties to the proceedings whose rights and interests have been brought before court by those entitled to represent them and initiate collective actions.[37] This general rule is supplemented by a specific rule dealing with collective actions undertaken by consumer associations.[38] While public bodies such as the public prosecutor and the Spanish Agency of Consumption, Food Safety and Nutrition, as well as consumer groups and even individuals are entitled to litigate regarding this type of interests, in practice the most significant representative claimants are consumer associations.[39]

Despite the significance of provisions on standing and *res iudicata* to pursue interests and rights on a collective basis, Royal Decree 231/2008 does not mention them. Article 58(1) of Royal Decree 231/2008 stipulates that collective arbitration is to be initiated by the president of the competent consumer arbitration board either on her own initiative, the initiative of the arbitration boards of inferior territorial jurisdictions or at the request of the relevant representative consumer association. However, this is not a rule on standing, i.e. indicating who is entitled to bring and represent collective interests before arbitral tribunals. In fact, once the decision has been taken and arbitral proceedings commence, the general rule on standing is applicable,[40] hence consumers have to claim or otherwise intervene in the proceeding for their legal or contractual rights to be arbitrated. Remarkably, there is no further reference to consumer associations which have a leading role in bringing collective actions before the courts in practice in Spain, i.e. in the absence of a specific provision, they are not entitled to pursue 'collective interests in arbitration'.[41] By the same token, Royal Decree 231/2008 does not address the binding effects of arbitral awards on third parties should the arbitral proceedings be truly collective; the usual principle of *res iudicata* is thus applicable, i.e. the award is only binding on parties to the arbitration.[42] In the light of this gap, it can be concluded that what is referred to as 'collective consumer arbitration' is a mechanism for dealing with large-scale disputes arising out of the same event, but is based upon the mere aggregation of individual claims. A closer look at the different stages will confirm this.

3 COLLECTIVE CONSUMER ARBITRATION IN SPAIN: FEATURES AND CRITIQUES

A. The Consumer Arbitration Board in Charge of Administering Collective Arbitration

CAS is administrative in nature, for which reason each arbitration board only operates in a given geographical area. Collective arbitration in particular is to be administered by the arbitration board with jurisdiction in the area where consumers whose legitimate economic rights and interests have been affected by the event brought to arbitration, are domiciled. Should affected consumers live in more than one autonomous region of Spain, the National Arbitration Board is competent to administer the arbitration procedure.[43] As will be seen in the following sections, the competent board pursuant to these clear-cut rules decides whether to initiate collective consumer arbitration, and if it decides to do so, takes the necessary steps to open the procedure, namely, obtaining the requisite acceptances from the parties to the arbitration and appointing the arbitration tribunal.

However, the jurisdiction issue is far from being settled, as the relevant board may have to make the decision to arbitrate on a collective basis at a time when the group has still not been determined. The make-up of the claimant group may therefore change during the arbitral proceedings, but nothing is said about how to proceed in these cases, i.e. whether the non-competent board should refer the arbitration to the newly competent board or not.[44] In contrast, it is only once the decision to arbitrate collectively has been made that a notice inviting interested consumers to join the proceedings is published in an Official Journal or by some other means. Furthermore, while pre-trial discovery is highly unusual in Spain and is limited to cases stipulated by law, the courts can be requested to help establish a group made of a determinable number of persons by adopting the appropriate measures, including requesting the respondent's cooperation.[45] However, Royal Decree 231/2008 makes no reference to this

LEC provision, and by default consumer arbitration boards are not allowed to resort to the courts for other than the usual support measures.[46]

The president of the competent consumer arbitration board is responsible for deciding whether to arbitrate on a collective basis or not. The initiative can come from her, from arbitration boards in inferior territorial areas or can be requested by the associations representing consumers in the area where the consumers' collective interests have been affected. It should be noted that the latter's participation is supposed to end at this point, as nothing is said about their intervening in the arbitral proceedings; otherwise, a truly collective arbitration would have been set up. There is also no further explanation of the meaning of 'representative associations' in Royal Decree 231/2008, although the notion is present in the Law on Consumer Protection, namely, only associations registered in a specific public registry are to be deemed 'representative'.[47] This requirement seems to be pointless, bearing in mind the fact that they do not actually join in the collective arbitration; while Spanish legislation requires registration to ensure an adequate representative claimant as far as possible, this provision is meaningless if this is not the case. In contrast, it would have made sense to entitle any association and, in particular, a group of affected consumers, to request collective arbitration.[48]

Finally, it is striking that access to collective arbitration is only granted to consumers domiciled in Spain and not to those domiciled in other countries, even when the businesses or professionals responsible for the matters in dispute are based in Spain.[49] In the light of Regulation (EC) 2006/2004 of the European Parliament and of the Council of 27 October 2004 on cooperation between national authorities responsible for the enforcement of consumer protection laws,[50] this geographical limitation is highly regrettable. In contrast, consumers domiciled in Spain can take advantage of this kind of arbitration to request arbitration against businesses or professionals based or domiciled in foreign countries.

B. Arbitration Agreements and Intervention Issues

Arbitration agreements can either be incorporated into contracts or separate contracts can be drawn up, but they always record the parties' willingness to submit their differences to CAS.[51] In line with Article II of the New York Convention on the recognition and enforcement of foreign arbitral awards, arbitration agreements must be written, signed by the parties or contained in an exchange of letters, telegrams, telexes, faxes and any other means of electronic communication allowing written documentation of the agreement, even when it is only electronically or optically available.[52] So far, nothing here stands out as being particularly innovative. However, there is one feature that makes the system unusual, and it is that companies and professionals can join CAS on an *ex ante* basis, meaning that they publicly declare themselves to be engaged in CAS, thereby accepting any arbitration requested by any consumers trading with them. The benefit in doing so lies in the fact that all those agreeing publicly to join the system can sell this as an extra service to consumers, who receive a clear signal that they can claim against the respective professional or business by resorting to CAS should conflict arise. Professionals and businesses who are interested in sending this signal have to offer publically to submit to CAS, and if accepted are then registered. Should a dispute arise later on, consumers simply have to request arbitration before the competent arbitration board.[53] Hence, the arbitration agreement may consist of an *ex ante* public offer to submit to CAS plus the consumer's request for arbitration. In cases where there had not been a public offer to submit to CAS, or this one had not been accepted, consumer's request is equally admitted, but the respondent must expressly accept arbitration. In short, CAS admits both pre- and post-dispute submission agreements.

The case of collective consumer arbitration is somewhat different because it must be specifically accepted by respondents; once the competent board decides to initiate collective arbitral proceedings, the professionals or businesses responsible for the event that has allegedly caused injury to consumers have to give their express consent to it,[54] otherwise, the case file is archived.[55] The 2008 statute provides no rationale for this requirement, and there is no plausible explanation for it in the light of the structure of this type of arbitration. In fact, it is surprising that it is not included in the scope of public offers to submit to CAS made by professionals and businesses, bearing in mind that collective arbitration only deals with consumers joining the proceedings and not with third parties to the arbitration.[56]

Should this procedure be accepted by the relevant professional or business, the collective proceedings still have to be accepted by individual consumers, who are literally invited to claim their legal or contractual rights arising out of the matter in dispute. To this end, the affected consumers are notified of the respondent's acceptance by information published in the Official Journal in the region where the dispute is taking place.[57] As will be seen later, if they do not join the arbitration, they are not bound by any arbitral award that may be rendered.[58]

This notification process raises many issues, in particular concerning its efficiency and effectiveness, bearing in mind how many consumers regularly read the wide range of Official Journals published in Spain. Admittedly, the president of the consumer arbitration board has the power to make the information public by other mean, although as this is a discretionary power, the president in question may choose not to do so or may resort to the newspapers; but it would certainly be strange if she gives individual notification, which is the best way to build a collective arbitration. Furthermore, the notification's content is very basic and consumers are only informed that the president agrees to the initiating of the action and that they have a period of two months to join the proceedings; otherwise they are allowed to intervene before the arbitral hearing, but only in the steps taken after the date of their intervention.[59]

Given these provisions, this is clearly not a version of collective actions; while the fact that consumers have to join the proceedings could call to mind an opt-in system, the issue of the standing to represent consumers in the arbitral proceedings is not addressed. While it is true that consumers do not need legal representation in arbitration, neither do they have to act on a collective basis during the proceedings. Hence, the legal understanding of 'collective arbitration' really amounts to aggregating as many claims as possible. To this end, consumers may join the arbitration in the two-month period following notification and intervene during the proceedings provided that the hearing has not yet taken place. Meanwhile, if the businesses or professionals involved accept collective arbitration, this has the effect of suspending any other procedure that could have been initiated by an individual request for arbitration arising out of the same factual scenario, and these requests have to be transferred to the board competent to handle the collective arbitration within 15 days after notification of the acceptance. It should be noted that this rule applies to the stage at which individual arbitral proceedings have not yet been opened, or the petition for arbitration has been transferred to the parties to the arbitration but the arbitrators have not yet been appointed; in this case, the claimant and respondent must be notified of the suspension and transfer of the proceedings.[60] Individual proceedings that have already been before an arbitral tribunal are not suspended, but an objection by the respondent at any time, including during the hearing, on the grounds that a collective arbitration has been opened, requires suspension and transfer; in other words, the decision to transfer the case effectively lies with the respondent.

The rationale for these provisions is that collective arbitration absorbs all individual arbitrations, including cases in which these have already been initiated. Consumers are not entitled to opt out, and neither can they initiate individual proceedings while the collective arbitration is underway. In principle, this could impair consumers' constitutional right to present their case.[61] A case in point is the one underlying a request for a preliminary ruling currently before the Court of Justice of the European Union, stemming from a collective action involving 101 banks that was brought before a commercial court in Madrid in 2010 by a consumer association, on the grounds that their mortgage contracts included unfair terms.[62] In view of the lengthy procedure involved, many consumers decided to litigate individually, but the defendants have applied for a stay of individual proceedings on the grounds that the judgment to be rendered in the collective action is a preliminary issue in relation to these individual claims.[63] While the system in Spain is neither an opt-in nor an opt-out system, a Barcelona commercial court decided to ask the Court of Justice whether the rule on preliminary issues and suspension of proceedings was consistent with EU consumer protection, arguing that 'the consumer is bound by the decision in those [collective] proceedings without having had the opportunity to put forward the appropriate pleas or adduce evidence with full equality of arms'.[64] However, while the Court of Justice decision may be of interest for collective actions and their structure in Spain, the same does not apply to collective arbitration, as consumers not joining the procedure can request arbitration immediately after the arbitral award has been rendered.[65]

C. Settlement Agreements

Businesses and professionals that accept collective arbitration can propose a settlement agreement with a view to complying with, wholly or in part, the rights at stake.[66] In this case, the notification advising affected consumers of the arbitration must also contain information on the settlement proposal.[67] However, nothing is said as to what happens next; the affected consumers may obviously accept or reject the proposal, but the issue is how the settlement interacts with the arbitral proceedings, and thus, whether it can gain preclusive effects. One option is that it has no effect on the arbitration, in which case this will simply continue with the consumers who do not accept the settlement. Another option would be to render the same number of arbitral awards as there are consumers that accept the settlement, thereby applying the rules on settlement agreements provided for individual arbitrations.[68] However, the option of taking the settlement into account within the collective arbitration seems to be preferable, i.e. the arbitral award will not only decide on the claims of consumers that have not accepted the settlement, but will also refer to the settlement agreement, and by this means it will gain preclusive effect, at least with regard to consumers that have accepted it.[69]

D. Arbitral Proceedings.

Once the affected consumers have been notified, the president of the competent consumer arbitration board has to appoint the arbitral tribunal,[70] which proceeds according to the general rules applicable to arbitral proceedings with regard to the parties' communications and proof, and the hearing. The arbitral award is generally rendered within a period of six months,[71] which begins the day after the two month period for affected consumers to join the proceeding expires.[72] No cases have been reported so far, but the proceedings' ambiguities and the extending of the deadline for rendering the award raises the question as to whether collective arbitration really does favour consumers, in the light of the delay involved in resolving cases.[73]

It should be pointed out here that there is no provision similar to Article 222 LEC. The applicable rule for the award's binding effects is thus that provided by the Spanish Law on Arbitration, which does not mention the special case of collective arbitration. Accordingly, awards rendered in collective consumer arbitrations are only binding on consumers that join the proceedings and do not have preclusive effects for consumers that were affected by the factual presumptions discussed during the proceedings but who remained outside them.[74] In other words, the latter are entitled to assert their rights, for example, by requesting an individual arbitration.

4 RECOGNITION AND ENFORCEMENT ISSUES

The previous sections have sought to explain that collective consumer arbitration in Spain is a procedural joinder but is not representative in nature, i.e. one that makes arbitrating on the rights of absent group members possible. For this reason, no objections other than the usual ones ought to be raised should an arbitral award rendered in this type of arbitral proceeding seek to be enforced in another state; although only consumers resident in Spain are entitled to resort to collective arbitration, it can be initiated against professionals or businesses that are domiciled or based in a foreign country.[75] In this case, the New York Convention on the recognition and enforcement of foreign arbitral awards would be applicable.[76] While different challenges to the recognition and enforcement of US class awards could be raised,[77] this does not apply to collective awards in Spain.

Objections regarding arbitration agreements in Spain are in principle inappropriate, since both parties have to expressly accept arbitration.[78] The same applies to objections regarding arbitral proceedings. While there are several that can be raised against US class arbitration,[79] — namely, the lack of agreement on class treatment, privacy and confidentiality issues, the composition of the arbitral tribunal, the lack of proper notice and the inability to present one's case — none of these are applicable to the procedure in Spain, as, apart from its initial stage, it is no different from individual arbitrations, including the application of the general rules on privacy and confidentiality. In particular, all affected consumers are able to present their cases, since there is no representative claimant.

The right to a fair trial/arbitration is protected under the public policy clause, and this objection could be raised to ensure that group members have been adequately represented, especially in cases of collective proceedings construed on an opt-out basis. But this is clearly not applicable in Spain, either, as everyone bound by the arbitral award is already a party to the arbitration. By the same token, it would be very difficult to raise the public policy clause on the grounds that a conflict of interest had led to a fraudulent award,[80] because the lack of a representative claimant prevents one interest from prevailing over others within the claimant position, in that the arbitral tribunal will have to assess all defences and objections raised during the proceeding.

5 CONCLUDING REMARKS

While there is no doubt that collective consumer arbitration is a procedural joinder, it is definitively not a mechanism by which absent group members can be bound by the arbitral award. The initial intention of establishing a collective action mechanism can be found in the provisions laid down by Royal Decree 231/2008, indicating that this type of arbitration deals with conflicts involving the collective interests of consumers and affecting a determined or determinable number of such persons. However, the procedural mechanism chosen involves aggregating claims, not a representative device.

Royal Decree 231/2008 also addresses the consolidation of claims where a number of arbitrations arising out of similar factual scenarios have been requested.[81] As the statute does not address the latter's interaction with collective arbitration, this silence amounts to an alternative, meaning that consumer arbitration boards and interested parties can choose between the two procedures. As a matter of fact, it should be pointed out that the consolidation of claims mechanisms can be more beneficial than collective arbitration, insofar as the respondent's acceptance is not specifically requested in this framework and the president of the arbitration board can mandatorily consolidate arbitrations on the grounds of procedural economy.[82] At any rate, in its current terms it is more practical than collective arbitration, whose reform ought to be considered.

In the light of the shortcomings highlighted in this chapter, current collective consumer arbitration needs a thorough overhaul which addresses the currently absent issues of standing, finance,[83] opt-in/opt-out rights,[84] and enhances the information given to the consumers affected by the event that gives rise to the damage. The termination of collective arbitration by settlement agreement ought to be tackled as well, in particular as it could turn arbitration into a preferable alternative to collective litigation; the LEC does not address this issue, and a settlement reached in the course of a collective action is thus not binding on third parties, even in spite of court approval.[85] In this regard, Royal Decree 231/2008 is to be seen as a missed opportunity, as termination by settlement agreement is not possible in collective arbitration; were the latter to be feasible, it would have made arbitration more attractive to stakeholders than collective litigation. However, the fact that Royal Decree 231/2008 is a piece of secondary legislation cannot be disregarded; while the amendments mentioned above involve the right to a fair trial, the lawmaker of Royal Decree 231/2008 was the Spanish government and not parliament. Hence, all that remains is to advocate a thorough revision of collective consumer arbitration by the Spanish legislature via, e.g. amending the Spanish Law on Arbitration. This would also have the benefit of opening a debate on whether to extend collective arbitration to other matters.

NOTES

1 See Article 20 of Law 26/1984 of 19 July on Consumer Protection (*Ley para la defensa de los consumidores y usuarios*), now Article 24 of Royal Legislative Decree 1/2007 of 16 November, which issued a consolidated text on the Law on Consumer Protection and other supplementary laws (*Texto refundido de la Ley General para la Defensa de los Consumidores y Usuarios y otras leyes complementarias*).

2 See Carballo Piñeiro, Laura, *Las acciones colectivas y su eficacia extraterritorial. Problemas de recepción y trasplante de las* class actions *en Europa*, 2009, pp. 36-96.

3 The key provisions are Articles 56-62 of Royal Decree 1/2007. An English translation can be found in Strong, SI, "Collective Consumer Arbitration in Spain: A Civil Law Response to US-Style Class Arbitration", *Journal of International Arbitration* 30(5), 2013, p. 508. On the system's general features and historical background, see Marín López, Manuel Jesús, "La nueva regulación del arbitraje de consumo: el Real Decreto 231/2008, de 15 de febrero", *Diario La Ley*, No 6905 of 17.3.2008.

4 See Article 51 of the Spanish Constitution.

5 See the Explanatory Introduction to Law 60/2003 on Arbitration. See UNCITRAL Model Law on International Commercial Arbitration (UN Resolution 40/72 of 11 December 1985), with amendments as adopted in 2006 (UN Resolution 61/33 of 18 December 2006).

6 See Cremades, Bernardo María and Cortés, Rodrigo, "Class Actions and Arbitration Procedures—Spain", in Billiet, Philip et al. (eds.) *Class Actions and Arbitration in the European Union*, 2012, pp. 155-156.

7 Articles 6, 11, 15, 15bis, 221, 222(2), 256(1)(6), 519 LEC.

8 The interaction between class actions and arbitration has been explored in the US by the inclusion of arbitration agreements in standard contracts. The aim is to avoid class actions, insofar as the Federal Arbitration Act favours arbitration over jurisdiction, even in consumer matters. See Byrne, Thomas A., "Class Actions", *Mercer Law Review*, 57, 2006, pp. 1031-1037. Critical, Gilles, Myriam E., "Opting Out of Liability: The Forthcoming, Near-Total Demise of the Modern Class Action", *Michigan Law Review*, 104, 2005, pp. 381-430. However, this trend has resulted in class arbitration being accepted, i.e. although the agreement excluding jurisdiction is honoured, arbitration may proceed on a class-wide basis and different arbitral organizations have issued rules on class arbitration proceedings, mainly by imitating class action proceedings to safeguard absent class members' due process rights. See *American Arbitration Association. Supplementary Rules for Class Arbitrations* (2003), **http://www.adr.org/sp.asp?id=21936** (last access, 1.9.2010) (hereafter, AAA Supplementary Rules); *Judicial Arbitration and Mediation Services Class Action Procedures* (2009),

http://www.jamsadr.com/files/Uploads/Documents/JAMS-Rules/JAMS_Class_Action_Procedures-2009.pdf; *National Arbitration Forum. Class Arbitration Procedures*, http://www.adrforum.com/users/naf/resources/Arbitration%20Class%20Procedures%202007.pdf.

9 Outside the United States, two collective arbitration cases have been reported, one issued by a Colombian arbitral institution [*Valencia v Bancolombia* (*Tribunal Arbitral de la Cámara de Comercio de Bogotá*), available at http://www.kluwerarbitration.com. Comments by Strong, SI, "Enforcing Class Arbitration in the International Sphere: Due Process and Public Policy Concerns", *University of Pennsylvania Journal of International Law*, 30, 2008, p. 1], and another by a Canadian arbitral institution [*Kanitz v Rogers Cable Inc.*, [2002] 58 O.R. (3d) 299, 21 B.L.R. (3d) 104, available at http://www.kluwerarbitration.com>]. In Canada, the issue has evolved in a similar way to the United States, and the Canadian Supreme Court issued a decision supporting arbitration and excluding class proceedings [*Dell Computer Corp. v Union des consommateurs*, 2 S.C.R. 801, 2007 SCC 34 (S.C.C. 2007).]. See, in general, Saumier, Genevieve, "Consumer Dispute Resolution: The Evolving Canadian Landscape", *Class Action Defence Quarterly*, p. 1 available at http://ssrn.com/abstract=1291960; Saumier, Genevieve, "Consumer Arbitration in the Evolving Canadian Landscape", *Penn State Law Review* 113, 2009, p. 1203; Strong, SI, "Class Arbitration Outside the United States: Reading the Tea Leaves", *Legal Studies Research Paper Series*, Research Paper No. 2009-36, University of Missouri, available at <http://ssrn.com/abstract=1517272.].

10 See n. 8 above.

11 See Article 11(2) and (3) LEC.

12 See Article 31 of Law 26/1984 on Consumer Protection.

13 The Consumer Arbitration System was set up by Royal Decree 636/1993 of 3 May 1993, now replaced by Royal Decree 231/2008. The Spanish government was entitled to issue the latter by Law 44/2006 of 29 December amending the Law on Consumer Protection. Other relevant rules are Articles 57 and 58 of Royal Legislative Decree 1/2007 of 16 November approving a text consolidating the General Law on Consumer Protection and other supplementary laws, and Law 60/2003 of 23 December on Arbitration.

14 Law 60/2003 replaced the 1988 Law on Arbitration which Royal Decree 636/1993 was in line with, i.e. the latter was supplementary to CAS and included specific references to the 1988 Law; once the 1988 Law on Arbitration had been abrogated, it was clear that new provisions on the arbitration system were necessary.

15 The aggregation of claims was feasible but it depended on a group of consumers actually requesting arbitration together or a consumer association doing so on their behalf; however, the 1993 Royal Decree made no mention of consumer arbitration boards bringing claims arising from the same event together. See Marcos Francisco, Diana, *El arbitraje de consumo y sus retos*, 2010, pp. 264-265.

16 See Articles 57(1) of Law 44/2006 and 2(2) of Royal Decree 231/2007. The latter is broader than the former in that it excludes from CAS tort liability arising out of the other exclusions indicated, such as events that show signs of crime. This exclusion contradicts Law 44/2006, a contradiction which is not in line with the principle of hierarchy of norms, not to mention the principle of consumer protection. See Pita Ponte, José María, "La implementación del Real Decreto 231/2008, de 15 de febrero, por el que se regula el Sistema Arbitral de Consumo", in González Pillado, Esther (Coord.), *Arbitraje y mediación en materia de consumo*, 2012), p. 26.

17 However, counterclaiming is feasible, a fact which is strongly criticized. See Pita Ponte, José María, n. 16 above, pp. 24-25 and pp. 40-43; Richard González, Manuel, "Análisis crítico del sistema y los procedimientos arbitrales y de mediación en España. Especial atención a la reforma de la Ley de Arbitraje (Ley 11/2011) y al proyecto de Ley de Mediación de 2011", in Richard González, Manuel, Riaño Brun, Iñaki and Rifá Soler, José María (eds.), *Estudios sobre arbitraje de consumo*, 2011, pp. 133-134.

18 Council Directive 93/13/ECC of 5 April 1993 on unfair terms in consumer contracts [1993] OJ L 95/29. Annex to Directive 93/13/ECC includes within the terms referred to in Art. 3(3)1, i.e. those that are null and void, terms '(q) excluding or hindering the consumer's right to take legal action or exercise any other legal remedy, particularly by requiring the consumer to take disputes exclusively to arbitration not covered by legal provisions, unduly restricting the evidence available to him or imposing on him a burden of proof which, according to the applicable law, should lie with another party to the contract'. This provision has been transposed to Article 90 of the 2007 Law on Consumer Protection.

19 Apart from specific sector-based arbitration systems, most consumer disputes are submitted to CAS.

20 At least, this is the official description of the system. An in-depth reading of Royal Decree 231/2008 reveals a different picture, inasmuch as many administrative formalities, *e.g.* concerning notification, are applicable; the more administrative formalities, the more grounds there are for challenging the arbitral awards. See criticism in Pita Ponte, José María, n. 16 above, p. 22 and p. 32. As to the system's being free of charge, parties to the arbitration proceedings only have to pay for gathering their own proof, as evidence requested *ex officio* is paid for by the state. See Article 45(3) of the Royal Decree 231/2008.

21 If several Consumer Arbitration Boards cover the same geographical area, the smallest is deemed competent. Should a geographical limitation be included in the public submission issued to CAS by the respective business, the Consumer Arbitration Board to which the business makes the submission is competent unless the business has made submissions to several boards, in which case the consumer can choose. See Article 8 of Royal Decree 231/2008.

22 Ibid, Article 11(1).

23 In the light of the neat separation between the administrative bodies responsible for handling CAS and the arbitrators, this Commission of Consumer Arbitration Board power is to be criticized. See Pita Ponte, José María, n. 16 above, pp. 34-37.

24 Compliance with requirements and qualifications is monitored by the president of the respective consumer arbitration board. See Article 17 of Royal Decree 231/2008.

25 See for a thorough account of all arguments contra and in favour of this type of arbitration Strong, SI, *Class, Mass, and Collective Arbitration in National and International Law*, 2013, *passim*.

26 For example, the Barcelona Provincial High Court rendered null and void an arbitral award ordering RENFE, the national railway service, to include some information on short distance train tickets. The court understood that the consumer did not have standing, as she was not claiming an individual right but a diffuse interest. See the *Audiencia Provincial (Sección 14ª) de* Barcelona judgment of 3 November 2003 (AC 2003, 1763).

27 See among others, Marcos Francisco, Diana, "¿Es posible la tutela de intereses colectivos y difusos en el arbitraje de consumo? El arbitraje colectivo de consumo en el Real Decreto 231/2008, de 15 de febrero, regulador del Sistema Arbitral de Consumo", *Revista Boliviana de Derecho* 11, 2011, p. 188.

28 Article 56 of Royal Decree 231/2008. (SI Strong translation. See n. 3 above)

29 The provision read as follows: 'If those injured by an event are a group of consumers or users whose members are determined or easily determinable, the standing to pursue the protection of those collective interests pertains to consumer associations, legal entities whose main objective is consumer protection and groups of the consumers affected by the said event'. (Author translation).

30 See Stadler, Astrid, "Collective Action as an Efficient Means for the Enforcement of European Competition Law", in Basedow, Jürgen, *Private Enforcement of EC Competition Law*, 2007, p. 211.

31 The number is expected to increase as a result of the Commission's Recommendation 'on common principles for injunctive and compensatory collective redress mechanisms in the Member States concerning violations of rights granted under Union Law' [C(2013) 3539 final].

32 Taking this approach, see Cappalli, Roberto and Consolo, Claudio, "Class Action for Continental Europe? A Preliminary Inquiry", *Temple International and Comparative Law Journal* 6, 1992, p. 217.

33 Such terms originate in Brazil's Consumer Protection Code, but the discussion about the meaning of collective and diffuse interests is still ongoing. See, among others, Bujosa Vadell, Lorenzo, *La protección jurisdiccional de los intereses de grupo*, 1995, pp. 59-62; Gutiérrez de Cabiedes e Hidalgo de Cabiedes, Pablo, *La tutela jurisdiccional de los intereses supraindividuales: colectivos y difusos*, 1999, *passim*; Pérez Ragone, Álvaro J. D., "¿Necesitamos los procesos colectivos? En torno a la justificación y legitimidad jurídica de la tutela de intereses multisubjetivos", *Revista de Derecho Procesal*, 2005, pp. 618-629.

34 See Carballo Piñeiro, Laura, n. 2 above.

35 See Carballo Fidalgo, Marta, *La protección del consumidor frente a las cláusulas no negociadas individualmente. Disciplina legal y tratamiento jurisprudencial de las cláusulas abusivas*, 2013, p. 243; Carballo Piñeiro, Laura, "La tipicidad de las acciones colectivas en el ordenamiento jurídico español", *Justicia. Revista de derecho procesal*, 2007, p. 63.

36 Royal Legislative Decree 1/2007 consolidating the 1984 Law on Consumer Protection and other consumer laws has reduced the number of these laws, of which there were over twenty-five. Some still remain, and include rules on collective actions, such as Articles 32 and 33 of Law 3/1991 of 10 January on Unfair Competition, and Article 6 of Law 34/1988 of 11 November on Advertising.

37 This provision specifically refers to Article 11 LEC inasmuch as this is also a rule about the standing to bring legitimate consumers' collective and diffuse rights before court. However, it also applies to any other person entitled to initiate collective actions in accordance with any consumer law dealing with this issue.

38 Article 221(1) LEC addresses the following cases: (1st) should the judgment decide on a redress collective action, the court must individually specify the affected consumers if possible; if not, it must at least enumerate all relevant elements to make their identification feasible at the enforcement stage; (2nd) if the judgment renders an act wrongful, usually providing for injunctive relief, the court must establish whether it is binding on third parties; (3rd) should individu-

al consumers have joined the collective proceeding, the judgment must reach a decision on those claims in addition to the collective claim presented by the respective consumer association. Article 221(2) refers to injunctive collective actions and the courts' power to make the judgment public by its preferred means and at the defendants' expense.

39 In fact, and in order to promote collective actions, Article 37(d) of Royal Legislative Decree 1/2007 laid down the right of consumer associations' to legal aid. Against this background, only some collective cases have made their way to court over the last thirty years, mostly injunctive actions; despite having been legally addressed in Spain, collective redress actions are rare in practice due to their cost and the difficulty involved first, in legally understanding what is needed to proceed with the action, and second, in gathering together group members and evidence and administering enforcement if the action is successful. However, an increase can be observed in recent years as a result of the economic downturn. See, addressing some cases, Carballo Piñeiro, Laura, "La construcción del mercado interior y el recurso colectivo de consumidores", in Esteban de la Rosa, Fernando (ed.), *La protección del consumidor en dos espacios de integración: Europa y América. Una perspectiva de Derecho internacional, europeo y comparado*, 2015, pp. 1055-1088.

40 See Article 34 of Royal Decree 231/2008.

41 See, among others, Cubillo López, Ignacio J., "El procedimiento para la tutela arbitral de consumidores", in Cubillo López, Ignacio J. (ed.), *Cuestiones actuales sobre la protección de los consumidores: tutela penal, civil y arbitral*, 2010, p. 292.

42 Because of this limitation, injunctive actions for consumer protection cannot be submitted to consumer arbitration either, inasmuch as they are binding on third parties and this *res iudicata* and preclusive effect cannot be granted by this type of arbitration.

43 See Article 57 of Royal Decree 231/2008.

44 See Marcos Francisco, Diana, n. 27 above, p. 191.

45 See Article 256(1)(6) LEC.

46 See Marcos Francisco, Diana, n. 27 above, p. 192.

47 See Article 22(1)(c) of the Law on Consumer protection. This law is now included in Royal Legislative Decree 1/2007, whose Title II, Book I, deals with the rights to stand, to counsel and participation, and the legal regime for consumer associations. Chapter II of Title II set up a State Registry of Consumer Associations under the supervision of the Spanish Agency for Consumption, Food Safety and Nutrition (Articles 33-36). To register, an association's main objective has to be the pursuit of consumer protection (Article 23) and it must not incur in the prohibitions laid down in Article 27, such as not being a for-profit corporation. Further requirements such as the length of time that the association has been operating, the number of stakeholders and activity programmes are included in other pieces of legislation [Article 33(2)].

48 See Marcos Francisco, Diana, n. 27 above, p. 195.

49 It should be noted that CAS involves consumer matters that arise out of trading in Spain, i.e. regardless of the parties' nationality or domicile, as that there is no other indication in Royal Decree 231/2008. See Cubillo López, Ignacio, n 41 above, p. 290.

50 [2004] OJ L 364/1.

51 Article 24 of Royal Decree 231/2008.

52 See ibid, second paragraph of Article 24. See also the Recommendation regarding the interpretation of Article II, paragraph 2, and Article VII, paragraph 1, of the Convention on the Recognition and Enforcement of Foreign Arbitral Awards, New York, 10 June 1958, adopted by the United Nations Commission on International Trade Law at its thirty-ninth session on 7 July 2006.

53 Unfortunately, some professionals and businesses do not honour arbitral awards, despite having publically offered to submit to the system, and Royal Decree 231/2008 does not address this problem; when professionals and businesses take advantage of CAS in this way, consumers are forced to initiate enforcement proceedings. See Pita Ponte, José María, n. 16 above, pp. 22-24. Further criticism concerns the fact that many businesses fail to establish their own claims services because of the existence of CAS. See Richard González, Manuel, n. 17 above, p. 74 and p. 89.

54 Giving rise to an ex post submission agreement, in S.I. Strong's words, n. 3 above, p. 498.

55 Article 58(2) of Royal Decree 231/2008. The competent board and any other interested persons, such as the representative consumer association requesting for this type of arbitration, have to be notified that this type of arbitration has not been accepted by the professional or business in question.

56 See Marcos Francisco, Diana, n. 27 above, p. 196.

57 See Article 59(1) Royal Decree 231/2008. It is important to note that, in addition to the Official Journal of the Spanish Parliament, the *Boletín Oficial del Estado*, every autonomous region and province in Spain publishes an Official Journal.

58 See below Section 3.D.

59 Ibid, Article 61.

60 Ibid, Article 60.

61 Raising this issue, see Strong, SI, n. 3 above, at 502-503.

62 The collective action is being handled by the *Juzgado de lo Mercantil* No. 11, Madrid, *juicio verbal* No. 471/2010, and involves 15,000 consumers who are represented by the consumer association ADICAE, although the key reason for the delay lies with the 101 defendants.

63 The European Central Bank set the interest rate at which it lent money to commercial banks very low, but Spanish mortgage lenders had not been taking advantage of this, due to what are known as 'floor clauses', the minimum interest rates that banks included in their mortgage contracts. This is why many consumers do not want to wait for the judgment on the collective action, because meanwhile they have to comply with the actual terms of the contract, including those whose nullity is being requested. To make the situation even more complicated, the Supreme Court judgment of 2013 ruled that these terms were null and void, but argued that the declaration only had *ex nunc* effects, i.e. the terms must be removed from contracts, but banks did not have to give back the money already paid on their account. The Supreme Court changed this doctrine in its judgment No 139/2015 of 9 March and clarified that banks do have to give back the money already collected, but only from 9 May 2013.

64 See Request for a preliminary ruling from the *Juzgado de lo Mercantil* No 9, Barcelona (Spain) lodged on 11 August 2014, *Jorge Sales Sinués v Caixabank, S.A.* (Case C-381/14). The opinion of Advocate General Szpunar on this case and the case of Yossouf Drame Ba v Catalunya Caixa, S.A. (Case C-385/14) was delivered on 14 January 2016, indicating that 'the staying, on grounds of civil procedural precedence, of individual actions brought in parallel to a collective action for an injunction pending the delivery of a final judgment concluding the

collective proceedings — provided that such a stay is neither mandatory nor automatic, and provided that the consumer concerned is able to dissociate herself from the collective action' is admissible. Should the CJEU follow this opinion, Spanish legislation ought to be updated to make opt-out rights available.

65 See below Section 3.D.

66 Article 58(2) of the Royal Decree 231/2008.

67 Ibid, Article 59(2).

68 Ibid, Article 49(2).

69 Ibid, Article 48(2) provides settlement agreements with preclusive effects. See Marcos Francisco, Diana, n. 27 above, p. 197.

70 Article 59(3) of Royal Decree 231/2008.

71 Ibid, Article 49. The arbitral tribunal can extend this period for two months, subject to the agreement of the parties to the arbitration.

72 Ibid, Article 62.

73 Highlighting the lack of consumer interest in these proceedings, see Richard González, Manuel, n. 17 above, p. 148.

74 See Domínguez Plata, Jesús, "El arbitraje colectivo", in Esteban de la Rosa, Fernando, and Orozco Pardo, Guillermo (eds.), *Mediación y arbitraje de consumo: una perspectiva española, europea y comparada,* 2010, p. 161; Gascón Inchausti, Fernando, *Tutela judicial de los consumidores y transacciones colectivas,* 2010, p. 177; Marín López, Manuel Jesús, n. 3 above, p. 17.

75 See Section 3.A. above.

76 See Strong, SI, "From Class to Collective: The De-Americanization of Class Arbitration", *Arbitration International*, 26, 2010, pp. 524-525.

77 This topic has been thoroughly studied by ibid; Strong, S. I., "The Sounds of Silence: Are U.S. Arbitrators Creating Internationally Enforceable Awards When Ordering Class Arbitration in Cases of Contractual Silence or Ambiguity?", *Michigan Journal of International Law*, 30, 2009, p. 1017, available at **http://ssrn.com/abstract=1359353.**

78 See Section 3.B. above.

79 See Strong, S. I., n. 76 above, pp. 528-547.

80 See Nagareda, Richard A., "Administering Adequacy in Class Representation", *Texas Law Review*, 82, 2003, pp. 324-330.

81 See Article 39(2) of Royal Decree 231/2008.

82 See Marcos Francisco, Diana, above n. 27, p. 199.

83 CAS is a cost-free system provided by the state; however, the parties to arbitration bear the costs of gathering proof at least. These can be particularly high when it comes to collective consumer arbitration, to say nothing of the fact that the representative claimant is acting on behalf of third parties. Royal Decree 231/2008 does not address these issues, as it does not establish any special competence for the arbitration tribunal or the fees payable taking into account the work to be done. Establishing a fund would be a good solution.

84 As the LEC does not tackle this issue, there is nothing in the Spanish legal system to oppose setting up an opt-out system. However, Principles 21 to 24 of the European Commission Recommendation on common principles for injunctive and compensatory collective redress mechanisms in the Member States concerning violations of rights granted under Union Law [C(2013) 3539 final] aim to severely curtail the opt-out system. This is to be criticized, though,

inasmuch as the inability to present one's case can be procedurally supplemented without infringing the right to a fair trial, and the opt-out system already works well in a number of countries.

85 To this end, the representative claimant ought to be entitled to negotiate on behalf of absent group members and the arbitration tribunal's approval ought to be made dependent on the examination of fraudulent conduct.

Chapter 8

Mass Arbitrations in International Investment Cases

Introductory Remarks

Eloïse M. Obadia*

Until a few years ago, the question of whether there could be 'mass' arbitrations in investment arbitration was non-existent. The question arose at the end of 2006, when more than 180,000 claimants presented a request for arbitration before the International Centre for Settlement of Investment Disputes (ICSID) against Argentina.[1] The ICSID Secretary-General registered the request five months later, in February 2007, under the name *Giovanna a Beccara and others v Argentine Republic*.[2] The majority of the tribunal's decision on preliminary issues of jurisdiction and admissibility was issued more than four years later, on 4 August 2011, and was followed by a dissenting opinion of the arbitrator appointed by Argentina in October 2011.[3]

Since then, mass arbitration has been the subject of numerous discussions and further decisions such as the ones issued in the two other "Italian bondholder" cases, namely *Ambiente Ufficio S.p.A. and others v Argentine Republic* (ICSID Case No. ARB/08/9)[4] and *Giovanni Alemanni and others v Argentine Republic* (ICSID Case No. ARB/07/8).[5] Nevertheless, some questions related to the subject remain unanswered, and the answers that have been proposed reflect the different approaches and reasonings that have been adopted in relation to mass arbitration.

In this paper, I will touch upon two questions: the relevance of the terminology used, and the nature of the issues raised by these types of proceedings.

1 TERMINOLOGY

The first obvious set of questions relate to terminology: What is mass arbitration? Is there any difference between mass arbitration and multiparty arbitration? Where does multiparty arbitration stop and mass arbitration begin?

As already discussed by the other contributors, mass arbitration is derived from the American concept of class action litigation which is defined as a lawsuit that allows a large number of people with a common interest in a matter to sue or be sued as a group. It is a vehicle generally used when a number of people have suffered the same or similar injuries, but the injuries being relatively minor, they might not pursue legal redress on their own. When applied to arbitration under US law, 'class arbitration' consists in proceedings in which individual claimants assert claims in arbitration on

* Partner, Derains & Gharavi PLLC. The views expressed in this article are the views of the author and do not necessarily reflect the views of Derains & Gharavi International or its clients. The author wishes to thank Clara Maghani for her assistance on this article.

behalf of a defined class of unnamed, similarly situated claimants.[6] This is closer to what has been called mass arbitration in the context of investor-State disputes, and yet it remains different. Indeed, in mass arbitrations in international investment cases, the representative element is missing in the sense that one individual claimant or several claimants cannot initiate a proceeding for an undetermined number of unidentified claimants. Under Article 25(1) of the ICSID Convention and under other arbitration rules as well as under the treaties that form the basis for the parties' consent, each claimant must have consented to arbitration. Therefore, the number of claimants must be established as well as their identity. Mass arbitration in such context is a proceeding initiated by unrelated individuals and juridical persons having similar claims arising from the same basic conduct of the State.

However, as underlined by the *Abaclat* tribunal, there may be some features of a representative action in an investor-State mass arbitration proceeding, in particular with respect to its conduct:

> Although Claimants made the individual and conscious choice of participating to the arbitration, their participation is thereafter limited to a passive participation in the sense that a third party, TFA, represents their interests and makes on their behalf all the decisions relating to the conduct of the proceedings. The high number of Claimants further makes it impossible for the representative to take into account individual interests of individual Claimants, and rather limits the proceedings to the defense of interests common to the entire group of Claimants.[7]

In fact, beyond a certain number of claimants, it is difficult to imagine a proceeding where each individual claimant would have to be consulted for the appointment of the arbitrators, or the procedural strategic choices, or the review of the draft pleadings. These representative aspects of the mass arbitration proceedings are further discussed by Luca G. Radicati di Brozolo in his contribution entitled "Representative aspects of 'mass claims' proceedings in investor-State arbitration."

As summarized by the *Abaclat* tribunal, these types of proceedings initiated by thousands of claimants are a "hybrid kind of collective proceedings, in the sense that it starts as aggregate proceedings, but then continues with features similar to representative proceedings due to the high number of Claimants involved."[8] The *Ambiente* tribunal agreed with the *Abaclat* tribunal in considering that these proceedings cannot be qualified as class actions;[9] however, it rejected the label of 'mass claims' or 'collective proceedings' to describe, instead, the situation it was confronted with as a 'multi-party proceeding.'[10]

It must be specified, however, that where the *Abaclat* case involved 180,000 claimants, the *Ambiente* tribunal was facing 90 claimants.[11] Accordingly, it is understandable for the *Ambiente* tribunal as well as the *Alemanni* tribunal, which was confronted with 74 claimants, to consider that the proceeding concerned was not a mass arbitration. While the distinction between 180,000 or even 60,000 claimants,[12] on the one hand, and 90, on the other hand, is clear, the *Ambiente* tribunal did not take the risk to specify when a claim would reach the critical level of a 'mass.'[13] The *Ambiente* tribunal and other tribunals that have dealt with this issue cannot be criticized for not defining such a level. This is because this 'terminological imbroglio'[14] (to borrow the term used by the *Ambiente* tribunal) has in any event no impact on the crucial issue of whether the relevant tribunal can hear the case as initiated. In other words, the number of claimants is irrelevant to the pivotal question of whether the tribunal can hear the claims brought on a joint or collective basis. The issue arises as soon as there is an unrelated second claimant. Therefore, this 'mass' level does not need to be clearly defined. This does not mean, however, that the mass aspect of a claim does not have any implications that merit consideration. As developed by Luca G. Radicati di Brozolo in his contribution, there are due process considerations as well as special procedural mechanisms that are to be taken into account, in particular for the assessment of evidence.

In a nutshell, as stated by the *Alemanni* tribunal:

> The present Tribunal sees no advantage whatsoever in entering into a battle of terminology. None of the terms that have been bandied about in argument is to be found in the two treaties that govern this Arbitration or in the applicable procedural rules, and none of them has a recognized and defined technical meaning in international law.[15]

Rather than a question of terminology, it is a question of consent, more specifically the respondent's consent facing multiple claimants. As the *Alemanni* tribunal concluded: "In a BIT case, therefore, where the consent of the respondent State is in issue, the question for consideration remains simply: on the proper interpretation of the BIT, has the respondent, or has it not, given a consent which is wide enough in scope to cover the proceedings brought (as in this case) by the multiple group of co-claimants?" This brings me to my second question: What are the issues linked to multiparty arbitration?

2 ISSUES LINKED TO MULTIPARTY ARBITRATION

The main question linked to multiparty arbitration involving unrelated claimants is whether the respondent's written consent to arbitration encompasses the possibility for the tribunal to hear the case in a single proceeding. The correlated question is whether this is an issue of jurisdiction, admissibility, or simply a matter related to the conduct of the procedure. These topics are addressed by Carolyn Lamm in her contribution that follows. For introductory purposes, three questions will be addressed: how were multiparty arbitrations treated in prior cases, what is the analysis of the Italian bondholder tribunals and why objections to one single proceedings have recently been successful?

Prior Cases

It is worth noting that multiparty arbitration is not new under the ICSID Convention. Authors and tribunals often cite as examples the *Klöckner*[16] or the *Goetz v Burundi* cases.[17] Nonetheless, mass arbitrations — such as the Italian bondholder cases — are not comparable to *Klöckner* and *Goetz*. In these latter cases, the claimants were either related entities or individuals and the dispute concerned the same investment or project. Particularly, the *Klöckner* case involved a German company and its subsidiaries with respect to agreements related to the delivery and management of a fertilizer plant. The Goetz case concerned six Belgian investors owning a company incorporated in Burundi involved in the production and marketing of precious metals. On the other hand, mass arbitrations involve unrelated claimants with distinct investments.

Prior cases comparable to the Italian bondholder proceedings include: *Bernardus Henricus Funnekotter and others v Republic of Zimbabwe*,[18] involving 13 Dutch investors owning different large commercial farms that were expropriated by Zimbabwe; *Bayview Irrigation District and others v United Mexican States*,[19] concerning 46 claimants in relation to the use of the waters of the Rio Grande river; *Piero Foresti, Laura de Carli and others v Republic of South Africa*,[20] involving 11 claimants — individuals and entities from two different nationalities (Italian and Luxembourgish) — against South Africa in relation to their mineral rights; *Alasdair Ross Anderson and others v Republic of Costa Rica*,[21] concerning 137 Canadians victims of a scheme organized by two brothers in Costa Rica. The claimants alleged that Costa Rica had failed to provide proper vigilance and governmental regulatory supervision over the national financial system.

In these cases, the respondent either did not raise any objection to the fact that there were multiple claimants joined in one single proceeding or agreed to have the individual claims heard in one proceeding for preliminary objection purposes. Those objections were upheld.[22] Therefore, the tribunals' decisions in those cases do not bring light on the scope of respondent's consent contained in the relevant bilateral or multilateral treaty (*'BIT'* or *'MIT'*). In the *Noble Energy v Ecuador* case, the tribunal examined the question of the respondents' scope of consent as the proceeding involved the joinder of three disputes. The tribunal considered that it was not a matter of jurisdiction but a matter relating to the conduct of the procedure. It further sought inspiration from the law and practice on consolidation to conclude that by analogy, the disputes submitted to it could be heard in one single proceeding.[23] Although informative, this case is once again distinct from mass arbitrations as the claimants were related (MachalaPower was a subsidiary of Noble Energy), and as underlined by the tribunal: "there is an obvious interdependence between the different disputes submitted to this Tribunal. They stem from the same facts, the same overall economic transaction, and the same measures. Moreover, the measures complained of and the relief sought under the different instruments offer significant similarities."[24]

The Italian Bondholder Cases

Therefore, the question of respondent's scope of consent with respect to multiparty proceedings was first tackled by the three tribunals that dealt with the Italian bondholder cases. However, the question is not definitively solved as these tribunals took different approaches. In *Abaclat*, the tribunal considered that the mass aspect of the proceeding was a question of admissibility.[25] According to that tribunal, the relevant question was whether claimants' claims were identical or sufficiently homogeneous:

> The only relevant question is whether Claimants have homogeneous rights of compensation for a homogeneous damage caused to them by potential homogeneous breaches by Argentina of homogeneous obligations provided for in the BIT.[26]

In *Ambiente*, the tribunal did not enter into the discussion of the distinction between jurisdiction and admissibility and reviewed the jurisdictional requirements. It considered that the question of number of claimants was one related to the manageability of the proceedings and due process.[27] As for the question of the homogeneity of the claims, the tribunal refused to give abstract conclusions but instead considered that the claims were sufficiently linked for them to be treated, and decided upon, by the tribunal in one single multiparty arbitration.[28]

In *Alemanni*, the tribunal treated the question as a jurisdictional one and considered that the distinction between jurisdiction and admissibility was irrelevant for the issues before it. The tribunal stated that what mattered under the ICSID Convention and the relevant bilateral treaty[29] was a substantive unity in the dispute submitted to arbitration.[30] The tribunal further considered that to decide whether there was a single dispute, it would have to determine the actual rights of the claimants and the actual effect on those rights of Argentina's conduct. It concluded that the substance of that jurisdictional issue was closely entwined with the factual and legal substantive disagreement between the parties and that accordingly the objection had to be joined to the merits.[31] Since the case was discontinued for lack of payment of the advances required,[32] we will not know the final outcome.

Given the disparities in the different approaches, it is difficult to draw clear conclusions on the question of whether a tribunal can hear multiple claims in a single proceeding when the claimants are unrelated, when there is no unity of investment and when the respondent objects to this setting. It seems that (i) all three tribunals agree that there is no additional consent needed from the respondent besides the written consent given in the relevant treaty. Although in practice, the reasoning followed by the tribunals seems to lead to the requirement of a double consent by the respondent State when it is concluded that there is lack of single dispute or homogeneity of the claims; (ii) two out of the three tribunals considered that it is a jurisdictional question related to the scope of consent; and (iii) two out of the three tribunals considered that there is a need for a homogeneity of the claims (rather than a single dispute).

Successful Objections

It is interesting to note that concomitantly or subsequently to these decisions, respondent States seem to have given more attention to this question, and when they objected to the joining of the different claims, they were successful. Three examples illustrate this trend.

First, in 2012, the ICSID Secretary-General refused to register a request for arbitration brought by two unrelated foreign companies that had lost national FM radio-broadcasting frequencies after a tender procedure organized by Hungary. The requesting parties had filed a joint request for arbitration with the Centre. Hungary, however, submitted several communications objecting to the registration of the request. The Secretary-General notified the parties that "[i]n the absence of consent by all disputing parties to join disputes relating to manifestly separate investments, the Secretary-General cannot proceed to register the Request for Arbitration as submitted to the Centre." The requesting parties then proceeded to submit two separate amended requests: one on behalf of investors in Danubius Radio and a second one of behalf of the investors in Slàger Rádió Műsorzolgáltató Zrt.[33] Following the reasoning of the Italian bondholder tribunals, the absence of homogeneity of the claims or the existence of distinct disputes justified the refusal to maintain a single proceeding. In addition, it should be specified that contrary to the Italian bondholder cases, these claims were based on three different bilateral investment treaties with Hungary (the United Kingdom, the Netherlands and Switzerland). As advanced by Zachary Douglas in his presentation, in cases where the unrelated claimants bring a joint claim based on different treaties, one cannot talk of one consent, but must note the existence of different written consents. Consequently, the respondent State is entitled to choose a different arbitrator for each claim, thereby procedurally refusing their joinder. This is what occurred in the second example described below.

Second, in 2013, the Permanent Court of Arbitration endorsed the Czech Republic's refusal to allow claims by 10 foreign investors to proceed under a single arbitral proceeding. The 10 claimants had filed a joint request for arbitration complaining of various measures allegedly affecting their investments on the photovoltaic (pv) sector in the Czech Republic. The request had been brought on the basis of the Energy Charter Treaty and Czech bilateral investment treaties with five different countries (the Netherlands, Germany, Cyprus, Luxembourg and the United Kingdom).[34] Here again, for the most parts, the claimants were unrelated, the investments, claims and disputes distinct as well as the source of consent. The issue is whether the Czech Republic should have appointed one arbitrator and raise the objection to the joinder of the claims once the tribunal was constituted, as argued by Luca G. Radicati di Brozolo or whether the Czech Republic was right in appointing different arbitrators for each claim as endorsed by the PCA and explained by Zachary Douglas. In any event, the result might have been the same (i.e., rejection of the joinder) as reflected in the third example below.

Third, in 2015, an UNCITRAL tribunal declined jurisdiction over an arbitration initiated by 22 Turkish claimants against Turkmenistan.[35] The majority of the tribunal considered that the question was a jurisdictional one that went to the issue of consent. The claims being entirely unrelated, raised by unrelated claimants, and in relation to different unrelated investments, they could not be heard jointly. The tribunal further specified that the claimants had not met their burden of proof, even on a prima facie basis, that Turkmenistan had adopted an anti-Turkish policy upon the coming to the office of President Berdimuhamedow in December 2006.

3 CONCLUSION

Rather than trying to solve legal inconsistencies, I suggest to offer a practical approach to the question. The issue arises when two unrelated claimants or more (whichever the number is) file a joint request for arbitration and the respondent State objects to this joinder. The legal question is: does the State's consent (in the bilateral or multilateral treaty) encompass joint claims? The practical answer is: the more elements of commonality exist, the higher the chances are that a tribunal will consider that it has jurisdiction. For instance, if the source of consent is identical (one BIT or MIT relied upon by the investors), the measure affecting the investors is the same, and the type of investment is similar, it is highly likely that a tribunal would consider that it could hear the claims in a single proceeding. On the contrary, if the investors rely on different BITs or MITs, the investments present significant variations and the measures are not exactly the same, then it is highly likely that the tribunal would refuse to hear the claims jointly. As to the question of the choice made by the respondent

State to accept or refuse the single proceeding, this is a strategic question that varies from one situation to another and could be the subject of another conference! The advice is to weigh the pros and the cons on a case-by-case basis rather than systematically refuse single proceedings only to create obstacles to the claimants.

NOTES

1 *Abaclat and Others v Argentine Republic* (ICSID Case No. ARB/07/5), Decision on Jurisdiction and Admissibility dated August 4, 2011, ¶¶1 and 98, available at http://www.italaw.com/sites/default/files/case-documents/ita0236.pdf ('*Abaclat*').

2 *Abaclat*, ¶641.

3 See ICSID website, Procedural details of *Abaclat and Others v Argentine Republic* (ICSID Case No. ARB/07/5), https://icsid.worldbank.org/apps/ICSIDWEB/cases/Pages/casedetail.aspx?CaseNo=ARB/07/5&tab=PRD.

4 *Ambiente Ufficio S.p.A. and others v Argentine Republic* (ICSID Case No. ARB/08/9), Decision on Jurisdiction and Admissibility dated February 8, 2013, available at http://www.italaw.com/sites/default/files/case-documents/italaw1276.pdf ('*Ambiente*').

5 *Giovanni Alemanni and others v Argentine Republic* (ICSID Case No. ARB/07/8), Decision on Jurisdiction and Admissibility dated November 17, 2014, available at http://www.italaw.com/sites/default/files/case-documents/italaw4061.pdf ('*Alemanni*').

6 Kent Rachael, String Marik, "Availability of Class Arbitration Under U.S. Law," in Albert Jan van den Berg (ed), *Legitimacy: Myths, Realities, Challenges, ICCA Congress Series*, Vol. 18, 2015, p. 853.

7 *Abaclat*, ¶487.

8 *Abaclat*, ¶488. The Tribunal defined the aggregate proceedings as individual claims arising out of the same fact pattern and assigned to the same judge (see ¶483).

9 *Ambiente*, ¶116.

10 *Ambiente*, ¶¶121-122.

11 *Ambiente*, ¶113. The request was filed by 119 claimants and the number dropped to 90 claimants after the exchange offer proposed by Argentina in 2010.

12 *Abaclat*, ¶216. The request was filed by 180,000 claimants and the number dropped to 60,000 claimants after the exchange offer proposed by Argentina in 2010.

13 *Ambiente*, ¶¶119-120.

14 *Ambiente*, ¶122.

15 *Alemanni*, ¶267.

16 *Klöckner Industrie-Anlagen GmbH, Klöckner Belge, S.A. and Klöckner Handelsmaatschappij B.V. v United Republic of Cameroon and Société Camerounaise des Engrais* (ICSID Case No. ARB/81/2), Award dated October 21, 1983, 111 Journal du droit international 409, ('Klöckner').

17 *Antoine Goetz and others v Republic of Burundi* (ICSID Case No. ARB/95/3), Award dated February 10, 1999, available at https://icsid.worldbank.org/ICSID/FrontServlet?requestType=CasesRH&actionVal=showDoc&docId=DC537_Fr&caseId=C151, ('Goetz').

18 *Bernardus Henricus Funnekotter and others v Republic of Zimbabwe* (ICSID Case No. ARB/05/6), Award dated April 22, 2009, available at http://www.italaw.com/sites/default/files/case-documents/ita0349.pdf.

19 *Bayview Irrigation District and others v United Mexican States* (ICSID Case No. ARB(AF)/05/1), Award dated June 19, 2007, available at http://www.italaw.com/sites/default/files/case-documents/ita0076_0.pdf, ('*Bayview*').

20 *Piero Foresti, Laura de Carli and others v Republic of South Africa* (ICSID Case No. ARB(AF)/07/1), Award dated August 4, 2010, available at https://icsid.worldbank.org/ICSID/FrontServlet?requestType=CasesRH&actionVal=showDoc&docId=DC1651_En&caseId=C90.

21 *Alasdair Ross Anderson and others v Republic of Costa Rica* (ICSID Case No. ARB(AF)/07/3), Award dated May 19, 2010, available at http://www.italaw.com/sites/default/files/case-documents/ita0031.pdf.

22 In the *Bayview* case, Mexico's consent to having the tribunal's jurisdiction determined for all claims in one single proceeding was indicated in Mexico's Memorial on Jurisdiction, ¶126, available at: http://www.economia.gob.mx/files/comunidad_negocios/solucion_controversias/inversionista-estado/casos_concluidos/Bayview/esc_excep_mxbv_060419_ing.pdf.

23 *Noble Energy, Inc. and MachalaPower Cia. Ltda. v Republic of Ecuador and Consejo Nacional de Electricidad* (ICSID Case No. ARB/05/12), Decision on Jurisdiction dated March 5, 2008, ¶¶ 185-207, available at http://www.italaw.com/sites/default/files/case-documents/ita0563.pdf, ('Noble Energy').

24 *Noble Energy*, ¶192.

25 *Abaclat*, ¶¶491-492.

26 *Abaclat*, ¶541.

27 *Ambiente*, ¶¶147-151.

28 *Ambiente*, ¶¶152-163.

29 Agreement between the Argentine Republic and the Italian Republic on the Reciprocal Promotion and Protection of Investments signed in Buenos Aires on May 22, 1990, available at http://investmentpolicyhub.unctad.org/Download/TreatyFile/99.

30 *Alemanni*, ¶287, ¶292.

31 *Alemanni*, ¶293.

32 See ICSID website, Procedural details of *Giovanni Alemanni and others v Argentine Republic* (ICSID Case No. ARB/07/8), https://icsid.worldbank.org/apps/ICSIDWEB/cases/Pages/casedetail.aspx?CaseNo=ARB/07/8&tab=PRD.

33 *Accession Mezzanine Capital L.P. and Danubius Kereskedöház Vagyonkezelö Zrt. v Hungary* (ICSID Case No. ARB/12/3), Decision on Respondent's Objection under Arbitration Rule 41(5), dated January 16, 2013, ¶9, available at http://www.italaw.com/sites/default/files/case-documents/italaw1292.pdf; and *Emmis International Holding B.V., Emmis Radio Operating B.V., MEM Magyar Electronic Media Kereskedelmi Szolgáltató Kft. v Hungary* (ICSID Case No. ARB/12/2), Decision on Respondent's Objection under ICSID Arbitration Rule 41(5), March 11, 2013, ¶9, available at http://www.italaw.com/sites/default/files/case-documents/italaw1239_0.pdf.

34 See *IA Reporter*, "Following PCA decision, Czech Republic thwarts move by solar investors to sue in single arbitral proceeding; meanwhile Spain sees new solar claim at ICSID," January 1, 2014, available at www.iareporter.com.

35 *Erhas Dis Ticaret Ltd. Sti and others v Turkmenistan*, Award dated June 8, 2015, unpublished. See *IA Reporter*, "An UNCITRAL tribunal declines jurisdiction over a joint treaty claim brought against Turkmenistan by a series of unrelated claimants," June 23, 2015, available at **www.iareporter.com.**

Chapter 9

Mass Claims in Investment Arbitration

Jurisdiction and Admissibility

Carolyn B. Lamm,* Eckhard R. Hellbeck and Onur Saka

Abaclat and others v Argentina, the ICSID arbitration brought under the Italy-Argentina Bilateral Investment Treaty ("BIT") in 2006 by tens of thousands of Italian retail holders of Argentine sovereign bonds, has become known as a landmark case for addressing novel issues in international investment arbitration.[1] In its 2011 Decision on Jurisdiction and Admissibility, the *Abaclat* tribunal concluded that Argentina's consent in the BIT to ICSID jurisdiction "includes claims presented by multiple Claimants in a single proceeding" and that "Claimants' claims are admissible."[2] This conclusion sparked a heated debate about how investment treaty-based tribunals should deal with mass claims, in particular whether and under what circumstances the numerosity of claimants should affect the tribunal's jurisdiction and/or the admissibility of claims.[3]

In subsequent decisions, the tribunals in two other ICSID arbitrations, *Ambiente and others v Argentina*[4] and *Alemanni and others v Argentina*,[5] which likewise concerned claims by multiple claimants based on the Italy-Argentina BIT with respect to Argentine sovereign bonds, reached similar conclusions as to the numerosity issue.

While all three arbitrations involved claims brought under the same BIT by multiple Italian claimants holding Argentine sovereign bonds and basing their claims on the same actions of Argentina, the *Abaclat* arbitration is unique because it alone involves 'mass claims.' In the *Abaclat* tribunal's words, "this appears to be the first case in ICSID's history that 'mass claims' are brought before it."[6] With approximately 180,000 claimants at the time the arbitration was initiated, and 60,000 claimants at the time of the Decision on Jurisdiction and Admissibility (due to a second Exchange Offer made by Argentina immediately following the jurisdictional hearing in April 2009),[7] the *Abaclat* arbitration differs substantially from both the *Ambiente* arbitration, which involved initially 119 claimants, later reduced to 90 claimants, and the *Alemanni* arbitration, which involved initially 183 claimants, later reduced to 74 claimants.[8] In this respect, the *Abaclat* tribunal has contributed to the international law jurisprudence by directly and comprehensively addressing the novel issue of mass claims in investment arbitration with key determinations on jurisdiction and admissibility, as well as the distinction between these two fundamental concepts in the context of a mass claim.

In this article, we will discuss the key findings of the *Abaclat* tribunal on jurisdiction and admissibility, with a particular focus on how these fundamental concepts are affected in the context of a mass claim. Before

* Partner, White & Case LLP, Washington, United States; Member, ICC Institute of World Business Law

doing so, it is useful to begin with a brief examination of how the tribunals defined the term 'mass claim.'

1 DEFINITION OF 'MASS CLAIM'

In an age where business streams around the world integrate and businesses offer products and services on a global basis, it is not surprising that a group of individuals with similar claims against a global actor will come together to seek a remedy. Thus, the International Bar Association has defined 'collective redress' as "a procedure designed to allow a group of individuals with similar claims to combine their claims in a single action, rather than require each individual to file his or her own lawsuit."[9]

Different forms of collective actions have developed in various legal systems. The two most common forms of such actions are representative proceedings, in which a named representative acts on behalf of a class of unnamed claimants, and aggregate proceedings, in which a group of individually named claimants jointly files a claim.[10]

Representative proceedings can be further divided into 'opt-in' and 'opt-out' actions. In an opt-in action, the class representative is required to inform the potential individual claimants that they must consent to participate in the collective action. If the potential individual claimants do not consent to participate, then any prospective judgment with respect to that action will not be binding on them, or on the defendant as to their claims. In an opt-out action, conversely, potential individual claimants are informed that they must specifically state their desire not to participate in the collective action. If the potential individual claimants do not make a statement refusing to participate, then any judgment in that action will be binding on them and on the defendant.

The term 'mass claim' has been used in international law to describe claims processes before international claims commissions and other international adjudication tribunals that were historically established to remedy the consequences of major international crises, such as the United Nations Compensation Commission, the Iran-United States Claims Tribunal, and the Commission for Real Property Claims of Displaced Persons and Refugees in Bosnia and Herzegovina.[11] Distinct features of mass claims have been found to be, first, a high number of claimants and claims, ranging from thousands to millions of claims and, second, sufficient similarity of the issues raised, such that it is more efficient to resolve the claims jointly rather than separately.[12]

In the investment arbitration context, the *Abaclat* tribunal, which to date has remained the only investment tribunal to rule on a mass claim, decided to qualify the proceedings as 'mass proceedings' based on "the high number of Claimants appearing together as one mass."[13] The tribunal found that "the present proceedings seem to be a sort of a hybrid kind of collective proceedings, in that it starts as aggregate proceedings, but then continues with features similar to representative proceedings due to the high number of Claimants involved."[14] In reaching this conclusion the *Abaclat* tribunal considered that each individual Claimant was aware of, consented to, and was identified in the arbitration, thus distinguishing the proceeding from a class action.[15] It also considered, however, that each Claimant's participation in the proceeding was passive in that each Claimant had delegated the right to make all decisions relating to the conduct of the proceeding to an agent who, due to the high number of Claimants could not take into account the particular interests of individual Claimants, but was limited to representing the interests that were common to all Claimants as a group.[16]

By contrast, the *Ambiente* and *Alemanni* tribunals considered that the significantly lower number of claimants before them did not warrant characterizing their claims as mass claims, regardless of where one might draw the line between mass claims and 'ordinary' multi-party claims.[17]

2 JURISDICTION AND ADMISSIBILITY IN GENERAL

Although there is not always a clear distinction between the two concepts, in general, as Keith Highet put it, "[j]urisdiction is the power of the arbitral tribunal to hear the case; admissibility is whether the case itself is defective – whether it is appropriate for the tribunal to hear it."[18] In *Hochtief v Argentina*, the tribunal stated that "jurisdiction is an attribute of a tribunal and not of a claim, whereas admissibility is an attribute of a claim but not of a tribunal."[19] In *PIATCO v Philippines*, the tribunal explained the "subtle distinction between jurisdiction and admissibility" as follows:

> A decision that a Tribunal lacks jurisdiction and a decision that a claim is not arbitrable both prevent the claim proceeding. However, the former is only a determination that the chosen Tribunal cannot hear the claim. In contrast, a decision of lack of admissibility is a decision that the claim should not be heard at all. Inadmissibility, therefore, encompasses those situations where the Tribunal possesses jurisdiction (as it does here) but where there is a substantive obstacle to the enforcement of the claim, such as illegality, or a procedural obstacle such as where a mandatory pre-condition to enforcing the claim, such as the giving of notice, has not been complied with.[20]

Admissibility thus concerns the appropriateness of a specific claim for adjudication, or, in other words, whether the "tribunal can exercise its adjudicative power in relation to specific claims submitted to it."[21]

The tribunal similarly explained the concepts as follows:

> Although a lack of jurisdiction or admissibility may both lead to the same result of a tribunal having to refuse to hear the case, such refusal is of a fundamentally different nature and therefore carries different consequences:
>
> i. While a lack of jurisdiction *stricto sensu* means that the claim cannot at all be brought in front of the body called upon, a lack of admissibility means that the claim was neither fit nor mature for judicial treatment;
>
> ii. Whereby a decision refusing a case based on a lack of arbitral jurisdiction is usually subject to review by another body, a decision refusing a case based on a lack of admissibility can usually not be subject to review by another body;
>
> iii. Whereby a final refusal based on a lack of jurisdiction will prevent the parties from successfully re-submitting the same claim to the same body, a refusal based on admissibility will, in principle, not prevent the claimant from resubmitting its claim, provided it cures the previous flaw causing the inadmissibility.[22]

Objections based on admissibility are frequently considered as "alleged impediments to consideration of the merits of the dispute which do not put into question the investiture of the tribunal as such."[23] In practice, it is critical for an international arbitral tribunal first to draw the boundaries of its jurisdictional power based on the parties' consent or agreement to arbitrate, and then to determine whether the specific claim submitted to it can be processed and resolved under the applicable procedural framework. A failure of an international arbitral tribunal to carefully determine the issues of jurisdiction and admissibility exposes its decisions to invalidation and unenforceability, although the specific legal consequences attached to a successful challenge to jurisdiction and a successful challenge to admissibility of the claim may vary.[24]

In ICSID arbitration, "[c]onsent of the parties is the cornerstone of ... jurisdiction."[25] Thus, under Article 25(1) of the ICSID Convention, each party to a dispute must "consent in writing" to submit the dispute to ICSID arbitration.

Where the host State's consent to submit investment disputes to ICSID arbitration is expressed in an investment treaty, such expression is generally interpreted as a standing offer of consent, which any investor that qualifies as such under the investment treaty may accept, thereby perfecting the consent.[26] In a recent decision, the tribunal in *Ickale v Turkmenistan*[27] took a somewhat different view of the nature of a State's consent to arbitrate contained in investment treaties. The *Ickale* tribunal criticized the concepts of 'standing offer' and 'perfection' as being based on privity of the parties under a contractual analogy. Rather, the *Ickale* tribunal explained, "the State's consent, which is addressed to an anonymous class of foreign investors meeting the relevant nationality requirements, and not specifically to any particular foreign investor, is expressed in a binding manner even before any dispute has arisen."[28] In comparison, "the investor's consent is usually ... expressed only after the dispute has arisen, often with a considerable time interval ...."[29] Based on this distinction, the tribunal concluded that a State's unilateral consent to arbitrate expressed in an investment treaty is binding on the State "without any further 'perfecting,' as a unilateral undertaking vis-à-vis a class of foreign investors."[30] The *Ickale* tribunal further concluded that the State's consent to arbitrate "can be invoked by a qualified investor once it has complied with and taken the procedural steps set out in the [dispute resolution] provision [of the investment treaty]."[31] Accordingly, "[a]n investor taking these steps in order to be able to invoke the State's consent does not affect the consent itself in any way; it only affects the investor's right to invoke it."[32] Under either interpretation, the terms of the investment treaty become part of the parties' agreement to arbitrate and, as such, may establish the terms and scope of the tribunal's jurisdiction.[33]

The ICSID Convention does not specifically mention any type of collective redress proceedings, nor does it contain any rules on multi-party proceedings. Article 25 merely requires the parties' written consent to submit the dispute to ICSID arbitration. While this requirement arguably bars opt-out representative proceedings, in which members of the class have not expressed their consent in writing, or may not even be aware of the proceeding, it does not exclude multi-party proceedings in which each party has consented in writing.

The practice of investment tribunals confirms this understanding. Thus, various tribunals have affirmed jurisdiction over claims of multiple and unaffiliated parties: in *Goetz v Burundi*, the ICSID tribunal accepted jurisdiction over a claim brought by six individual Belgian shareholders in a

Burundian company; in *Suez et al. v Argentina*, the ICSID tribunal found jurisdiction over a claim brought under two BITs by a French and two Spanish shareholders in an Argentine water company; in *Urbaser et al. v Argentina*, the ICSID tribunal heard a claim of two Spanish shareholders in an Argentine water company; in *OKO Pankki Oyj et al. v Estonia*, the ICSID tribunal exercised its jurisdiction over a claim brought under two BITs by a German and two Finnish banks; and in *Funnekotter et al. v Zimbabwe*, the ICSID tribunal decided a claim brought by fourteen unaffiliated Dutch investors in different farms in Zimbabwe.[34] In *Amco Asia v Indonesia*, there were three claimants from three different jurisdictions.[35] Similarly, arbitral jurisdiction was not precluded by the number of claimants in the investment treaty cases of *Anderson et al. v Costa Rica*, where there were 137 claimants; in *Bayview Irrigation District et al. v Mexico*, with 46 claimants; or in Canadian Cattlemen for *Free Trade v United States*, with 109 claimants, although each of these three cases was dismissed on grounds other than the claimants' numerosity.[36]

3 JURISDICTION AND ADMISSIBILITY AS APPLIED IN THE *ABACLAT* DECISION

The *Abaclat* tribunal found that each of the approximately 60,000 Claimants was individually named in the request for arbitration and had executed a written consent to ICSID arbitration accompanied by a power of attorney and delegation of authority.[37] Each Claimant also presented information on, and evidence of, his or her bond holdings and nationality. The request for arbitration in *Abaclat* thus contained each claimant's evidence of nationality, investment, and consent.

Given the large number of Claimants and the resulting high volume of information and documentation submitted to the tribunal, all documents relating to consent, nationality, and investment of each Claimant, including millions of pages of documents, were reviewed and organized in an electronic database that enabled the parties, the tribunal, and the experts to search, group and produce in spreadsheets the various groups of Claimants, and also to review the underlying evidence the Claimants submitted with regard to their consent, nationality and investment.

The *Abaclat* tribunal rejected Argentina's objection that its offer of consent expressed in the Italy-Argentina BIT did not extend to disputes in the form of mass proceedings, and that the tribunal lacked jurisdiction absent Argentina's specific consent to the conduct of mass proceedings.[38] The tribunal did so on the following two grounds: First, the tribunal reasoned that, assuming it had jurisdiction over the claims of a single Claimant or several Claimants, looking at them individually, it was "difficult to conceive why and how the Tribunal could [lose] such jurisdiction where the number of Claimants outgrows a certain threshold."[39] Second, the tribunal found that "the collective nature of the present proceeding derives primarily from the nature of the investment made," which in this case was bonds "which are susceptible of involving in the context of the same investment a high number of investors."[40] Given that the Italy-Argentina BIT expressly covered investments in bonds,[41] the tribunal concluded:

> [W]here such investments require a collective relief in order to provide effective protection to such investment[s], it would be contrary to the purpose of the BIT and to the spirit of ICSID [to promote and protect

investments] to require, in addition to the consent to ICSID arbitration in general, a supplementary express consent to the form of such arbitration. In such cases, consent to ICSID arbitration must be considered to cover the form of arbitration necessary to give efficient protection and remedy to the investors and their investments, including arbitration in the form of collective proceedings.[42]

Additionally, the language of the Italy-Argentina BIT, including its dispute settlement clauses, is replete with references to "investors" in the plural form:

- Article 8: "Settlement of disputes between the investors and the Contracting Parties"
- Article 8(3): "If a dispute still exists between investors and a Contracting Party, ..."
- Preamble: "[F]or the making of investments by investors of one Contracting Party ..."
- Article 2(1): "Each Contracting Party shall encourage investors of the other Contracting Party ..."
- Article 2(2): "Investments of investors of each Contracting Party shall at all times ..."
- Article 3(1): "Neither Contracting Party shall in its territory subject investments made by the investors ..."
- Article 4: "Investors of one Contracting Party ..."
- Article 5(1)(a): "Each Contracting Party undertakes not to adopt provisions limiting ... the rights of ownership ... relating to the investments made by the investors ..."
- Article 5(1)(b): "The investments of the investors of ..."
- Article 6(1): "Upon satisfaction by investors of all tax obligations ... each Contracting Party shall guarantee to investors ..."
- Article 6(4): "[E]ach Contracting Party shall, at any time, guarantee to investors ..."
- Article 10(1): "[T]he Contracting Parties and their investors ..."
- Article 10(2): "In the event that one Contracting Party, ... has adopted for investors of the other Contracting Party ..."
- Article 11: "This Agreement shall also apply to investments ... by investors of one Contracting Party ..."

The Italy-Argentina BIT thus clearly contemplated that multiple investors might act jointly with respect to their investments.

Having established that Argentina's consent to ICSID arbitration as expressed in the Italy-Argentina BIT "includes claims presented by multiple Claimants in a single proceeding,"[43] and that the numerosity issue thus was one of admissibility and not of consent,[44] the *Abaclat* tribunal proceeded to interpret the silence of the ICSID Convention and Arbitration Rules with respect to collective proceedings. The tribunal found that it would be contrary to the purpose of the BIT and the spirit of the ICSID framework to interpret this silence as one that prohibited collective proceedings given that collective proceedings were virtually unknown at the time the ICSID Convention was concluded and that the ICSID procedure could be adapted to ensure due process and a balance of the parties' procedural rights and interests.[45] The tribunal also found that it had the power, under Article 44 of the ICSID Convention and ICSID Arbitration Rule 19, to fill the gap left by the ICSID framework's silence.[46]

The *Abaclat* tribunal adopted a practical approach to determine whether the numerosity of Claimants was an obstacle for it to hear the case. The Tribunal simply asked itself whether an ICSID arbitration could be conducted in the form of "mass proceedings."[47] Implicitly drawing a line between jurisdiction and admissibility, the *Abaclat* tribunal determined that in the event the ICSID arbitration could be conducted as a mass proceeding by adapting certain procedural rules under the ICSID framework, then Argentina's consent to ICSID arbitration included arbitration of mass claims; but in the event the ICSID arbitration could not be conducted as a mass proceeding, then "ICSID arbitration [would not be] possible, not because Argentina did not consent thereto but because mass claims as the ones at stake are not possible under the current ICSID framework."[48] On this basis, the *Abaclat* Tribunal found that "the 'mass' aspect of the present proceedings relates to the modalities and implementation of the ICSID proceedings and not to the question whether Respondent consented to ICSID arbitration. Therefore, it relates to the question of admissibility and not to the question of jurisdiction."[49]

Based on ICSID Arbitration Rule 19, the *Abaclat* tribunal decided that it could conduct the proceeding as it deemed proper and sufficient for processing and resolving each individual claim of the investors while safeguarding both parties' due process rights. Indeed, the tribunal mentioned the possibility that denying jurisdiction on these grounds might leave the Claimants with no choice but to bring tens of thousands of separate claims, which would result in a *de facto* deprivation of Claimants' substantive and due process rights:

> The Tribunal finds it appropriate to compare the consequences of these implications to the consequences of rejecting the claims for lack of admissibility and requesting each Claimant to file an individual ICSID claim. In this regard, the Tribunal finds that not only would it be cost prohibitive for many Claimants to file individual claims but it would also be practically impossible for ICSID to deal separately with 60,000 individual arbitrations. Thus, the rejection of the admissibility of the present claims may equal a denial of justice. This would be shocking given that the investment at stake is protected under the BIT, which expressly provides for ICSID jurisdiction and arbitration.[50]

The tribunal found that this also would present a greater challenge for Argentina to exercise its due process rights: "The measures that Argentina would need to take to face 60,000 proceedings would be a much bigger challenge to Argentina's effective defense rights than a mere limitation of its right to individual treatment of homogeneous claims in the present proceedings."[51]

The tribunal accordingly examined the implications of making the adaptations required to deal with the collective aspect of the claims. It noted the implications were twofold: "(i) It will not be possible to treat each Claimant as if he/she was alone and certain issues, such as the existence of an expropriation, will have to be examined collectively, i.e., as a group; and (ii) the implications will likely limit certain of Claimants' and Argentina's procedural rights to the extent that Claimants will have to waive individual interests in favor of common interests of the entire group of Claimants, while Argentina will not be able to bring arguments in full length and detail concerning the individual situation of each of the Claimants."[52]

In determining whether the claims could be subjected to 'group treatment,' the *Abaclat* tribunal focused on whether the Claimants had 'homogeneous' claims.[53] In this regard, the tribunal emphasized that the claims before it concerned only treaty claims under the Italy-Argentina BIT, and not any contractual claims that individual Claimants might have against Argentina under the bond instruments.[54] The tribunal concluded that, as a result, "the specific circumstances surrounding individual purchases by Claimants of security entitlements are irrelevant."[55] The tribunal found that "[t]he only relevant question is whether Claimants have homogeneous rights of compensation for a homogeneous damage caused to them by potential homogeneous breaches by Argentina of homogeneous obligations provided for in the BIT."[56] In this regard, the tribunal found that the nature of each Claimant's claims was homogenous because all claims were based on the same alleged conduct by Argentina in connection with its default on its sovereign bonds. Likewise, the tribunal found that "the potential damage caused to Claimants is, by nature, the same for all Claimants, although the scope of such damage will of course depend on the scope of their individual investment."[57]

Recognizing the difficulties in examination of the voluminous elements and evidence underpinning the Claimants' claims, the tribunal emphasized the need for a special mechanism for efficient and fair examination of evidence. The tribunal pointed out that it would "need to implement mechanisms allowing a simplified verification of evidentiary material, while this simplification can concern either the depth of examination of a document (e.g., accepting a scanned copy of an ID document instead of an original), or the number of evidentiary documents to be examined, and if so their selection process (i.e. random selection of samples instead of a serial examination of each document) ...."[58] Then, to address any concerns about this mechanism, the *Abaclat* tribunal appointed an independent expert to examine and verify every single piece of information that was contained in the Claimant database, including documentation related to Claimants' forms of consent to ICSID arbitration and power of attorney, documents of nationality and residency of Claimants on various key dates, and bank certificates confirming each Claimant's bond ownership, value, and purchase date.[59]

By enabling utilization of an electronic claimant database for organization of claims and underlying evidence and appointing an independent expert to examine and verify the database and the evidence contained therein, the *Abaclat* tribunal implemented the mechanism necessary to effectively adjudicate a mass claim within the ICSID framework while safeguarding the parties' due process rights. In 2013, the independent expert found that "[t]he information contained in the Claimants' Database and the documents relating thereto are comprehensive and are organized in a way which allows a reliable verification of the information in the Claimants' Database against the documents on which this information is based."[60]

By contrast, when the *Ambiente* tribunal affirmed jurisdiction and admissibility, it expressly avoided "draw[ing] a neat dividing line between these two concepts" or "giv[ing] an answer as to whether the legal issues at stake are to be classified as questions of jurisdiction or admissibility."[61] The *Ambiente* tribunal adopted a result-oriented approached concluding that "all claims of lack of jurisdiction and admissibility . . . will have to be perused and, if considered as not justified, rejected before the dispute could proceed to the merits phase. In no way would the distinction between jurisdictional and admissibility issues suggest a different degree of 'bindingness'."[62]

The *Alemanni* tribunal, having reviewed the decisions of the *Abaclat* and *Ambiente* tribunals, concluded that it remained unconvinced that "the distinction between the two concepts, such as it may be, raises any major difficulty; but nor is it convinced that the distinction is of any particular importance in disposing of the issues presently before it."[63] Nonetheless, the *Alemanni* tribunal drew a fine line between jurisdiction and admissibility. It stated that while jurisdictional objections "raise the issue whether the Parties have duly consented to the dispute being brought to ICSID arbitration," admissibility objections "raise the question whether, even if the Parties have duly consented, there nevertheless exist reasons why the Tribunal should decline to hear the dispute in the form in which the dispute is brought before it, even though it possesses the formal competence to do so."[64]

4 CONCLUSION

While the increased globalization of investment flows may entail a greater need for investment tribunals to effectively adjudicate collective redress actions, the answer to the question of whether mass claims are permissible as a matter of jurisdiction or as a matter of admissibility may vary depending on the language of the particular investment treaty that applies. Generally, so long as the parties' consent to arbitrate is established and the applicable arbitral procedures do not expressly disallow adjudication of a mass claim, it would be contrary to the fundamental notions of justice and fairness to effectively preclude an otherwise legitimate claim merely because the arbitral mechanism requires some adjustment. Thus, as the *Abaclat* tribunal held, "[c]ollective proceedings emerged where they constituted the only way to ensure an effective remedy in protection of a substantive right provided by contract or law; in other words, collective proceedings were seen as necessary, where the absence of such mechanism would *de facto* have resulted in depriving the claimants of their substantive rights due to the lack of appropriate mechanism."[65] It is important to keep in mind, however, that the *Abaclat* tribunal reached its decision in the context of a particular type of investment that was specifically geared by the host State to a large number of investors and that was expressly covered by the applicable BIT's definition of investment. While most investment treaties contain very similar language, there are subtle differences, which may cause a tribunal to reach divergent conclusions.

NOTES

1 OGEMID named the Decision on Jurisdiction and Admissibility the "Most Influential Award," "The Arbitration Decision of the Year 2011," and "The 'most controversial or surprising' Arbitration Decision of the Year 2011," Transnational Dispute Management, OGEMID Awards, *available at* https://**www.transnational-dispute-management.com/ogemidawards/.** Carolyn Lamm was lead counsel for the Claimants in *Abaclat*, and Eckhard Hellbeck and Onur Saka were members of the Claimants' legal team in that case.

2 *Abaclat and others v Argentine Republic*, ICSID Case No. ARB/07/5, Decision on Jurisdiction and Admissibility (4 Aug. 2011), ¶ 713, *available at* **http://www.italaw.com/sites/default/files/case-documents/ita0236.pdf.** The Tribunal did not render an award on the merits of the dispute as the proceeding was suspended until 19 July 2016 pursuant to the parties' agreement on 21 March 2016, as noted on the ICSID website. *See* https://icsid.worldbank.org/apps/ICSIDWEB/cases/Pages/casedetail.aspx?CaseNo=ARB/07/5. On 21 April 2016, the Argentine Republic signed a final settlement agreement with Task Force Argentina acting on behalf of the Claimants. *See* Global Arbitration Review, *Argentina pays out to end sovereign debt claim* (25 Apr. 2015), *available at* **http://globalarbitrationreview.com/news/article/35261/argentina-pays-end-sovereign-debt-claim/.**

3 Indeed, this was one of the issues on which Arbitrator Abi-Saab based his dissent. *See Abaclat and others v Argentine Republic*, ICSID Case No. ARB/07/5, Dissenting Opinion of Georges Abi-Saab (28 Oct. 2011), ¶¶ 122-127, *available at* **http://www.italaw.com/sites/default/files/case-documents/ita0237.pdf.**

4 *Ambiente Ufficio S.p.A. and others v Argentine Republic*, ICSID Case No. ARB/08/9, Decision on Jurisdiction and Admissibility (8 Feb. 2013), *available at* **http://www.italaw.com/sites/default/files/case-documents/italaw1276.pdf.** The proceeding was discontinued on 28 May 2015.

5 *Giovanni Alemanni and others v Argentine Republic*, ICSID Case No. ARB/07/8, Decision on Jurisdiction and Admissibility (17 Nov. 2014), *available at* **http://www.italaw.com/sites/default/files/case-documents/italaw4061.pdf.** The proceeding was discontinued on 14 December 2015.

6 *Abaclat et al. v Argentine Republic*, ICSID Case No. ARB/07/5, Decision on Jurisdiction and Admissibility (4 Aug. 2011) ¶¶ 294, 295.

7 A considerable number of Claimants accepted Argentina's 2010 Exchange Offer and withdrew from the proceeding. *See Abaclat et al. v Argentine Republic*, ICSID Case No. ARB/07/5, Decision on Jurisdiction and Admissibility (4 Aug. 2011) ¶¶ 97, 216.

8 *Abaclat and others v Argentine Republic*, ICSID Case No. ARB/07/5, Decision on Jurisdiction and Admissibility (4 Aug. 2011) ¶ 294; *Ambiente Ufficio S.p.A. and others v Argentine Republic*, ICSID Case No. ARB/08/9, Decision on Jurisdiction and Admissibility (8 Feb. 2013) ¶ 113; *Giovanni Alemanni and others v Argentine Republic*, ICSID Case No. ARB/07/8, Decision on Jurisdiction and Admissibility (17 Nov. 2014) ¶¶ 1, 267.

9 IBA Legal Practice Division, *Guidelines for Recognising and Enforcing Foreign Judgments for Collective Redress* (2008) ¶ 2.

10 *Abaclat and others v Argentine Republic*, ICSID Case No. ARB/07/5, Decision on Jurisdiction and Admissibility (4 Aug. 2011) ¶ 483; Strong, SI, Class, Mass, and Collective Arbitration in National and International Law 6 (2013).

11 Hans Das, "The Concept of Mass Claims and the Specificity of Mass Claims Resolution", in *Redressing Injustices Through Mass Claims Processes: Innovative Responses to Unique Challenges* 3, 6-7 (International Bureau of the Permanent Court of Arbitration, ed. 2005); *see also International Mass Claims Processes: Legal and Practical Perspectives* (Howard M. Holtzmann and Edda Kristjàhsdòttir, eds. 2007); Veijo Heiskanen, *Arbitrating Mass Investor Claims: Lessons of International Commissions*, in Multiple Party Actions in International Arbitration 297 (B. MacMahon and Permanent Court of Arbitration staff eds., 2009).

12 Hans Das, "The Concept of Mass Claims and the Specificity of Mass Claims Resolution", in *Redressing Injustices Through Mass Claims Processes: Innovative Responses to Unique Challenges* 6-7 (International Bureau of the Permanent Court of Arbitration, ed. 2005).

13 *Abaclat and others v Argentine Republic*, ICSID Case No. ARB/07/5, Decision on Jurisdiction and Admissibility (4 Aug. 2011) ¶ 480.

14 *Abaclat and others v Argentine Republic*, ICSID Case No. ARB/07/5, Decision on Jurisdiction and Admissibility (4 Aug. 2011) ¶ 488.

15 *Abaclat and others v Argentine Republic*, ICSID Case No. ARB/07/5, Decision on Jurisdiction and Admissibility (4 Aug. 2011) ¶ 486.

16 *Abaclat and others v Argentine Republic*, ICSID Case No. ARB/07/5, Decision on Jurisdiction and Admissibility (4 Aug. 2011) ¶ 487.

17 *Ambiente Ufficio S.p.A. and others v Argentine Republic*, ICSID Case No. ARB/08/9, Decision on Jurisdiction and Admissibility (8 Feb. 2013) ¶¶ 119-121; *Giovanni Alemanni and others v Argentine Republic*, ICSID Case No. ARB/07/8, Decision on Jurisdiction and Admissibility (17 Nov. 2014) ¶ 267.

18 *Waste Management, Inc v United Mexican States*, ICSID Case No. AR-B(AF)/00/3, Dissenting Opinion of Keith Highet (8 May 2000) ¶ 58.

19 *Hochtief AG v Argentine Republic*, ICSID Case No. ARB/07/31, Decision on Jurisdiction (24 Oct. 2011) ¶ 90.

20 *Philippine International Air Terminals Co., Inc. [PIATCO] v The Government of the Republic of the Philippines*, ICC Case No. 12610/TE/MW/AVH/JEM/MLK, Award (22 July 2010) ¶ 572 (citing Jan Paulsson, *Jurisdiction and Admissibility*, in Global Reflections on International Law, Commerce and Dispute Resolution, Liber Amicorum in honour of Robert Briner 601, 617 (Gerald Aksen *et al.*, eds. 2005)).

21 Zachary Douglas, *The International Law of Investment Claims* ¶ 293 (2009).

22 *Abaclat and others v Argentine Republic*, ICSID Case No. ARB/07/5, Decision on Jurisdiction and Admissibility (4 Aug. 2011) ¶ 247.

23 Jan Paulsson, *Jurisdiction and Admissibility*, in Global Reflections on International Law, Commerce and Dispute Resolution, Liber Amicorum in honour of Robert Briner 601, 617 (Gerald Aksen *et al.*, eds. 2005).

24 Jan Paulsson, *Jurisdiction and Admissibility*, in Global Reflections on International Law, Commerce and Dispute Resolution, Liber Amicorum in honour of Robert Briner 601 (Gerald Aksen *et al.*, eds. 2005).

25 Report of the Executive Directors on the Convention on the Settlement of Investment Disputes between States and Nationals of Other States (18 Mar. 1965) ¶ 23.

26 *See* Jeswald Salacuse, The Law of Investment Treaties 422-423 (2d ed. 2015) ("Unlike the arbitration clauses used in contracts, these treaty provisions could not be considered an arbitration agreement with the investor because the investor, while a national of a contracting state, was not a party to the treaty. Conceptually, such a provision constitutes an irrevocable offer to arbitrate disputes concerning the interpretation and application of the treaty. An investor may accept that offer in different ways, including the submission of a request for arbitration or some other mechanism offered in the treaty. The offer includes the various terms and conditions contained in the applicable investment treaty.").

27 *Ickale Insaat Limited Sirketi v Turkmenistan,* ICSID Case No. ARB/10/24, Award (8 Mar. 2016).

28 *Ickale Insaat Limited Sirketi v Turkmenistan,* ICSID Case No. ARB/10/24, Award (8 Mar. 2016) ¶ 244.

29 *Ickale Insaat Limited Sirketi v Turkmenistan,* ICSID Case No. ARB/10/24, Award (8 Mar. 2016) ¶ 244.

30 *Ickale Insaat Limited Sirketi v Turkmenistan,* ICSID Case No. ARB/10/24, Award (8 Mar. 2016) ¶ 244.

31 *Ickale Insaat Limited Sirketi v Turkmenistan,* ICSID Case No. ARB/10/24, Award (8 Mar. 2016) ¶ 244.

32 *Ickale Insaat Limited Sirketi v Turkmenistan,* ICSID Case No. ARB/10/24, Award (8 Mar. 2016) ¶ 244.

33 *See* Carolyn B. Lamm, *Jurisdiction of the International Centre for Settlement of Investment Disputes*, 6 ICSID Rev.-Foreign Inv. L.J. 462, 464, 466 (1991).

34 *See Goetz v Burundi*, ICSID Case No. ARB/95/3, Award (10 Feb. 1999); *Suez, Sociedad General de Aguas de Barcelona S.A. and InterAguas Servicios Integrales del Agua S.A. v Argentine Republic*, ICSID Case No. ARB/03/17, Decision on Jurisdiction (16 May 2006); *OKO Osuuspankkien Keskuspankki Oyj and others v Republic of Estonia*, ICSID Case No. ARB/04/6, Award (19 Nov. 2007); *Bernardus Henricus Funnekotter and others v Republic of Zimbabwe*, ICSID Case No. ARB/05/6, Award (22 Apr. 2009).

35 *See Amco Asia Corporation and others v Republic of Indonesia*, ICSID Case No. ARB/81/1, Decision on Jurisdiction (25 Sept. 1983) (the three claimants were: Amco Asia Corporation (incorporated in Delaware, U.S.), Pan American Development Limited (established in Hong Kong), P.T. Amco (established in Indonesia)).

36 *See Alasdair Ross Anderson v Republic of Costa Rica*, ICSID Case No. ARB(AF)/07/3, Award (19 May 2010) ¶ 15 (dismissing on other jurisdictional grounds, without any objection to or discussion of the number of claimants); *Bayview Irrigation District et al. v United Mexican States*, ICSID Case No. ARB(AF)/05/1, Award (19 June 2007); *Canadian Cattlemen for Fair Trade v United States of America*, (UNCITRAL), Award on Jurisdiction (28 Jan. 2008).

37 *Abaclat and others v Argentine Republic*, ICSID Case No. ARB/07/5, Decision on Jurisdiction and Admissibility (4 Aug. 2011) ¶¶ 1-2.

38 *Abaclat and others v Argentine Republic*, ICSID Case No. ARB/07/5, Decision on Jurisdiction and Admissibility (4 Aug. 2011) ¶ 490.

39 *Abaclat and others v Argentine Republic*, ICSID Case No. ARB/07/5, Decision on Jurisdiction and Admissibility (4 Aug. 2011) ¶ 490.

40 *Abaclat and others v Argentine Republic*, ICSID Case No. ARB/07/5, Decision on Jurisdiction and Admissibility (4 Aug. 2011) ¶ 490.

41 *See* Italy-Argentina BIT, Art. 1(1) ("'Investment' shall mean, in compliance with the legislation of the receiving State and independent of the legal form adopted or any other legislation of reference, any conferment or asset invested or reinvested by an individual or corporation of one Contracting Party in the territory of the other Contracting Party, in compliance with the laws and regulations of the latter Contracting Party. In particular, investment includes, without limitation ... bonds, private or public financial instruments or any other right to performances or services having economic value, including capitalized revenues ....").

42 *Abaclat and others v Argentine Republic*, ICSID Case No. ARB/07/5, Decision on Jurisdiction and Admissibility (4 Aug. 2011) ¶ 490.

43 *Abaclat and others v Argentine Republic*, ICSID Case No. ARB/07/5, Decision on Jurisdiction and Admissibility (4 Aug. 2011) ¶¶ 500-502.

44 *Abaclat and others v Argentine Republic*, ICSID Case No. ARB/07/5, Decision on Jurisdiction and Admissibility (4 Aug. 2011) ¶ 515.

45 *Abaclat and others v Argentine Republic*, ICSID Case No. ARB/07/5, Decision on Jurisdiction and Admissibility (4 Aug. 2011) ¶ 519.

46 *Abaclat and others v Argentine Republic*, ICSID Case No. ARB/07/5, Decision on Jurisdiction and Admissibility (4 Aug. 2011) ¶¶ 520-528; *see* ICSID Conven-

tion, Art. 44 ("Any arbitration proceeding shall be conducted in accordance with the provisions of this Section and, except as the parties otherwise agree, in accordance with the Arbitration Rules in effect on the date on which the parties consented to arbitration. If any question of procedure arises which is not covered by this Section or the Arbitration Rules or any rules agreed by the parties, the Tribunal shall decide the question."); ICSID Arbitration Rule 19 ("The Tribunal shall make the orders required for the conduct of the proceeding.").

47 *See Abaclat and others v Argentine Republic*, ICSID Case No. ARB/07/5, Decision on Jurisdiction and Admissibility (4 Aug. 2011) ¶¶ 491-492.

48 *Abaclat and others v Argentine Republic*, ICSID Case No. ARB/07/5, Decision on Jurisdiction and Admissibility (4 Aug. 2011) ¶ 491.

49 *Abaclat and others v Argentine Republic*, ICSID Case No. ARB/07/5, Decision on Jurisdiction and Admissibility (4 Aug. 2011) ¶ 492.

50 *Abaclat and others v Argentine Republic*, ICSID Case No. ARB/07/5, Decision on Jurisdiction and Admissibility (4 Aug. 2011) ¶ 537.

51 *See Abaclat and others v Argentine Republic*, ICSID Case No. ARB/07/5, Decision on Jurisdiction and Admissibility (4 Aug. 2011) ¶ 545.

52 *Abaclat and others v Argentine Republic*, ICSID Case No. ARB/07/5, Decision on Jurisdiction and Admissibility (4 Aug. 2011) ¶ 536.

53 *Abaclat and others. v Argentine Republic*, ICSID Case No. ARB/07/5, Decision on Jurisdiction and Admissibility (4 Aug. 2011) ¶¶ 540-544.

54 *Abaclat and others. v Argentine Republic*, ICSID Case No. ARB/07/5, Decision on Jurisdiction and Admissibility (4 Aug. 2011) ¶ 541.

55 *Abaclat and others. v Argentine Republic*, ICSID Case No. ARB/07/5, Decision on Jurisdiction and Admissibility (4 Aug. 2011) ¶ 542.

56 *Abaclat and others v Argentine Republic,* ICSID Case No. ARB/07/5, Decision on Jurisdiction and Admissibility (4 Aug. 2011) ¶ 541.

57 *Abaclat and others v Argentine Republic,* ICSID Case No. ARB/07/5, Decision on Jurisdiction and Admissibility (4 Aug. 2011) ¶ 543.

58 *Abaclat and others v Argentine Republic,* ICSID Case No. ARB/07/5, Decision on Jurisdiction and Admissibility (4 Aug. 2011) ¶ 531.

59 *See Abaclat and others v Argentine Republic,* ICSID Case No. ARB/07/5, Procedural Order No. 15 (20 Nov. 2012) and Procedural Order No. 17 (8 Feb. 2013).

60 Task Force Argentina Press Release, *Independent Expert Report Verifies Bondholder Claim Procedure and Individual Claims Before World Bank* (1 Oct. 2013), *available at* http://www.tfargentina.it/download/TFA%20Comunicato%201%20ottobre%202013_eng.pdf.

61 *Ambiente Ufficio S.p.A. and others v Argentine Republic*, ICSID Case No. ARB/08/9, Decision on Jurisdiction and Admissibility (8 Feb. 2013) ¶¶ 573-574.

62 *Ambiente Ufficio S.p.A. and others v Argentine Republic*, ICSID Case No. ARB/08/9, Decision on Jurisdiction and Admissibility (8 Feb. 2013) ¶ 575.

63 *Giovanni Alemanni et al. v Argentine Republic*, ICSID Case No. ARB/07/8, Decision on Jurisdiction and Admissibility (17 Nov. 2014) ¶ 257.

64 *Giovanni Alemanni et al. v Argentine Republic*, ICSID Case No. ARB/07/8, Decision on Jurisdiction and Admissibility (17 Nov. 2014) ¶ 260.

65 *Abaclat and others v Argentine Republic*, ICSID Case No. ARB/07/5, Decision on Jurisdiction and Admissibility (4 Aug. 2011) ¶ 484.

Chapter 10

Representative Aspects of "Mass Claim" Proceedings in Investor-State Arbitration

Luca G. Radicati di Brozolo* and Flavio Ponzano**

1 INTRODUCTION

The title chosen by the organizers for this presentation is revealing of the uncertainties and complexities of the topic.

To begin, the expression 'mass claims' is not a term of art.[1] The term 'mass' is used, alongside others — such as group, collective, aggregate, large-scale, multiparty, multiple and representative — to refer generally to proceedings with a plurality of claimants. Each term emphasizes different features and aspects of the types of claim and proceedings falling under the broad category that encompasses a wide spectrum of types of proceedings with considerably different features.[2]

The general and perhaps most neutral term 'collective' proceedings will be used here to refer to all types of proceedings with a plurality of claimants.

As to the other expression in the title of this presentation, which refers to the 'representative aspects' of what we have decided to call collective claims, the term 'representative' is most often associated with class action-like proceedings. That type of proceeding is usually not considered possible in ICSID or investor-State arbitration in general, or for that matter even in commercial arbitration, except in the United States. This is because class actions pose complex problems in the identification of the proper parties to the arbitration, or in other words in the identification and definition of the class of plaintiffs, which largely have to do with the issue of consent[3]. It is generally felt that proceedings of this type require specific rules which, at least in the current phase, are not available for investor-State arbitration.[4]

There would therefore seem to be little scope to speak about 'representative aspects' of collective proceedings in investor-State arbitration. Nonetheless, as discussed below, at least in certain cases also investor-State proceedings may have a representative component. As was

* Professor, Catholic University of Milan; Arblit - Radicati di Brozolo Sabatini Benedettelli, Milan; Fountain Court Chambers, London. Luca Radicati di Brozolo was counsel for the claimants in *Ambiente Ufficio S.p.A. and Others v The Argentine Republic* (case formerly known as *Giordano Alpi and Others v The Argentine Republic*), ICSID Case No. ARB/08/9 and in *Giovanni Alemanni and Others v The Argentine Republic*, ICSID Case No. ARB/07/8, and is currently representing the claimants in *Natland Investment Group N.V., Natland Group Limited, G.I.H.G. Limited and Radiance Energy Holding S.A.R.L. v The Czech Republic*, PCA Case No. 2013-35; *Antaris Solar GmbH & Dr. Michael Göde v The Czech Republic*, PCA Case No. 2014-1; *WA Investments-Europa Nova Limited v The Czech Republic*, PCA Case No. 2014-19; *Voltaic Network GmbH v The Czech Republic*, PCA Case No. 2014-20; *Photovoltaik Knopf Betriebs-GmbH v The Czech Republic*, PCA Case No. 2014-21; I.C.W. *Europe Investments Limited v The Czech Republic*, PCA Case No. 2014-22, all mentioned in this article.

** Senior Associate, Arblit - Radicati di Brozolo Sabatini Benedettelli, Milan; Ph.D. candidate, Catholic University of Milan.

recognized in *Abaclat* [5], at least in some cases collective proceedings in investment arbitration can raise certain issues akin to those of proper representative actions.

The subject of collective proceedings in investment arbitration is still fluid. There are no rules regarding these types of proceedings in the ICSID Convention or in the BITs or in the ICSID Rules which either permit or forbid or in any other way govern them. The case-law is still quite scarce and there are even fewer accepted principles. The relatively few investor-State awards in what can be classified as collective proceedings[6] dealt with cases with significant differences, both in terms of the number of claimants (ranging from a handful or less to the initially 180,000 in *Abaclat*) and of the relations between the claimants (for instance, in *Antoine Goetz and others v Burundi* the claimants were all Belgian shareholders of the same Burundian company, while in *Alasdair Ross Anderson and others v Costa Rica* and in *Erhas v Turkmenistan* they were unrelated respectively Canadian and Turkish nationals).

This piece will touch briefly upon a few of the problems which arise in connection with these proceedings, and in particular those relating to the possibility of bringing multiple claims within the same proceedings and those relating to the conduct and management of the proceedings. The aim is only to provide a preliminary overview of these problems and of the solutions that have been considered by the case law.

2 THE CONDITIONS FOR BRINGING MULTIPLE CLAIMS IN THE SAME PROCEEDINGS

The crucial threshold question that presents itself in relation to collective proceedings is that of whether, and under what conditions, an aggregation of claims in a single set of proceedings is possible.

As indicated above, the ICSID Convention, BITs and the ICSID Rules provide no guidance.[7] Although it does not deal directly with collective proceedings, the NAFTA contains a provision (Article 1126[8]) permitting consolidation in certain circumstances, which could be of assistance in some cases. Provisions on consolidation are also found in other investment treaties[9] and in the chapters on investment protection of the economic and trade treaties currently being negotiated by the European Union with some of its trade partners.[10]

In principle, guidance could be sought in domestic civil procedure, which in all legal systems contains a wealth of rules on multiparty proceedings. However, as with many aspects of investor-State proceedings, there is not much that one can borrow from national civil procedure because of the differences between court litigation and arbitration, in particular investor-State arbitration, and because even the rules of domestic laws on this type of issue may differ considerably across legal systems. This was emphasized by the *Ambiente Ufficio* tribunal which "caution[ed] against importing domestic standards in this respect and [recalled] that the decision on jurisdiction within the ICSID framework is a question to be answered on the basis of international law".[11]

Not even the rules on multiparty proceedings applicable to commercial arbitration offer any meaningful guidance, largely because of the different way in which consent operates in commercial and in investment arbitration. The question must therefore be addressed having regard to the specific features of investor-State arbitration.

The discussion on this topic often starts from a consideration of the reasons for aggregating in the same proceedings the claims of a plurality of claimants. There is no doubt that in many cases such an aggregation can be justified on grounds of efficiency, consistency of outcomes, cost saving and, more significantly, access to justice. The cogency of each one of these justifications will of course vary depending on the circumstances, such as the nature of the individual claimants and of their claims, the similarities, differences and relations between them, the aggregate amounts involved and those of the individual claims and so on, and must be assessed on a case-by-case basis. For instance, the argument of access to justice is likely to be more compelling in situations such as the Argentine bondholder cases where, given the amounts of the individual claims, most of the claimants would not have been in a position to bring claims on their own, than in cases where there the claimants are sophisticated investors and the amounts at stake are high.

The link between permitting collective proceedings and access to justice in a broad sense was recognized by the *Abaclat* tribunal, which held that:

> [...] it appears that all these various forms of collective proceedings share a common 'raison d'être': collective proceedings emerged where they constituted the only way to ensure an effective remedy in protection of a substantive right provided by contract or law; in other words, collective proceedings were seen as necessary, where the absence of such mechanism would *de facto* have resulted in depriving the claimants of their substantive rights due to the lack of appropriate mechanism.[12]

The existence of a sound justification for aggregating multiple claims is obviously not of itself a sufficient ground for allowing the claims to be brought together.[13] It is therefore necessary to identify an adequate legal parameter.

As in all matters relating to arbitration, the starting point has to be the consent of the parties. Obviously, an agreement to permit or exclude the participation of multiple claimants in the same arbitral proceedings would be dispositive of the issue. The problem is that seldom, if ever, is there any clear indication as to an intention of the parties, and in particular of the State, on this point. The consequence is that one has to resort to attempts at interpreting the meaning of the parties' agreement. When the agreement consists of a treaty, as is very often the case, recourse has to be had to the rules of interpretation of the Vienna Convention on the Law of Treaties.[14]

Textual arguments will rarely be of assistance. In particular, it is difficult to draw any meaningful conclusion on this point in either direction from the use of the singular or the plural (for instance 'investor' as opposed to 'investors') in the relevant treaty or arbitration clause[15]. In *Ambiente Ufficio* the majority pointed to the *travaux préparatoires* of the ICSID Convention, which contained traces of an inconclusive discussion on multiparty proceedings, to dispute Argentina's contention that such proceedings were "way beyond 'the horizon of foreseeability' of the drafters of the ICSID Convention."[16]

Given the absence of specific indications as to the parties' intentions, there may be a temptation to rely more or less openly on assumptions or presumptions as to those intentions. Such an approach is not unusual in arbitration, particularly commercial arbitration where it is resorted to when specific considerations weigh in favor of broadening the personal or subject-matter scope of arbitration agreements. A typical example of this is the evolution that has occurred in relation to the subject matter of arbitration in commercial arbitration, which now are generally interpreted as encompassing all disputes arising in connection with the contractual relationship for which arbitration is stipulated, including non-contractual aspects. One of the reasons usually put forward in that regard is that the parties are assumed to have opted for a rational solution that allows the bringing of all related claims together, avoiding the complexities inherent in the need to parse the different types of issues that may or may not be subject to the jurisdiction of the arbitrators. A similar, although somewhat more controversial and complex, evolution occurs with regard to the extension of arbitration agreements to non-signatories in commercial arbitration. As is well known, in these situations there is a tendency to rely on different, mostly contract law, techniques to bring non-signatories within the scope of the agreement to arbitrate, which has spurred an interesting debate on the role of consent in arbitration[17]. Although this debate may take on different connotations in relation to commercial and to investment arbitration, since the consent of States may raise greater concerns, there is one difference between the two that could militate in favor of a less strict interpretation of the number of addressees of the offer to arbitrate that can be permitted to bring claims jointly. This is the fact that, while in commercial arbitration, the parties to the arbitration agreement are, at least in principle, identified or identifiable from the beginning, in investment arbitration the offer to arbitrate is very broad and directed to an undetermined number of potential parties.

The issue of consent to the bringing of single proceedings by a plurality of claimants arises in respect of both the number and the type of claims that can be brought together, although the two aspects are in several ways related.

The question of the number of the claims that can be brought together, which was touched upon in several earlier awards,[18] was addressed particularly in the three Argentine bondholder cases. The *Abaclat* and *Ambiente Ufficio* majorities held that specific consent was not required for the "mass aspect" of the cases before them. *Abaclat* held that

> Assuming that the Tribunal has jurisdiction over the claims of several individual Claimants, it is difficult to conceive why and how the Tribunal could lose such jurisdiction where the number of Claimants outgrows a certain threshold. First of all, what is the relevant threshold? And, second, can the Tribunal really 'lose' a jurisdiction it has when looking at Claimants individually?[19]

This reasoning was buttressed with a further argument based on the nature of the investment at issue:

> In addition, the collective nature of the present proceeding derives primarily from the nature of the investment made. The ICSID Convention aims at promoting and protecting investments, without however further defining the concept of investment and leaving this task to the parties through

> relevant instruments such as BITs (see §§ 257 and 362 et seq. above). Thus, where the BIT covers investments, such as bonds, which are susceptible of involving in the context of the same investment a high number of investors, and where such investments require a collective relief in order to provide effective protection to such investment, it would be contrary to the purpose of the BIT and to the spirit of ICSID, to require in addition to the consent to ICSID arbitration in general, a supplementary express consent to the form of such arbitration. In such cases, consent to ICSID arbitration must be considered to cover the form of arbitration necessary to give efficient protection and remedy to the investors and their investments, including arbitration in the form of collective proceedings.[20]

The sum of these two arguments led the *Abaclat* majority to conclude that the mass aspect of the proceedings did not relate to consent, but to the modalities and implementation of the ICSID proceedings, given the need to ensure that the proceedings could be carried out respecting due process requirements despite the number of claimants. This meant that the issue was not one of jurisdiction but rather one of admissibility. As one author has noted, the implication of the *Abaclat* majority's position is that mass claims are not fundamentally incompatible with investor-State arbitration, but more simply a possible consequence of the general and abstract nature of the type of consent contained in investment treaties.[21]

The *Ambiente Ufficio* majority came to the same conclusion having analyzed a number of other cases involving multiple claimants, where the issue had not been fully debated. It held that

> it is evident that multi-party arbitration is a generally accepted practice in ICSID arbitration, and in the arbitral practice beyond that, and that the institution of multi-party proceedings therefore does not require on the part of the respondent Government beyond the general requirements of consent to arbitration[22]

and that

> nothing [...] militate [...] in favour of interpreting the 'silence' of the ICSID Convention as standing in the way of instituting multi-party proceedings. Quite to the contrary, not only are multi-party arbitrations not excluded by the pertinent provisions of ICSID law, but they are perfectly compatible with them.[23]

Exactly like *Abaclat*, *Ambiente Ufficio* concluded that the ICSID Convention, the relevant BIT and the other applicable rules were not opposed to a plurality of claimants jointly submitting an ICSID claim and do not require "specific or additional consent" on the part of the State beyond the one required under Article 25(1) of the ICSID Convention.[24]

This issue was apparently decided in the opposite direction by the majority in *Erhas v Turkmenistan*[25] which seems to have held that specific consent by the State to collective adjudication could not be inferred without more and that it therefore lacked jurisdiction. One may wonder whether this conclusion was not in part influenced by the lack of commonality between the claims, since the case involved disparate "entirely unrelated claims" advanced by unrelated claimants, which is what ultimately led the dissenting arbitrator to hold that, although the tribunal had jurisdiction, the claims were inadmissible.

The need for a special, or secondary, consent for collective actions, which is not covered by a mere acceptance to arbitrate, is postulated by Professor Abi-Saab in his vigorous dissent in *Abaclat*.[26]

Giovanni Alemanni addressed the issue rather differently. Like its two companion awards, it reasoned that there is no basis for implying into the text of Article 25(1) of the ICSID Convention ("dispute arising directly out of an investment, between a Contracting State ... and a national of another Contracting State") the qualification "one, *but only one*, national of another Contracting State", which would imply some form of special consent on account of the collective nature of the claims.[27] However, *Giovanni Alemanni* parted ways with its sister awards because it added a further level of analysis. It noted for a start that arbitration with a multiplicity of parties is possible in three situations,[28] i.e. when it is specifically provided for in the applicable rules (for instance Article 1226 of NAFTA), when it is specifically agreed to in relation to the given situation, as was in its view the case in several of the ICSID cases with multiple claimants, and in a third, intermediary, category of situation (which was the one at hand) where the instrument setting up the arbitration or establishing the State's consent can be properly interpreted on the facts of the case as covering a multiplicity of claimants within the consent.

In the tribunal's view this required an analysis of the provision providing for arbitration of the relevant BIT (Article 8 of the Argentina-Italy BIT), which makes reference to a "dispute relating to investments". From this the Tribunal derived the conclusion that, whether there is one or more than one investor, there must be "a dispute," which it considered to be the element that most satisfactorily defines the link that must exist between a group of claimants and their claims in order for them to be heard together, in the absence of specific consent by the State.[29] *Giovanni Alemanni* held that the relevant treaty clauses

> provide for a mechanism for the settlement of individual disputes; they do not (absent either special agreement to that effect or joinder) provide a mechanism for the joint settlement of a collection of separate disputes. This does not however mean that the concept of 'dispute' has to be given a narrow or over-technical meaning. The Tribunal has already indicated that it is perfectly possible, in its opinion, for a 'dispute' to have more than one party on the claimant's side. But the interest represented on each side of a dispute has to be in all essential respects identical for all those involved on that side of the dispute.[30]

On this premise the *Alemanni* tribunal concluded that the necessary analysis into whether

> the actual rights of all of the Claimants [...] and whether the actual effect [...] on those rights (or associated expectations) of Argentina's conduct were sufficiently the same as to amount to a single 'dispute' over Argentina's obligations under the BIT, even within the broad and non-technical understanding of a 'dispute' that is appropriate to Article 8 of the BIT read in conjunction with Article 25 of the ICSID Convention

could only be conducted in light of a close analysis of the facts of the individual claims, which related to Argentine public bonds under different issues, with different maturities, governing laws, currencies, interest rates. This led the tribunal to join this issue to the merits.[31]

The conclusion that can be drawn from investment jurisprudence is therefore that there is no obstacle of principle to multiple claimants bringing the same arbitration, unless there is an explicit exclusion of this possibility in the relevant instruments.[32] The debate thus shifts to the relation that must exist between the different claimants and their claims in order for them to be aggregated in a single proceeding. It is in fact intuitive that, if claims are to be brought together, there must be some form of homogeneity between them.[33]

This position was clearly expressed by the *Ambiente Ufficio* majority which held that it "would [...] have its doubts whether completely unrelated claims could be brought by a plurality of persons in one and the same arbitral proceeding."[34] The *Abaclat* majority, which considered the question from the angle of the "preconditions for group treatment"[35] and viewed it as one of admissibility, held that "group examination of claims is acceptable where claims raised by a multitude of claimants are to be considered identical or at least sufficiently homogeneous."[36] In assessing homogeneity, *Abaclat* had regard to the claims arising under the Italy-Argentina BIT and not to the contractual claims of the individual claimants under the respective loan instruments they were claiming under. Using the adjective 'homogenous' four times in the same sentence, it held that

> the only relevant question is whether the Claimants have homogenous rights of compensation for homogenous damage caused to them by the potential homogenous breaches by Argentina of homogenous obligations provided for in the BIT.[37]

Abaclat held that in the case at hand the rights deriving from the bondholders' investments and Argentina's obligation to protect them were the same, the events leading to the alleged disregard of the rights and obligations were the same and the legislative acts of Argentina and their implementation were the same, as was the potential damage caused by them to the claimants. It therefore decided that the claims were "sufficiently homogenous to justify a simplification of the examination method and procedure".[38]

This approach was criticized in Prof Abi-Saab's extensively reasoned dissent which noted that

> homogeneity is in the eyes of the beholder. One can always reach a sufficient degree of homogeneity, i.e. common denominators, by climbing up the ladder of abstraction and/or by weeding out all the specificities of the claims that appear inconvenient. And that is precisely what the majority award does with the claims under consideration.[39]

The *Ambiente Ufficio* tribunal declined to consider *in abstracto* the question of the required links between the different claims, and specifically whether it is required that the claims be 'homogenous' or it suffices that they be 'sufficiently comparable,'[40] but came to the same conclusion as *Abaclat*.

As noted above, the majority of the *Giovanni Alemanni* tribunal was skeptical of the approach of the other two tribunals and preferred to rely on the element of 'dispute'. Unfortunately, the *Giovanni Alemanni* tribunal was not given the opportunity to carry out its analysis from this angle because the case never reached the merits phase. It would have been interesting to see whether its 'dispute' test — which would have required it to decide whether the factual and legal peculiarities of each claim, such as the timing and circumstances of each claimant's acquisition of its investment and the specificities of the individual loan instruments, were sufficiently similar to permit the conclusion that all were part of the same dispute — would have led to a different outcome to that of *Abaclat* and *Ambiente Ufficio*.

It seems that not even *Giovanni Alemanni*'s 'dispute' criterion is of itself capable of overcoming all the questions that can arise when it comes to assessing the nature and the intensity of the link between the different claims that is required to allow their aggregation in a single proceeding. Here one can only list some of the questions that can arise in this connection. For a start, is it necessary that all the claims arise from the same allegedly illegal measure of the host State? This in turn leads to other questions. For example, in what sense can a measure affecting one investor be considered the 'same one' as a measure that affects another investor? Does it have to be exactly the same measure? Or can measures sharing some common features qualify as well? For example, expropriatory measures with similar characteristics (for example targeting different assets, but of the same kind, say two or more oil concessions) arising from distinct, but in some way similar, administrative measures of the host State. Another example could be measures of the same type, but enacted at different times, such as a reiteration or an extension of the same law, or measures that target the same investment.

It is probably also reasonable to require some type of link or commonality of position between the individual claimants seeking to bring a collective claim, but here too there may be doubts as to what that should be. Does there have to be a legal relation of some kind between the different claimants, such as for instance the one between shareholders of the same company or companies of the same group or members of the same family? Must they have made the same investment? Should the claims share a common legal basis or cause of action, or can claims with different causes of action (for example one claim for expropriation and one for breach of the FET standard) or different requests for relief be brought together?

Another delicate question is whether claims arising from different investment protection agreements can be brought together. The issue was considered in *Guaracachi America and Rurelec v Bolivia* where the tribunal held that the submission by two claimants of identical claims based on the alleged violation of two different BITs (US-Bolivia BIT and UK-Bolivia BIT) "is not subject to the qualified express consent of the Respondent".[41] The tribunal reasoned as follows:

> The offers of arbitration contained in the BITs were not subject to any condition or limitation in their scope that would prevent the two Claimants from submitting a single, joint arbitration case against the Respondent. Nor were they subject to any condition that claimants in arbitration proceedings must ground their claims in just one BIT. Each of the Claimants accepted the offer of arbitration in the precise terms in which it was given by the Respondent, notably, providing consent by the Respondent that disputes over the application of the Treaties were to be settled by recourse to arbitration.
>
> One cannot therefore interpret the Treaties — using the well-known rules of treaty interpretation of Article 31 of the VCLT — as if they contained some limitation of scope preventing a claimant from submitting an arbitral claim together with another claimant when both claims are based on the same alleged facts and on the same alleged breaches although brought under

different BITs, provided that each claimant provides its own independent matching consent to arbitration.[42]

This issue arose also in the pending PCA cases against the Czech Republic relating to the measures enacted by that State which reduced the incentives allegedly promised to the investors as an inducement to invest in the renewables energy sector. In that case ten investors began an arbitration seeking compensation for the harm inflicted to their investments as a consequence of the host State's measures in violation of the Energy Charter Treaty and five different BITs (with Germany, Cyprus, United Kingdom, the Netherlands and Luxembourg).[43] The case was brought as a single UNCITRAL arbitration, but the Czech Republic responded by appointing different arbitrators, maintaining that the claims had to be decided in six different arbitration, four or which by different tribunals with the same composition on condition that the Claimants would not seek consolidation. The Claimants considered that such a move, which they considered purely tactical and aimed at increasing the procedural hurdles for them, was impermissible, as the Respondent should have appointed only one arbitrator and then subsequently contested the jurisdiction of the arbitral tribunal to hear all the claims together. This is, the position that would have been taken under most arbitration rules, and in particular the ICC Rules (Article 6). The investors accordingly asked the PCA to appoint a single arbitrator on the grounds that the Czech Republic had failed to do so as it should have, but the PCA very questionably washed its hands of the matter. The upshot is that the claims are now being prosecuted in separate parallel arbitrations and the issue of whether the claims could have been brought together was completely sidestepped and could not be subject to a proper adjudication.[44]

The appointment by the State of different arbitrators, which would signal its lack of consent to the aggregation of the proceedings, is obviously not relevant to the decision as to whether such an aggregation is admissible. It is of course permissible for the State to give its consent to the aggregation once the claims are brought, if such consent is clearly lacking or is in doubt (as may have been the case in some of the earlier cases). However, since as shown above a specific consent by the State to the aggregation of proceedings is not required, the satisfaction of the conditions for the aggregation has to be assessed regardless of the State's position on consent at the time when the claims are brought.

Added to all the issues sketched above is the further, procedural, problem, of whether the decision on the aggregation of the claims can be taken in a preliminary phase on jurisdiction or admissibility, as was held in the majority of the decided cases, notably in *Abaclat*, *Ambiente Ufficio* and *Guaracachi*, or whether it has to be deferred to the merits phase, as held by *Giovanni Alemanni*, which of course from a practical point of view can be quite unsatisfactory.

3 THE CONDUCT AND MANAGEMENT OF THE PROCEEDINGS

The second broad set of issues that arises in connection with proceedings involving a plurality of claimants relates to more practical issues related to the commencement, conduct and management of the proceedings.

At the commencement of the proceedings the problems can relate to the constitution of the group of claimants and to ensuring that consent to arbitration on the claimants' side is properly obtained and documented, to the instruction of counsel and to the determination of the method for such instructions and of governing the proceedings. The problems may be different if, in purely practical terms, the initiative of the arbitration comes directly from the claimants or if, instead, it comes from a third party, usually a third party funder. This was the case in all three Argentine bondholder cases, but with some differences between them. In the two smaller cases the entity behind the bringing of the proceedings was a pure third party funder. In *Abaclat* the promoting entity, the Task Force Argentina, an entity sponsored and funded by the Italian banks that had sold the defaulted bonds to the claimants, had a more direct interest, in that it agreed to fund the proceedings only for those claimants who expressly waived any claims against the banks who had sold the bonds.[45]

In this connection there arise practical problems of documentation, powers of attorney to counsel and mandate to the entity that organizes the proceedings. In the bondholder cases, Argentina even raised issues relating to the law governing the relations between the claimants and their counsel, arguing that they had to conform with domestic law. *Ambiente Ufficio* and *Giovanni Alemanni* rightly disposed of the problem on the basis that national law has no role to play in these aspects of ICSID proceedings.[46]

The presence of a plurality of claimants poses the problem of how to maintain the unity of strategy, of the degree of control that each individual claimant can maintain over the conduct of the proceedings and of the proper level of information of the claimants. The entity that directs the proceedings, where there is one, will inevitably have a crucial role and the rules governing this function can be equally crucial. The notion itself of collective proceedings is at odds with the ability for each claimant to have its say and to make its own decisions and adopt its own strategy. It is in this respect that collective proceedings take on an element of representative proceedings, as was noted in *Abaclat*, where the tribunal held that

> [...] one cannot ignore that some features of the present proceedings, in particular the way it is conducted, resemble representative actions: *Although Claimants made the individual and conscious choice of participating to the arbitration, their participation is thereafter limited to a passive participation in the sense that a third party, TFA, represents their interests and makes on their behalf all the decisions relating to the conduct of the proceedings*. The high number of Claimants further makes it impossible for the representative to take into account individual interests of individual Claimants, and rather limits the proceedings to the defense of interests common to the entire group of Claimants.
>
> In summary, the present proceedings seem to be a sort of a hybrid kind of collective proceedings, in the sense that it starts as aggregate proceedings, but then continues with features similar to representative proceedings due to the high number of Claimants involved (emphasis added).[47]

However, the absence of overarching rules governing this representative aspect, which unlike in true representative proceedings, is left to the contractual relations between the claimants, can make this difficult. What if there are differences between different claimants as to the conduct of the proceedings? What if some claimants want to change counsel and there is a difference of opinion between the different groups of counsel? What if counsel is subject to different rules?

A related, and perhaps even more complex, problem is due process, since collective proceedings may entail changes and adaptations to procedural mechanisms that could be held to entail a compression of due process rights of the parties. This issue has to be considered from the perspective of both the claimants and the respondent State.

The point was heavily debated in the Argentine bondholder cases in relation to the proposed adoption of special mechanisms could be adopted for the assessment of the evidence.[48] The *Abaclat* tribunal reasoned that

> [...] it is understood that adaptations made to the standard procedure must be done in consideration of the general principle of due process and must seek a balance between procedural rights and interests of each party.[49]

Considering the question both from the perspective of the respondent State and of the claimants, the *Abaclat* tribunal asked itself

> (ii) to what extent are Argentina's defense rights affected in comparison to 60,000 separate proceedings; and (iii) is it admissible to deprive Claimants of certain procedural rights, such as provided for under the TFA Mandate Package?[50]

The *Abaclat* majority weighted both parties' interests and found the balance to be in favor of adaptations to the procedure in the interests of both parties, and of just and fair settlement. As to the effects on Argentina's defense rights it held that

> (ii) Effects on Argentina's defense rights: It appears that the effect of such examination method and procedure on Argentina's defense rights is limited and relative. Whilst it is true that Argentina may not be able to enter into full length and detail into the individual circumstances of each Claimant, it is not certain that such approach is at all necessary to protect Argentina's procedural rights in the light of the homogeneity of Claimants' claims. In addition, the only alternative would be to conduct 60,000 separate proceedings. The measures that Argentina would need to take to face 60,000 proceedings would be a much bigger challenge to Argentina's effective defense rights than a mere limitation of its right to individual treatment of homogeneous claims in the present proceedings.[51]

Considering the matter from the perspective of the claimants, the *Abaclat* majority in essence held that, by initiating a mass claim, they had waived certain of their due process rights:

> It is undeniable that the TFA Mandate Package has the effect to depriving Claimants of a substantial part of their procedural rights, such as the decision on how to conduct the proceedings, the right to instruct the lawyers, etc. However, as mentioned above (see §§ 457-465), the setting of strict boundaries in relation to Claimants' procedural rights has been consciously accepted by Claimants in order to benefit from the collective treatment of their claims before an ICSID tribunal. In addition, the Tribunal did not find that such agreement was affected by any vice which would render it invalid. Consequently, the Tribunal sees no reason to disregard — as a matter of principle — Claimants' conscious choice.[52]

Prof. Abi-Saab dissented also on this point on the grounds that

> i) Justifying the abridgement and curtailment of the procedural rights of the Respondent, particularly as concerns the individual examination of claims

(and claimants) by the argument that the mass claims in question are sufficiently homogeneous, does not stand scrutiny [...].

This is because it is an absolute due process right of a respondent in a judicial or arbitral proceeding, to have every element of the claim or claims presented against him, examined by the tribunal, through adversarial debate that affords him full opportunity to contest and refute these elements one by one, if he can [...].

[...] although these mass-claims can be considered as arising 'out of the same fact pattern,' and thus share some common features (whence a degree of homogeneity), they are not identical and preserve some individualized features that distinguish them from one another. To the extent that the individual claims in the mass differ from each other, it is the absolute due process right of the defense, and the obligation of the Tribunal, to have them examined individually and adversarially by the Tribunal. The Tribunal has also to address and pass judgment on each of them and state the reasons on which it bases its judgment (Article 48/3 of the ICSID Convention). Failure to meet these requirements is a cause of annulment under the ICSID Convention (Art. 52/d).

A 'group examination' of mass claims that feature certain individual differences among themselves, can at best deliver rough or approximate justice. It may satisfy the due process requirements of an emergency mass claims program or an administrative compensation commission. But it definitely falls well below the stringent due process standard of judicial or arbitral proceedings.[53]

In *Corn Products International v Mexico*[54] the issue of due process was raised by the claimants, rather than by the State as occurred in the Argentine cases. In that case the claimants opposed consolidation under NAFTA Article 1126 by which they claimed they would have been prejudiced since, being "direct and fierce competitors," they would have been prevented from adequately presenting their cases with the attendant compression of their due process rights. The claimants' objection to consolidation was upheld by the arbitral tribunal.

In addition to the question of whether, in principle, recourse to special procedural mechanisms for the assessment of the evidence is admissible, there is the more practical question of which procedural mechanisms and case management techniques can be resorted to in practice. There is of course a variety of possible solutions. The only precedent for the moment is once again *Abaclat* where initially recourse to a 'sampling procedure' was contemplated. Faced with the parties' objection that such a procedure could jeopardize their rights to address all circumstances surrounding the investment of each claimant, the tribunal decided to examine each single document by appointing an expert and setting up a 'Database Verification process' with the following reasoning:

At this stage, the aim of the Database Verification is to verify the information available with regard to facts of nationality/incorporation, residence and date of purchase of the security entitlements, which are relevant to determine the Arbitral Tribunal's jurisdiction over the case (para 501(iii) of the Decision). While this process will allow to spot inconsistencies and irregularities in the information and documents submitted (such as inconsistencies in signatures), if any, it will be the Arbitral Tribunal's task to determine how to deal with such inconsistencies and irregularities, if any. The purpose of the Database Verification is not to proceed with an overall analysis of the circumstances surrounding the Claimants' consent or the validity of the documents on which such consent is based. This is and will remain the task of the Arbitral

> Tribunal. It, therefore, only constitutes a starting point for the Arbitral Tribunal to decide to what extent an individualized review of claims or documents will be necessary and how to best address such review. Therefore, Respondent's objections as to the necessity to review surrounding circumstances and the validity of the documentation submitted are inapposite and miss the point.[55]

It is in principle conceivable to adopt other techniques to deal with a plurality of claims, in particular ones borrowed from class actions, such as so-called pilot or bell-weather proceedings and simplified evidentiary rules, but their applicability in investment arbitration remains to be assessed. More broadly the question is how to identify and manage the issues that can be treated collectively and those that call for a specific treatment for each individual claimant.

Among the host of other potential problems, mention can be made of those that would arise in the event of a counterclaim by the respondent State and of a cost award in its favor. To mention only the most obvious ones, these include the apportionment of the liabilities among the different claimants and the existence of joint and several liabilities. At the moment there no clear responses, but these problems certainly loom in the background and will emerge if this type of proceedings will have a future.

4 CONCLUSIONS

The above discussion has merely scratched the surface of the issues related to whether and when the claims of multiple claimants can be aggregated in a single arbitration. The simple conclusion that can be drawn at this stage is that there are very few, if any, principles and that there are even fewer answers to the myriad problems that can arise in this connection.

Perhaps the only point as to which there is sufficient consensus is that there is no obstacle of principle to the aggregation of claims. There is of course also agreement that such aggregation is subject to the consent of the parties and it seems generally, albeit not unanimously, accepted that consent to aggregation does not have to be explicitly given. The discussion thus tends to focus not so much on the number of claims that can be brought together, but on the type of link that must exist between the different claims for their aggregation in a single proceeding to be possible. Beyond this, there is not much certainty. While at first sight providing a useful tool, the criterion proposed by the *Giovanni Alemanni* tribunal, which relies on the existence of a single 'dispute,' probably does not provide clear-cut solutions capable of eliminating uncertainties.[56] In order to decide whether the claims of multiple claimants form part of a single dispute that can be brought in a single arbitration, it will always be necessary to analyze the relations existing between the claims and the claimants. The outcome will thus be very fact-specific and will depend to a considerable extent on the appreciation of the arbitrators.

The introduction of special rules in the ICSID Convention on the consolidation of claims has been proposed.[57] Insofar as such rules were to mirror the one of NAFTA Article 1126 or the ones foreseen in the investment protection chapters of the agreements being negotiated by the European Union with its partners, they are unlikely to improve the situation dramatically by removing uncertainty and discretion. For instance, under NAFTA Article 1126 consolidation would require a decision on whether the case presents questions of law or fact in common. This would still leave it to the arbitrators to make the assessment on a case-by-case basis,[58] and is little more than a variation of the assessment of the homogeneity and commonality of claims in terms of which the issue has been framed so far. In any event a provision on consolidation would certainly not of itself do away with the need to balance the interests of the parties, the need to safeguard due process and so on. The situation would therefore not be significantly different from the one prevailing today, which ultimately rests largely on consent.[59]

The aggregation of claims might be facilitated if the arbitration is brought under rules such as the ICC Rules, which are an option available to the investor under a significant number of investment protection instruments. Article 10 of the ICC Rules which provides for the possibility of consolidation, in particular when all the claims are made under the same arbitration agreement, might lend itself to some creative thinking, but it would be illusory to expect it to eliminate all problems.

There thus remains a considerable tension between the specificities of arbitration, with its bedrock in consent[60], and of investment arbitration in particular, and the possibility of bringing together the claims of a large number of claimants. It remains to be seen whether the decisions of future arbitral tribunals will be more or less overtly influenced by policy considerations of some type, foremost among which access to justice, which can militate in favor of allowing the bringing of collective actions by large numbers of potential claimants who would not have the ability and the resources to prosecute their claims individually. In the case of violations by States, investment arbitration is the only dispute settlement mechanism capable of ensuring a fair treatment of the claims. In this respect, the situation is different from commercial arbitration, where also there is an increasing focus on attempting to make some form of collective arbitration possible (for example for antitrust follow-on claims), but where the plaintiffs have an alternative to arbitration (and possibly a much more effective one). It is true that, as indicated by some tribunals,[61] policy considerations should not hold much sway in this discussion. Nevertheless, in the absence of clear indications in the applicable rules, such considerations may creep into the reasoning of arbitral tribunals.[62] Given the present turmoil regarding investor-State arbitration and the risk of a backlash against it, it is advisable that arbitrators exercise restraint in pushing the boundaries of jurisdiction over States.[63]

NOTES

1 See V. Heiskanen, *Mass Claims in ICSID Arbitration*, in M. N. Kinnear, G. R. Fischer, *et al.* (eds), *Building International Investment Law: The First 50 Years of ICSID*, Kluwer Law International, 2015, p. 613-614 explaining that there is no agreed legal definition of "international mass claims" and that, as a technical term, "*mass claims refers to a level of numerosity in which statistical methods become available in claims proceedings*". *Contra*, H. van Houtte and B. McAsey, *Abaclat and Others v Argentine Republic — ICSID, the BIT and Mass Claims*, in ICSID Review, vol. 27 n. 2, 2012, p. 231-232, according to whom "*Abaclat is not a 'mass claims' process in the traditional sense*". See also the dissents of Prof. Abi-Saab in *Abaclat and Others v The Argentine Republic*, ICSID Case No. ARB/07/5, § 180, and Dr. Torres-Bernárdez in *Ambiente Ufficio S.p.A. and*

Others v The Argentine Republic, ICSID Case No. ARB/08/9, § 99 holding that international "mass claims" proceedings are different from collective ones commenced by investors.

2 See S. I. Strong, *Class, Mass and Collective Arbitration in National and International Law*, Oxford University Press, 2013, § 1.12-1.36 who distinguishes three types of "large-scale" arbitral proceedings: class, mass and collective arbitrations. While class arbitration is a specific product of the U.S. experience with judicial class actions, the now famous *Abaclat and Others v The Argentine Republic* (the first investment arbitration commonly labelled as "mass proceedings") would be "*a new form of large-scale arbitration unlike that which had evolved in the United States*" (*Id.*, § 1.30). As to the general term "collective arbitration", for S. I. Strong it "*includes a variety of different large-scale procedures unified only by the fact that they are private (non-treaty based) mechanism that do not bear the hallmarks of U.S.-style class arbitration*" (*Id.*, § 1.31). An example of the latter would be the arbitral procedure to resolve shareholders' disputes under the Supplementary Rules for Corporate Law Disputes of the German Institution of Arbitration ("DIS", according to the German acronym). In *Abaclat v Argentina* the tribunal recognized that "*there is no uniform terminology concerning the various kinds of proceedings involving a high number of parties, and that various jurisdictions, courts and authors refer to different terms and meanings*" (ICSID Case No. ARB/07/5, Decision on Jurisdiction and Admissibility, 4 August 2011, § 480). The tribunal decided to use the expression "mass proceedings" simply due to the high number of claimants involved, but without any elaboration on the "*procedural classification of the present proceedings as a specific kind of collective proceedings recognized under any specific legal order*" (*Id.*, § 480). In the parallel *Ambiente Ufficio S.p.A. and Others v The Argentine Republic*, where the number of claimants (initially 120 which dwindled to about 90) was far less that in *Abaclat* (60,000 claimants down from an initial 180,000), the tribunal advised against the use of the concept of "mass claims" and "mass proceedings", "*especially insofar as the use of the term 'mass claim' or 'mass proceedings' might convey the connotation that already the sheer number of claimants in itself calls for modifications or adaptations of the procedural arrangements to guarantee the manageability or fairness of the case*" (ICSID Case No. ARB/08/9, Decision on Jurisdiction and Admissibility, 8 February 2013, § 120). To avoid a "*terminological imbroglio*", the tribunal preferred to qualify that action as a "multiparty" arbitration (*Id.*, § 122). On terminology see also the third of the Argentine bondholder cases, *Giovanni Alemanni and Others v The Argentine Republic*, ICSID Case No. ARB/07/8, Decision on Jurisdiction and Admissibility, 17 November 2014, § 267.

3 On the problems of this type of arbitration see L. G. Radicati di Brozolo, *Class Arbitration in Europe?*, in A. Nuyts and N. E. Hatzimihail (eds.), *Cross-Border Class Actions. The European Way*, Sellier, 2014, p. 209 ff.

4 Specific institutional rules, such as the AAA Supplementary Rules and the JAMS Class Action Procedures, have developed in the U.S. to deal with "class arbitration". These provide for a "system" of partial final awards, subject to immediate court review, on whether the arbitration agreement permits class treatment (Rule 3 of the AAA Supplementary Rules and Rule 2 of the JAMS Class Action Procedures) and whether such treatment is appropriate under the circumstances, and therefore whether the class must be certified (Rules 4-5 of the AAA Supplementary Rules and Rule 3 of the JAMS Class Action Procedures). See S. I. Strong, *supra* fn 2, § 2.26-2.120.

5 See *Abaclat*, *supra* fn. 2, § 486-488:

> Looking at the way the present arbitration was initiated, the present proceedings appear to be aggregate proceedings, in which each individual Claimant is aware of and consented to the ICSID arbitration. [...] However, one cannot ignore that some features of the present proceedings, in

> particular the way it is conducted, resemble representative actions: Although Claimants made the individual and conscious choice of participating to the arbitration, their participation is thereafter limited to a passive participation in the sense that a third party, TFA [Task Force Argentina], represents their interests and makes on their behalf all the decisions relating to the conduct of the proceedings. The high number of Claimants further makes it impossible for the representative to take into account individual interests of individual Claimants, and rather limits the proceedings to the defense of interests common to the entire group of Claimants. In summary, the present proceedings seem to be a sort of a hybrid kind of collective proceedings, in the sense that it starts as aggregate proceedings, but then continues with features similar to representative proceedings due to the high number of Claimants involved.

6 The cases generally referred to in this connection (without any consistent reasoning as to why they are considered "collective") are *Erhas Dis Ticaret Sti and others v Republic of Turkmenistan*, Award, 8 June 2015 (involving 22 claimants; the decision is unpublished but reported in **www.iaireporter.com**); *Alasdair Ross Anderson and others v Costa Rica*, ICSID Case No. ARB(AF)/07/3, Award, 19 May 2010 (involving 137 claimants); *Bernardus Henricus Funnekotter and others v Zimbabwe*, ICSID Case No. ARB/05/6, Award, 22 April 2009 (involving 14 claimants); *Canadian Cattlemen for Fair Trade v United States*, NAFTA/UNCITRAL case, Award on Jurisdiction, 28 January 2008 (involving 109 claimants); *Bayview Irrigation District and others v Mexico*, ICSID Case No. ARB(AF)/05/1, Award, 19 June 2007 (involving 46 claimants); *Antoine Goetz and others v Burundi*, ICSID Case No. ARB/95/3, Award, 10 February 1999 (involving 6 claimants). In many of those cases the issue of whether claims by multiple claimants could be brought together was not addressed in and the *Ambiente Ufficio* tribunal advised caution regarding attempts to draw definitive conclusions from those decisions (*Ambiente Ufficio*, *supra* fn. 2, § 138; see also *Giovanni Alemanni*, *supra* fn. 2, § 288). The *Ambiente Ufficio* tribunal also recognized that "*multi-party arbitration is a common feature in ICSID arbitration*" since, at the time of the award, the ICSID's case list revealed that in almost forty reported cases there were at least three claimants (*Ambiente Ufficio*, *supra* fn. 2, § 135).

7 Also the investment chapters of the trade agreements that the European Union is negotiating with Canada, Singapore and the United States provide no specific rules. Interestingly, they all include "bonds" in the definition of protected investments. Bonds are a form of investment that by nature can give rise to collective claims, as the Argentinian cases under discussion demonstrate (see for instance Article 8.1 of the CETA, definition of "investment", let. c). For an overview of the substantive and procedural rules in these investment chapters, as well as a discussion of future evolution of investor-State protection and arbitration, see L. G. Radicati di Brozolo, *Where is Investor-State Arbitration Heading? Reflections on the Debate over EU Investor Protection Agreements*, in A. Carlevaris, L. Lévy, *et al.* (eds), *International Arbitration under Review. Essays in Honour of John Beechey*, ICC Publishing, 2015, p. 319 ff. and L. G. Radicati di Brozolo and F. Iorio, *Arbitration Under Investment Protection Agreements between the EU and Non-Member States*, in *World Arbitration Reports*, Rel. 8-2015.

8 Article 1126.2 of NAFTA:

> Where a Tribunal established under this Article is satisfied that claims have been submitted to arbitration under Article 1120 that have a question of law or fact in common, the Tribunal may, in the interests of fair and efficient resolution of the claims, and after hearing the disputing parties, by order: (a) assume jurisdiction over, and hear and determine together, all or part of the claims; or (b) assume jurisdiction over, and hear and determine one or more of the claims, the determination of which it believes would assist in the resolution of the others.

9 See, for instance, Article 33 of the US-Uruguay BIT; Article 15.24 of the US-Singapore Free Trade Agreement; and Article G27 of the Canada-Chile Free Trade Agreement.

10 See Article 8.43 of the CETA (the text is available online at **http://trade.ec.europa.eu/doclib/docs/2014/september/tradoc_152806.pdf**); Article 9.29 of the EU-Singapore FTA (the text as at May 2015 is available at **http://trade.ec.europa.eu/doclib/press/index.cfm?id=961**; and Section 3, Article 27 of the TTIP (the European Union's proposal made public on 12 November 2015 is available at **http://trade.ec.europa.eu/doclib/docs/2015/november/tradoc_153955.pdf**).

11 *Ambiente Ufficio*, *supra* fn. 2, § 153. On the relevance of the expectations that can be drawn from domestic law, and in particular that of the law of the host State, as to the bringing of collective proceedings see *Id.*, § 133-134.

12 *Abaclat*, *supra* fn. 2, § 484.

13 The irrelevance of policy goals and efficiency considerations for this analysis is underscored by *Ambiente Ufficio*, *supra* fn. 2, § 145.

14 *Ambiente Ufficio*, *supra* fn. 2, § 129; *Giovanni Alemanni*, *supra* fn. 2, § 269-270. On the relevance for this discussion of the notion of consent and on its formation in international law, see *Giovanni Alemanni, supra fn. 2,* § 284.

15 *Ambiente Ufficio*, *supra* fn. 2, § 131; *Giovanni Alemanni*, *supra* fn. 2, § 270, noting that the Vienna Convention's canon of interpretation according to good faith can "*by no stretch of the imagination be read as imposing a sort of lexicographical literalism*".

16 *Ambiente Ufficio*, *supra* fn. 2, § 132.

17 *See* S. Brekoulakis, *The role of non-signatories in international commercial arbitration: rethinking the concept of consent*, forthcoming.

18 See fn. 6 above. Most of these awards are discussed in *Ambiente Ufficio*, *supra* fn. 2, § 136 ff. and *Giovanni Alemanni*, *supra* fn. 2, § 285.

19 *Abaclat*, *supra* fn. 2, § 490.

20 *Abaclat*, *supra* fn. 2, § 490.

21 See V. Heiskanen, *supra* fn. 1, p. 619.

22 *Ambiente Ufficio*, *supra* fn. 2, § 141.

23 *Ambiente Ufficio*, *supra* fn. 2, § 146.

24 *Ambiente Ufficio*, *supra* fn. 2, § 146.

25 *Erhas v Turkmenistan*, *supra* fn. 6. The tribunal apparently also held that since arbitration (in that case UNCITRAL arbitration) is a private and consent-based process and designed to solve a single dispute, the parties have a legitimate expectation of separate processes.

26 Dissent of Prof. Abi-Saab, *supra* fn. 1, § 122 ff., especially § 146-190.

27 *Giovanni Alemanni*, *supra* fn. 2, § 270.

28 *Giovanni Alemanni*, *supra* fn. 2, § 285-286.

29 *Giovanni Alemanni*, *supra* fn. 2, § 288 ff.

30 *Giovanni Alemanni*, *supra* fn. 2, § 292.

31 *Giovanni Alemanni*, *supra* fn. 2, § 293.

32 As seen above, the outlier on this point may be *Erhas v Turkmenistan*, *supra* fn. 6.

33 The complete lack of homogeneity between the claims and the claimants seems to have been at the heart of the decision in *Erhas v Turkmenistan*, *supra* fn. 2.

34 *Ambiente Ufficio*, *supra* fn. 2, § 490, 153.

35 *Abaclat*, *supra* fn. 2, § 540.

36 *Abaclat*, *supra* fn. 2, § 540.

37 *Abaclat*, *supra* fn. 2, § 540. This type of analysis was not engaged in by earlier tribunals.

38 *Abaclat*, *supra* fn. 2, 542-544.

39 Dissent of Prof. Abi-Saab, *supra* fn. 1, § 142.

40 *Ambiente Ufficio*, *supra* fn. 2, § 154 and § 161.

41 *Guaracachi America, Inc. and Rurelec plc v The Plurinational State of Bolivia*, PCA Case No. 2011-17, Award, 31 January 2014, § 334. Claims under two different BITs in relation to the same investment were adjudicated in the same proceedings in *Flughafen Zürich A.G. and Gestión e ingeniería IDC S.A. v Bolivarian Republic of Venezuela*, ICSID Case No. ARB/10/19, Award, 18 November 2014.

42 *Guaracachi America, Inc. and Rurelec plc v The Plurinational State of Bolivia*, PCA Case No. 2011-17, Award, 31 January 2014, § 336-337.

43 These cases are mentioned *supra*, in fn. (*).

44 The issue was addressed in a much more satisfactory manner in *Guaracachi America*, *supra* fn. 41, § 338-340, which distinguished *ab initio* multiparty proceedings from the different situation of consolidation, which requires specific consent from all the parties:

> In the Tribunal's view, the issue raised by the Respondent of whether express consent regarding the form of the present arbitration is required is also not an issue of 'consolidation of proceedings'. Indeed, in the instant case, the Claimants did not commence two separate arbitrations in respect of two independent arbitral claims that have subsequently been consolidated. The Claimants submitted, *ab initio* and in the same arbitration, two claims by two claimants against one respondent, regarding the same dispute and involving the same set of facts, albeit allegedly in violation of two different BITs concluded by the Respondent with the UK and the US, respectively. It is clear that the object of both claims is the same, since the allegedly unlawful action by Bolivia was also a single one, notwithstanding the fact that, in practice, the present case concerns two identical and overlapping claims by two claimants against the same respondent in the same arbitration proceeding.
>
> On the other hand, in cases of consolidation of proceedings, the matching of consents with respect to each of the arbitrations has already occurred. As such, the case law and literature hold—as both Parties in this proceeding have also affirmed—that consent is required from all parties involved in order to allow the merger of the two arbitrations into one. The Tribunal considers that there is, therefore, no valid analogy to be made between this case and cases of consolidation of proceedings.
>
> The Tribunal therefore considers that, even if it would have been possible for the Claimants to submit separate arbitral proceedings, nothing precludes them—given the obvious link between both Claimants and the identity of the facts alleged—from deciding to jointly submit a single arbitration case, albeit invoking different BITs.

45 See *Abaclat*, *supra* fn. 2, § 65, 84 ff.

46 *Ambiente Ufficio*, *supra* fn. 2, § 242; *Giovanni Alemanni*, *supra* fn. 2, § 277.

47 *Abaclat*, *supra* fn. 2, § 487-488.

48 See R. Kabra, *Has Abaclat v Argentina left the ICSID with a 'mass'ive problem?*, in *Arbitration International*, vol. 31 no. 3, 2015, § 444: "*Due process is not an end in itself, but merely a means to achieve a just and fair settlement of a dispute.*

[...] making 'mass claims' inadmissible results in a frustrating situation for both investors and states since the former is denied an effective remedy and the latter becomes susceptible to potentially conflicting decisions".

49 *Abaclat, supra* fn. 2, § 519.

50 *Id.*, § 539.

51 *Id.*, § 545. See also *Ambiente Ufficio*, *supra* fn. 2, § 166; *Giovanni Alemanni*, *supra* fn. 2, § 324.

52 *Abaclat, supra* fn. 2, § 546. See also *Ambiente Ufficio*, *supra* fn. 2, § 168; *Giovanni Alemanni*, *supra* fn. 2, § 324.

53 Dissent of Prof. Abi-Saab, *supra* fn. 1, § 235-239.

54 *Corn Products International, Inc. v United Mexican States*, ICSID Case No. ARB (AF), Award (not public), 18 August 2009 analyzed in E. Silva Romero, *Consolidation and Parallel Proceedings*, in M. N. Kinnear, G. R. Fischer, *et al.* (eds), *Building International Investment Law: The First 50 Years of ICSID*, Kluwer Law International, 2015, p. 601 ff. Consolidation under NAFTA Article 1126 was instead admitted in *Canfor Corporation, Tembec Inc., Tembec Investments Inc. and Tembec Industries Inc. v United States*, UNCITRAL, Order of the consolidation Tribunal of September 7, 2005 (see E. Silva Romero, *op. cit.*, p. 607 ff.).

55 *Abaclat*, Procedural Order No. 17 of 8 February 2013, by majority, § 21.

56 Interestingly, the notion of dispute borrowed from *Alemanni* is proposed by S. Brekoulakis (*The role of non-signatories in international commercial arbitration*, *supra* fn. 17) as a more appropriate construct to deal with multiple claims and multiple parties in commercial arbitration and to overcome the problems with the traditional approach to this subject which improperly relies on putative consent.

57 V. Heiskanen, *supra* fn. 1, p. 624-625.

58 See E. Silva Romero, *supra* fn. 54, p. 607 ff.

59 See E. Silva Romero, *supra* fn. 54, p. 609.

60 There seems to be little room for importing into investor-State arbitration the "rethinking of the concept of consent" for which S. Brekoulakis (*The role of non-signatories in international commercial arbitration*, *supra* fn. 17) makes a very convincing case in relation to commercial arbitration. This is because investor-State arbitration involves States, whose amenability to submit to arbitration is less than that of private parties, and because it is not possible to conceive of arbitration in investor-State relations as a default dispute settlement mechanism, as commercial arbitration arguably is in relation to international business disputes.

61 See *supra*, fn. 13.

62 The pervasiveness of such considerations is evident in the two awards analyzed by E. Silva Romero, *supra*, fn. 54.

63 See L. G. Radicati di Brozolo, *Where is Investor-State Arbitration Heading?*, *supra* fn. 7, p. 342.

Chapter 11

Incentives for Large-Scale Arbitration

How Policymakers Can Influence Party Behaviour

S.I. Strong*

1 INTRODUCTION

Interest in large-scale arbitration has grown exponentially in recent years, and the international legal community has seen the development of a variety of types of procedures. Class arbitration is perhaps the most well-known of these devices and is most closely associated with the United States due to the procedure's resemblance to US-style class actions.[1] However, two other countries — Colombia and Canada — have also considered adopting the procedure.[2] The second large-scale device, collective arbitration, exists in a number of jurisdictions, including the United States, Spain and Germany.[3] Ireland has also adopted a number of large-scale collective procedures that can be considered arbitral or at least quasi-arbitral in nature.[4] Although each country has developed its own unique procedural approach, all of these mechanisms involve individual as opposed to representative claims, as is the case in class arbitration. The final large-scale mechanism, mass arbitration, is seen exclusively in treaty-based investment disputes and includes elements of both class and collective arbitration.[5]

Some people attribute the development of large-scale arbitration exclusively to the US experience.[6] However, other influences exist, most notably in the form of the increased attention being given to large-scale litigation around the world.[7] Numerous countries, including those that once scorned the US class action as (yet) another form of American exceptionalism, have now developed their own means of providing large-scale judicial relief. These mechanisms, often referred to as 'collective redress' so as to avoid confusion with US-style class actions, can provide useful models for new forms of large-scale arbitration.[8]

At this point, the future of large-scale arbitration can best be described as mixed. On the one hand, class arbitration has been curtailed in the United States as a result of two US Supreme Court decisions upholding waivers of large-scale suits in arbitration.[9] On the other hand, mass and multiparty arbitration appears to be on the rise in the investment context, with claims arising not only against Argentina but also against Cyprus.[10] Collective arbitration appears to exist somewhere between these two extremes. While various procedures exist, parties do not appear to pursue these actions very frequently.

* D.Phil., University of Oxford; Ph.D. (law), University of Cambridge; J.D., Duke University; Master in Professional Writing, University of Southern California; B.A., University of California, Davis. The author, who is admitted to practice as an attorney in New York and Illinois and as a solicitor in England and Wales, is the Manley O. Hudson Professor of Law at the University of Missouri and Senior Fellow at the Center for the Study of Dispute Resolution.

The fragmented nature of the legal environment involving large-scale arbitration gives rise to questions about the legal and social environments in which these procedures exist. In particular, doubts exist as to whether parties have sufficient incentives to pursue large-scale arbitration and whether states can or should do more to promote this particular form of dispute resolution. Questions also exist as to whether large-scale arbitration can arise in jurisdictions that do not provide for some type of large-scale legal relief in their national courts.[11]

This chapter attempts to address these concerns by considering the issue of incentives for large-scale arbitration and in particular whether and to what extent policymakers can and should attempt to influence party behaviour through various mechanisms such as the use of default rules.[12] Although questions relating to incentives and defaults have been considered in the context of large-scale judicial actions,[13] this research has not yet been applied to arbitration. Furthermore, to the extent commentary regarding party motivation in large-scale arbitration does exist, it focuses on US-style class arbitration and does not consider other types of large-scale proceedings.

The structure of this chapter is as follows. First, section 2 considers party-oriented incentives and disincentives to large-scale arbitration. Section 3 considers these issues from the perspective of the state to determine whether and to what extent a particular jurisdiction may want to either oppose or promote large-scale arbitration. Section 4 then considers what types of default rules and procedures might be used to generate an arbitral regime that best suits party and state interests. Section 5 contains various concluding remarks.

2 PARTY INCENTIVES AND DISINCENTIVES TO LARGE-SCALE ARBITRATION

The consensual nature of arbitration[14] means that parties will not adopt class, mass or collective proceedings unless they have sufficient incentives to do so. As a result, it is useful to consider the various reasons why parties might wish to proceed in large-scale arbitration as opposed to either large-scale litigation or bilateral arbitration.[15]

Over the years, commentators have identified a number of reasons why parties might want to engage in large-scale proceedings. Although some of these rationales are somewhat limited in scope (in that they apply only to particular jurisdictions or only to one side of the dispute), it is still useful to consider them all so as to generate a comprehensive analytical framework.

A number of incentives for large-scale arbitration duplicate those seen in litigation. The most well-known of these involves efficiency, since a single large-scale proceeding can often be resolved in less time and for less money than a series of bilateral proceedings conducted either simultaneously (which would be difficult or impossible for both the respondent and any administering institution) or seriatim.[16] Although this benefit inures most markedly to the respondent, there are also advantages to the claimants, since working together can reduce the time spent drafting pleadings and researching the law and the facts. Indeed, information-sharing among claimants has long been considered a benefit of large-scale litigation.

Joining multiple claims into a single forum also avoids the possibility of inconsistent determinations, something that respondents typically appreciate more than claimants.[17] The concept of inconsistent determinations could arise on a cross-border basis (based on differences in the underlying law)[18] or within single jurisdictions (based on differences in how the dispute is presented to the decision-maker). However, respondents may not view this feature in an entirely positive light, since the combination of claims into a single proceeding means that in the respondents lose, they lose big.

Commentators have long supported the use of large-scale dispute resolution devices based on the various benefits associated with a global settlement (ie, single resolution of all claims associated with a particular incident). To some extent, this perspective is justifiable, since respondents have been empirically shown to support global settlements. However, respondents only favour broad resolution of group claims after it becomes clear that the matter will be adjudicated on a large-scale basis. Up until that point, most respondents adopt a strategy that seeks either to have the claims thrown out of court or arbitration based on alleged 'frivolity'[19] or to limit the number of persons who may assert a claim. Limitations can be substantive (as would be the case if a respondent were able to demonstrate that certain types of claims were legally insufficient) or procedural (as would be the case if a respondent were able to demonstrate a waiver of class or collective proceedings). In many cases, respondents believe (correctly) that their legal liability will be eliminated if they can eliminate the possibility of a group action, since many claimants will be unable or unwilling to proceed on a bilateral basis.[20]

These types of defensive strategies are particularly predominant in the United States, where broad pre-trial discovery can sometimes allow claimants to obtain information about other victims or other possible types of wrongdoing and significantly expand the respondent's legal exposure. Respondents in the United States are also eager to limit or avoid large-scale suits because the broad availability of punitive or treble damages make class and collective claims a threat to the respondent's continued existence and viability. However, if a class proceeding cannot be avoided, US parties should want to be in arbitration rather than litigation, since the obligation to exchange information is far less onerous in arbitration than in litigation.[21] Furthermore, arbitration does not use juries, which are often seen as one reason why class action judgements are so high.[22]

Respondents in countries that do not contemplate the use of juries, broad pre-trial discovery or punitive damages may not see as many benefits to large-scale arbitration as respondents who may be sued in US state courts. However, parties in these jurisdictions may nevertheless identify other incentives (confidentiality, speed, cross-border coordination, etc.) involving large-scale arbitration.

One key incentive for large-scale arbitration that has not been considered in the literature involves the likelihood that most class, mass and collective suits will be resolved through settlement rather than adjudication.[23] If this is indeed the case, then parties — particularly respondents — have a significant interest in being in arbitration, since the privacy associated with arbitration should help avoid the disclosure of information that would be embarrassing or legally problematic to the respondent. This is not to say that all types of large-scale arbitral proceedings can or should be entirely private and confidential (indeed, some arbitral institutions have already identified the various ways in which information about class, mass or collective proceedings should be made public), but the amount of publicity nevertheless appears to be more limited than in many types of litigation. [24]

The likelihood that large-scale claims will settle before final resolution of the claims in arbitration or litigation identifies another reason why parties should prefer to initiate such matters in arbitration. At this point, it is very difficult to enforce a negotiated or mediated settlement agreement across national borders. While parties could seek to proceed under the Dutch Act on Collective Settlements (WCAM), which provides judicial confirmation to large-scale settlement agreements,[25] not all parties will wish to invest the time and money associated with the Dutch proceeding. Instead, they may simply prefer to memorialize their agreement between themselves and hope that no dispute relating to the settlement agreement arises in the future. While there is currently no mechanism for enforcing such agreements in case of breach,[26] some commentators have suggested that these types of settlement agreements could be deemed to be arbitral awards and enforced under the United Nations Convention on the Recognition and Enforcement of Foreign Arbitral Awards (New York Convention).[27] This approach is as yet unproven, although commentators have suggested that it is important that any settlements that are intended to be enforced under the New York Convention be subject to a pre-existing arbitration agreement.[28]

Although some parties, practitioners and commentators consider the above-mentioned incentives to large-scale arbitration significant, there are a number of disincentives to consider. The first and perhaps most significant concern for respondents is that by allowing large-scale arbitration, they open themselves up to larger numbers of claims and thus larger damages awards.[29] This issue is perhaps most obvious in proceedings based on the Spanish statute for collective consumer arbitration, which requires notice of a large-scale proceeding to be given to the public at large.[30] Similar concerns might arise in collective proceedings under the DIS Supplementary Rules for Corporate Law Disputes, although the notice given in those matters is much more limited than in the Spanish example.[31] However, other types of actions — such as mass arbitration in the investment realm and class arbitration under the US model — do not involve a significant expansion of the number of claimants after the matter has been filed. In those cases, respondents attempt to have the entire matter deemed inadmissible, as reflected by battles over jurisdiction, admissibility and propriety of the underlying substantive claims.

As the preceding suggests, large-scale claims, however formulated, are often seen as 'bet the company' types of disputes. However, the nature of the issue is essentially the same in both litigation and arbitration, which means that large-scale arbitration cannot be considered inherently worse than large-scale litigation. Instead, the two procedures can be seen as largely analogous.

Although respondents are often the most vocal opponents to large-scale arbitration, claimants have their own sets of concerns. For example, claimants can often obtain a better outcome by proceeding individually than collectively, which should logically lead them to opt out or refuse to opt in to certain types of large-scale proceeding.[32] However, many claimants fear the time, cost and energy associated with pursuing an individual litigation or arbitration and therefore prefer to proceed on a group basis.

Interestingly, one purported disincentive of arbitration involves the lack of a substantive appeal. This issue is raised most often by respondents, although defendants in large-scale judicial actions lose on appeal far more often than plaintiffs do, at least in the United States.[33] As a result, this purported disincentive should actually be viewed by respondents as an incentive.

3 STATE INCENTIVES AND DISINCENTIVES TO LARGE-SCALE ARBITRATION

Although arbitration is traditionally framed as a party-driven procedure, states also have a significant interest in arbitral proceedings.[34] Furthermore, states are capable of either encouraging or discouraging parties to engage in arbitration by altering the legal environment in which arbitration operates. These influences can be the result of judicial decisions (as has been the case in both Germany[35] and the United States[36]) or statutory enactments (as has been the case in Spain[37] and, to a lesser extent, Ireland[38]).

State incentives to class, mass, and collective arbitration can in some cases mirror incentives for similar types of judicial actions. For example, states would be just as concerned about inconsistent determinations in the arbitral context as in the judicial setting. However, some issues require a slightly different analysis due to the private nature of arbitration. For example, judicial efficiency is often touted as one of the primary motivations for both large-scale litigation and large-scale arbitration. However, the concept of judicial efficiency is slightly different in the arbitral setting because large-scale arbitration does not consolidate numerous types of similar cases in a single court but instead removes those cases from the judicial system altogether. This particular feature might be extremely attractive in jurisdictions with extremely overburdened courts. Furthermore, as the Irish experience suggests, large-scale arbitration might be possible in counties that do not currently allow group actions in court, since the arbitration can sometimes provide for procedures that are not sanctioned in the judicial setting.[39]

Arbitration might also be a way for states to make sure that large-scale disputes are heard by decision-makers with the necessary substantive and procedural expertise. To some extent, this conclusion may seem counterintuitive, since judges are often considered to be somehow superior to arbitrators. However, the evolution of international commercial arbitration suggests that states are willing to admit that arbitrators are at least as well-qualified as judges in matters involving cross-border commercial disputes. While it is unclear whether the confidence in arbitral competence relates to procedural matters associated with arbitration's special blend of common law and civil law procedures or substantive concerns associated with arbitration's frequent reliance on foreign law, the fact is that numerous states have promoted arbitration in international disputes, even in cases where domestic arbitration would not be appropriate.[40]

Another potential incentive to large-scale arbitration involves the way in which class, mass and collective proceedings can be used as an *ex post* regulatory device.[41] Using arbitration as a means of regulating certain behaviour may be particularly appropriate in international disputes, given the difficulties associated with traditional forms of international regulation.[42] While some states may see this technique as inherently risky, the availability of the 'second look' doctrine would allow states to avoid enforcement of any award that violated a relevant public policy.[43]

Although these incentives to allow large-scale arbitration are in many ways compelling, there are also a number of reasons why states may not wish to support class, mass, or collective arbitration.[44] The first rationale involves the desire to avoid 'secret' proceedings on matters of wide social significance. Not only is arbitration seen as limiting the public debate about certain matters, but arbitration can also be seen as hindering the development of the law through judicial precedent. Confidential proceedings can also be considered as diminishing the deterrent value of large-scale actions, since other potential wrongdoers will not be aware of the consequences of improper behaviour.

States might also object to large-scale arbitration based on concerns about the parties' procedural rights. Many of these concerns involve the use of representative mechanisms such as those seen in US-style class arbitrations. However, some types of mass and collective arbitrations can also give rise to potential problems not only with respect to the claimants' ability to decide when, where, how and whether to assert a legal claim but also with respect to the ability of the respondent to defend against large-scale suits.[45] Commentators have also raised concerns about collusion, particularly in the context of US class actions.[46] Many of these issues have been addressed through various procedural protections,[47] but in some cases the stigma associated with US-style class suits can lead states to oppose large-scale arbitration without undertaking a detailed analysis as to whether the procedure in question gives rise to the types of concerns at issue. Notably, not all concerns are relevant to all types of large-scale arbitration.[48]

4 HOW STATES CAN AFFECT PARTY BEHAVIOUR

States can affect party behaviour in a variety of ways. For example, a state can adopt a particular law or regulation that explicitly prohibits or requires certain acts and can provide a penalty for non-compliance. However, this kind of direct approach may not be possible in cases where the state is not authorized to act.[49] Thus, a law requiring a corporate entity to enter into a particular type of contract (such as an arbitration agreement) would be impermissible, since it exceeds the state's ability to compel a particular action.

However, this is not to say that states cannot encourage parties to adopt certain behaviour that the state would be unable to control through direct regulation. Thus, a state can 'encourage' particular types of private activity by (1) creating a default regime that the parties would find difficult or expensive to change, even if change is technically or legally possible, (2) providing certain incentives to act in a particular manner, and/or (3) adopting certain disincentives to act in a particular manner. Each of these approaches can be used in the arbitral setting.

States that wish to undertake these types of actions can do so judicially or legislatively. At this point, the only legislature to have positively acted in favour of large-scale arbitration is Spain, which passed a statute providing for collective arbitration in consumer cases in 2008.[50] However, at least one Canadian province has considered statutory action in the area of class arbitration[51] and Ireland has enacted a number of statutes allowing for various types of quasi-arbitral proceedings against the state.[52]

Courts have also been involved in developing various forms of large-scale arbitration.[53] The most notable example has been the United States, which has generated several types of class arbitration[54] as well as various forms of collective arbitration.[55] Colombia has also adopted class arbitration by judicial decision.[56] In 2009, the German Federal Court of Justice (Bundesgerichtshof or BGH) declared shareholder disputes arbitrable, thereby opening the door to large-scale arbitration of certain types of corporate disputes.[57] Interestingly, the BGH only acted after the German legislature failed to address such issues following an invitation from the BGH in 1996 to consider such matters.[58]

Before a state takes any direct or indirect steps to promote large-scale arbitration, it must decide that such a goal is desirable. Only after the determination to move forward with a particular policy has been made can the state identify the best means of achieving the enunciated goal. Each of these steps is considered below.

A. Step One Determining Whether to Encourage Large-Scale Arbitration

When considering whether and to what extent to support large-scale arbitration, courts and legislatures must first determine whether there is a need for such a mechanism.[59] This analysis is in many ways similar to the debate about the need for various forms of large-scale relief in the judicial context. Traditionally, common law jurisdictions (most notably the United States, Canada and Australia) considered large-scale litigation to be a necessary and appropriate means of supplementing the state's regulatory scheme,[60] while civil law jurisdictions (with a few exceptions, most notably Brazil) tended to view large-scale relief as both unnecessary and inappropriate.[61] However, various changes in law and society have led numerous civil law jurisdictions to adopt various forms of collective redress. Thus, for example, more than half of the Member States of the European Union (EU) now offer some form of large-scale judicial relief as a domestic matter.[62] Furthermore, the EU has identified a need to develop some form of cross-border collective relief so as to address the growing number of large-scale disputes involving claimants located in different countries.[63]

These developments suggest a growing need for large-scale relief as a general concern. However, states must determine whether such relief can and should be offered in arbitration. In so doing, states must weigh the various incentives and disincentives identified in section two above.

The first thing to note when conducting this analysis is that a number of disincentives (namely, those relating to concerns about representative relief and those involving adequate protection of procedural rights) can be overcome through the adoption of proper procedures.[64] Furthermore, some policy-related concerns about the use of large-scale arbitration (such as those relating to the need to develop precedent or the decreased ability to provide a deterrent effect) are inapplicable in those jurisdictions that do not use litigation as a means of developing law and policy or as a deterrent measure.[65]

The diminished power of the various disincentives to large-scale arbitration suggests that states should be disposed to look favourably on the procedure. However, it is still necessary to consider the relative weight of the various state incentives to large-scale arbitration, since the mere lack of a disincentive is not enough to inspire a state to take a particular action. As it turns out, a number of the incentives discussed above (such as the ability of large-scale arbitration to reduce the burden on courts or regulatory enforcement mechanisms) are undeniable and can lead to significant public savings.[66] While the strength of some potential incentives are subject to debate (for example, whether and to what extent arbitrators are better able than judges to manage large-scale disputes and whether large-scale arbitration can provide an equally or less expensive means of resolving mass disputes than litigation), many of the underlying concerns can be addressed through proper procedures (such as the requirement that at least one of the tribunal members be experienced in large-scale dispute resolution and specific provisions about cost-sharing among parties).[67]

When considering these matters, states might find it useful to distinguish between domestic and international disputes, since large-scale arbitration may be particularly useful in cross-border matters. Thus, commentators have noted the way in which class, mass, and collective arbitration can overcome problems associated with (1) obtaining jurisdiction over all the parties, (2) determining and applying the governing law pursuant to a conflict of laws analysis, (3) harmonizing different national procedures and (4) facilitating international enforcement of the final decision.[68]

Another issue that states may wish to consider when conducting this analysis involves the likelihood that most large-scale disputes are resolved by either a negotiated or mediated settlement.[69] Although the Netherlands offers a relatively innovative means of enforcing international settlement agreements, the ability of a party to enforce other types of settlement agreements across national borders is very much in doubt.[70] However, it has been suggested that parties to a pre-existing arbitration agreement may be able to have a settlement agreement declared to be a type of arbitral award that would be enforceable under the New York Convention.[71] Thus, there may be benefits to having a pre-existing arbitration agreement in international disputes that are likely to settle.[72]

Those states that decide to encourage large-scale arbitration can do so through a variety of means, as discussed in the next subsection. However, the situation does not require an all-in or all-out solution. Jurisdictions that are still undecided about the propriety of large-scale arbitration can adopt an intermediate step similar to that taken in Germany in cases involving corporate disputes. There, the BGH did not take affirmative steps to encourage collective arbitration but instead simply declared such matters arbitrable in theory and identified certain basic procedural protections that had to exist for a particular arbitration agreement or award to be considered valid.[73] Thus, a court or legislature that wished to adopt a moderate approach to large-scale arbitration could declare such matters arbitrable (as Germany, Spain, Colombia and the United States have done, either explicitly or implicitly) and allow the precise procedures to evolve organically over time. Indeed, the task of creating detailed procedures for use in large-scale arbitrations might best be delegated to arbitral institutions that have the subject-matter expertise and the incentive to develop workable procedures.

While there is some risk associated with allowing arbitral institutions to develop large-scale procedures (since it might initially be unclear whether the arbitral institution has met all of the criteria considered necessary by the state), that task has been successfully carried out in both Germany and the United States.[74] Furthermore, the current international arbitral regime evolved as a result of this type of trial and error process, so this approach is not without precedent. While it is impossible to discuss each of the relevant issues in the current chapter, states will likely pay particular attention to a variety of factors ranging from the nature of claimant participation (ie, whether parties proceed in a representative or aggregative (individual) capacity and whether participation proceeds on an opt-in or opt-out basis); how notice is to be provided to potential claimants; what alterations, if any, are to be made to the presumptions of privacy and confidentiality; how respondent consent may arise; and whether arbitral or judicial approval must be given to any settlements generated by the dispute.

B. Step Two
Determining How to Encourage Large-Scale Arbitration

At this point, several jurisdictions have demonstrated support for large-scale arbitration, although the level and type of support can vary both between different states and over time. When considering how best to encourage a particular procedure, states must consider whether to (1) create a default regime that the parties would find difficult or expensive to change, even if change is technically or legally possible; (2) provide incentives to adopt the procedure in question; and/or (3) adopt disincentives to adopting a procedure other than the one the state wishes to encourage. Each of these approaches is considered below.

4.B.1 Creating a Default Regime that the Parties Would Find Difficult or Expensive to Change

The legal literature is rife with information about how states can and do use default rules to affect party behaviour.[75] Although these default rules are intended to maximize state interests, the rules do not operate as a traditional top-down regulatory mechanism. Instead, default rules operate in a coercive and often invisible manner to encourage parties to choose behaviours that the state wants to encourage.

Notably, the mere existence of legislation concerning large-scale arbitration does not necessarily constitute a default rule. Thus, for example, Spain has enacted a statute regarding collective consumer arbitration, but that provision does not operate as a default, since it does not drive the parties toward a particular procedure.[76] Instead, the statute simply offers the parties an alternative means of resolving their disputes.

A different approach is reflected in a proposal that Gary Born made recently regarding a new international treaty that would make arbitration the default for all international commercial disputes.[77] What makes this mechanism a default rule is the way in which the law requires parties to take certain affirmative steps to change the standard procedural regime. Rather than opting into a particular method of dispute resolution (as is the case with the Spanish statute), the parties would have to opt out of the proposed treaty regime. Since opting out requires some effort and incurs a certain amount of transaction costs, parties will be more likely to use the default mechanism, even if they might not otherwise choose to do so.[78]

Default rules can often be recognized by the phrase 'unless the parties agree otherwise' and are extremely common in institutional rules on arbitration.[79] Default rules on arbitration also exist, albeit to a more limited degree, in certain national laws[80] and international treaties.[81] Thus, it would be possible for a state that wanted to encourage large-scale arbitration to do so through the creation of default rules. Indeed, one way to increase the use of the Spanish statute on collective arbitration would be to turn it into a default rule.[82] Party autonomy would still be respected if the parties were allowed to opt out of the procedure, but the use of the procedure would likely increase if it were the default process.

These examples provide some basic illustrations of how a default rule relating to large-scale arbitration might be constructed. However, states only use default rules when they have a relatively high commitment to a certain mode of behaviour. At this point, it is unclear whether any particular jurisdiction has determined that large-scale arbitration is so useful that it should exist as the default in certain categories of cases.

This having been said, some states might be willing to consider a default rule on large-scale arbitration if they are presented with a concrete proposal on what that rule might entail. Unfortunately, that analysis cannot be conducted in the abstract. Instead, it is necessary to consider a variety of questions relating to the context and nature of the dispute (national or international), the mechanism in question (class, mass or collective), the relevant legal environment (common law or civil law) and whether the procedure is offered on a trans-substantive basis (as is the case with class and collective arbitration in the United States) or only with respect to certain subject matters (as is the case with collective arbitration in Spain and Germany and mass arbitration in the investment realm). It is also necessary to understand the legal and regulatory environment in which any proposed rule would operate, since any new procedure must work in tandem with existing procedures.

When thinking about whether to impose a default rule, states will likely be highly influenced by questions of timing, since default rules are typically imposed only in situations where the state has had some prior experience with a particular issue and can weigh the relative benefits of different approaches. Given the relative novelty of most forms of large-scale arbitration, it is unlikely at this point that states will adopt default rules encouraging class, mass or collective procedures. Instead, it is more likely that states will move gradually into this field and will begin by either increasing the incentives or decreasing the disincentives to group arbitration, since that approach allows the state to gather more evidence about the propriety of a particular rule or procedure before creating a default regime.

4.B.2 Providing Certain Incentives to Act in a Particular Manner

States often seek to affect party behaviour by providing incentives to act in a particular manner. Thus, for example, states wishing to minimize disputes about the service of process in litigation may give parties who waive formal process of service a longer time to respond to a complaint than parties who demand full and proper service.[83] This approach encourages parties to avoid preliminary disputes about service without creating a default rule that could be seen as infringing on the parties' procedural rights.

Incentives to party behaviour can be more difficult to identify than default rules. Indeed, some incentives have become so well-established that they are virtually invisible. However, such measures can nevertheless be found in the world of international commercial arbitration. Perhaps the most successful of these incentives involves the strong pro-enforcement policy reflected in the New York Convention.[84] This policy has been one of the major reasons why parties have been attracted to arbitration over both litigation (which is the default regime) and mediation (which is another alternative mechanism that was more popular than arbitration in the years prior to the enactment of the New York Convention).[85] States have consciously sought to incorporate this particular incentive into their national arbitration regime by joining the New York Convention.[86] Use of incentives can also be seen on the domestic level in cases involving the United Nations Commission on International Trade Law (UNCITRAL) Model Law on International Commercial Arbitration (MAL).[87] Although parties are still able and indeed entitled to seek judicial redress in international commercial disputes, adoption of the MAL makes arbitration so attractive that parties are likely to incur the necessary transaction costs (i.e., the cost of establishing an arbitration agreement) so that they can enjoy the benefits of this particular procedure.

One easy way for states to increase the incentives for large-scale arbitration would be to declare class, mass and collective procedures arbitrable as a matter of national law, thereby increasing the possibility that awards and agreements relating to such disputes will be deemed enforceable under the New York Convention.[88] However, other types of incentives are also possible.

The most powerful measures would focus on expanding or solidifying existing reasons for parties to use large-scale arbitration. Thus, for example, actions that would decrease the costs associated with class, mass or collective dispute resolution would be effective in encouraging parties to adopt group procedures. These efforts could relate to measures to save litigation costs or increase the speed or finality of the process. Arbitration already offers some such measures (such as limits on the exchange of information and the ability to appeal on the merits), but additional actions might be adopted for large-scale disputes. For example, many respondents claim that the limited ability to have the claims dismissed during the preliminary stages of arbitration increases their transaction costs and results in more 'strike suit' settlements.[89] Several arbitral institutions based in the United States have attempted to address that concern in class arbitration by creating two types of preliminary awards that could allow the dispute to be dismissed before the matter is heard on the merits.[90] This system, which is somewhat similar to that adopted in investment proceedings,[91] could be adapted for use in non-class proceedings.

Previously, this chapter suggested that respondents might be inclined to embrace large-scale arbitration as a means of avoiding inconsistent determinations, but only if having a single proceeding does not increase their financial exposure by bringing more claimants into the action than already exist or by allowing punitive damages.[92] Thus, respondents might be encouraged to participate in large-scale arbitration if states found a way to limit the number of potential claimants[93] or eliminated the possibility of damages multipliers. While this latter option might not be much of an incentive in states that already limit recovery to consequential damages, there are enough countries in the world that allow punitive, exemplary or aggravated damages to make this proposal worth considering.

When adopting measure such as the elimination of damages multipliers, states must take care that they are not affecting the overall effectiveness of a particular system of justice. For example, commentators have noted that limiting the availability of punitive damages could be problematic in jurisdictions that typically fund large-scale dispute resolution through the use of contingency fees, since an attorney may not be willing to take a case where the final award is not calculated by reference to a multiplier.[94] However, some of those difficulties might be addressed through the use of third party funders who may be willing to support a case even in the absence of punitive or exemplary damages.[95] This is particularly true in the investment context, where the awards are often significant enough to generate the interest of third party funders even though damages are awarded on a compensatory basis. The same might be true of a large-scale competition law or cross-border consumer case.[96]

Another potential incentive that the state might offer would be to allow parties in arbitration to use procedures that are not available in litigation. This measure might be particularly attractive in jurisdictions that have not yet adopted judicial forms of class or collective redress. Although some states might be concerned about the legitimacy of this approach, parties have long been allowed to consent to certain procedures in arbitration (such as fast-track or documents-only arbitration) that are not available in litigation.[97]

States might also consider whether parties could be encouraged to use class, mass, or collective arbitration as a result of the principle of arbitral privacy and confidentiality. While many of the large-scale proceedings currently in place contemplate some derogation from the standard understanding of arbitral privacy and confidentiality, some degree of privacy or confidentiality nevertheless exists, thereby making arbitration more attractive than litigation. Certain additional provisions might also be put into place, such as measures prohibiting information that was disclosed in a large-scale arbitration from being used in other proceedings.[98]

These are just a few of the possible ways to provide positive incentives to parties who might wish to engage in large-scale arbitration. Again, it is impossible to provide a comprehensive list of such measures in the abstract, since such recommendations must be made within the context of a particular legal environment. However, these types of policies could be combined with more general measures (such as the lengthening of time limits, as discussed in the context of the service of process) to encourage class, mass and collective procedures in appropriate circumstances.

4.B.3 Minimizing Any Disincentives to Act in a Particular Manner

States can also seek to affect party behaviour by minimizing any disincentives to act in a particular manner. Disincentives can be as difficult to identify as incentives, since they are often taken for granted in a well-established legal regime. However, it is possible to identify certain policy choices that eliminate or minimize disincentives that might otherwise limit parties' willingness to use a particular procedure.

One example might be the way in which states allow arbitral institutions to require corporate entities to pay all or most of the fees and costs associated with consumer or employment arbitration.[99] In so doing, the state helps remove one of the disincentives (cost) to claimants who might otherwise be inclined to enter into arbitration. While this measure could be seen as creating a disincentive to the respondent, most corporations prefer to have certain types of disputes (such as consumer, labour, employment and insurance matters) heard in arbitration for reasons ranging from savings of time and cost to avoidance of negative publicity and precedent. Therefore, the imposition of a small disincentive to the corporation is offset by the removal of a significant disincentive to the claimant.

Again, when considering how to encourage the use of large-scale arbitration, it is helpful to consider which disincentives are most problematic to the parties. The biggest concern appears to arise on the respondents' side and is associated with the way in which group arbitration appears to expand the number of claims beyond that which would arise on a bilateral basis. Respondents have fought against this particular phenomenon by either requiring potential claimants to waive the right to proceed as a class or collective[100] or by declining to opt into systems that could result in an unknown number of claimants.[101] The one type of large-scale arbitration that appears to avoid this problem involves corporate law disputes in Germany. However, the nature of those types of cases involves a relatively stable number of claimants, so the use of collective arbitration does not expand the respondent's liability in any discernible way.[102]

In many ways, questions of how to decrease disincentives are more difficult than those relating to increasing incentives, since a number of potential measures (such as reducing damages awards to eliminate respondents' concerns about unlimited liability) could result in a violation of claimants' procedural or substantive rights. Of course, this is not to say that solutions may not be found. For example, it might be possible to justify certain actions through analogies to other procedures (such as those relating to settlement agreements or insolvency actions, where creditors accept a percentage of what they would normally be entitled to receive in order to facilitate resolution of the dispute).

Other economically oriented solutions might look to the English Civil Procedure Rules for inspiration. Under those rules, a party may make a special type of settlement offer (a 'Part 36' settlement offer) to the court.[103] If the offeree chooses not to accept a Part 36 offer, the offeree may continue to litigate the matter, although the offeree will be typically liable for the offeror's litigation costs after the date of the settlement offer if the final judgment is less advantageous to the offeree than the proposed settlement.[104] States might encourage both settlement and arbitration of large-scale disputes if they created a similar mechanism whereby the respondent was allowed to make a certified settlement offer to the arbitrator that capped damages at a particular sum. If the claimants chose to move forward with the arbitration, all costs after the date of the settlement offer would be borne by the claimants if the final award was greater than proposed settlement amount. This device may be particularly attractive in arbitration, where fees and costs can include not only attorneys' fees but also arbitration fees and costs. The procedure encourages respondents to identify a reasonable amount for settlement, since an offer that is too low will easily be bettered after determination on the merits.

The other major disincentive to respondents is the relative difficulty of terminating an arbitration during the early stages of the dispute. However, that issue can be resolved by formalizing several intermediate stages where the matter might be dismissed, as discussed previously.[105]

4.B.4 Balancing Measures

When considering various incentives and disincentives, it is important to consider how the proposed procedure works together as a whole. Commentators have noted that many judicial procedures offering collective redress are ineffective because they fail to provide parties on both sides of the dispute with sufficient rationales to use the mechanism.[106] This problem usually arises because drafters are primarily concerned with avoiding the shortcomings of the US class action system.[107] However, in many cases, reformers failed to appreciate how certain aspects of the US class action system made large-scale suits worthwhile to both plaintiffs and plaintiffs' counsel. Without such incentives, neither victims nor lawyers may find it feasible to bring a large-scale suit.[108]

States considering the possibility of large-scale arbitration should bear these issues in mind when seeking to create their own forms of class, mass, or collective arbitration. The system must be sufficiently even-handed to attract parties while also offering certain reasons to choose arbitration over litigation.

5 CONCLUSION

For years, the international community has wondered whether large-scale arbitration would become popular and what that procedure would look like. Up until this point, the development of large-scale arbitration has been delayed by two different obstacles.

First, lawyers and policymakers have been unsure as to whether there is actually a need for such mechanisms. Many commentators and policymakers took the view that *ex ante* regulation was in fact sufficient to control improper behaviour and provide redress to injured individuals. However, the evolution of judicial forms of class and collective relief around the world suggests that there is in fact a growing need to address large-scale legal injuries. While it is possible that some jurisdictions' domestic courts provide adequate protection for injured individuals, there may be times when arbitration offers a superior method of dispute resolution. One such example might be in cases involving cross-border disputes. In those situations, large-scale international arbitration offers the same significant benefits as international arbitration in bilateral proceedings.[109] The recent increase in large-scale international disputes and the problems in developing inexpensive means of bilateral dispute resolution (such as through online dispute resolution (ODR))[110] suggests that new alternatives need to be developed.

The second obstacle to the development of large-scale arbitration involves the presumption that all such proceedings will reflect the norms used in US-style class arbitration.[111] That presumption appears largely incorrect, given the criticism of both US-style class actions and US-style class arbitration. Furthermore, that presumption ignores the wide variation of collective redress procedures seen around the world and the growing number of mass and collective procedures in different jurisdictions.

At various times the preceding discussion has referred to the need to consider the precise shape of the proposed procedures before evaluating how to construct default rules and party incentives. Although this chapter does not take a view on what types of large-scale procedures are appropriate (since that question should be answered by reference to the particular type of legal injury the procedure is seeking to address and the legal environment in which the procedure is to operate), there are a variety of alternatives to consider as potential models: mass arbitration in the investment realm, collective consumer arbitration in Spain, collective corporate arbitration in Germany, and trans-substantive collective arbitration in the United States, just to name a few.[112] Existing procedures can be blended, amended and transformed for use in other jurisdictions and other contexts.[113]

Although states have an important role to play in the development of large-scale arbitration, it is unlikely that they will become involved at a detailed level. Instead, states will and likely should focus primarily on acts (legislative or judicial) that confirm the arbitrability of large-scale disputes and that identify any procedural minimums that must be met to allow such disputes to be arbitrated.[114] Although it is possible for a state to participate in the creation of the precise procedures to be used,[115] there are certain benefits to allowing the arbitral community to take the lead in developing procedures. Not only can arbitration experts be both innovative and efficient (as was the case in Germany, where the DIS created the Supplementary Rules for Corporate Law Disputes in a matter of months), but arbitral rules are more easily amended than laws, which allows the relevant procedures to evolve over time.

At this point, it may be useful for the arbitral community to seek to create international rules of procedure relating either to trans-substantive claims (ie, rules addressing any possible subject matter) or subject-specific claims (such as consumer, online or competition/antitrust disputes). Not only will such a process be useful to parties seeking to decide whether they wish to adopt such a procedure, it will also be useful to states seeking to determine whether and to what extent they wish to promote large-scale arbitration. Once a basic procedure is in place, the relevant stakeholders — states, parties, practitioners, institutions — can work to fine-tune the details over time, as has been the standard practice in both national and international arbitration.

The lead for this sort of initiative could come from a private institutional body with significant experience in both international and large-scale proceedings. While this recommendation may lead some people to think of the American Arbitration Association (AAA), which admittedly has a great deal of experience with class arbitration,[116] that is a national institution that has close ties to a particular national procedure. Instead, a more international institution such as the International Chamber of Commerce (ICC) might be better placed to devise a truly international procedure that takes into account the predilections of both common law and civil law countries.

Public entities might also become involved in this discussion. While it is likely too early to ask UNCITRAL to develop a set of rules, since UNCITRAL works by international consensus and there is quite likely no consensus at the interstate level regarding the need for or form of international large-scale arbitration, the Permanent Court of Arbitration (PCA) might be amenable to developing a set of procedures that could be used in international disputes.[117] In many ways, the PCA appears to be an ideal choice, since the PCA not only has the trust of the international community but also has significant experience in administering mass claims through various claims tribunals.[118] Indeed, the PCA has already assisted with the resolution of a large-scale international claim that was originally filed as a US class action.[119] Although the PCA's mass claims procedures are somewhat different from what is at issue in this discussion, in that the PCA procedures typically do not attempt to resolve all claims at a single time, in a single forum, there may nevertheless be some overlap between the two processes.[120] Additional rules for large-scale matters might also be developed by the International Centre for Settlement of Investment Disputes (ICSID), particularly given the increasing incidence of such disputes in the investment context.[121] Such an initiative would reduce the debate about the jurisdiction of the tribunal and the admissibility of the claims in ICSID proceedings and would therefore save the parties time and money.

Although the international legal and business communities may be concerned about the spread of large-scale arbitration, the situation is very different than it was in 2003, when the US Supreme Court decision in *Bazzle v Green Tree Financial Corp* shook the arbitral world to its very foundations.[122] The development and expansion of large-scale arbitration has been gradual and well-considered, and there is every indication that future reforms will be taken with equal thoughtfulness. Furthermore, it seems likely that the fear and misapprehensions that often surround new procedural mechanisms are on the wane, and the national and international legal community can begin to discuss the future of class, mass and collective arbitration in a measured and thoughtful manner. It is hoped that this chapter has contributed to that discussion.

NOTES

1 Strong, SI, *Class, Mass, and Collective Arbitration in National and International Law* (Oxford University Press 2012) 6-16, 38-42, 43-74 (hereinafter Strong, *Class, Mass, and Collective Arbitration*).

2 ibid 14-15 (noting Colombia has seen at least one class arbitration and Canada has considered the procedure both judicially and legislatively).

3 ibid 17-19, 36-37, 84-104; Strong, SI, "Collective Consumer Arbitration in Spain: A Civil Law Response to US-Style Class Arbitration," *Journal of International Arbitration* 30, 2013, 495 (hereinafter Strong, Spanish Statute) (discussing and

translating Ley 231/2008); Strong, SI, "Collective Arbitration Under the DIS Supplementary Rules for Corporate Law Disputes: A European Form of Class Arbitration?" *ASA Bulletin*, 29, 2011, 45.

4 Strong, SI, "Large-Scale Dispute Resolution in Jurisdictions Without Judicial Class Actions: Learning From The Irish Experience," *ILSA Journal of International & Comparative Law*, 22, 2016, __ (hereinafter Strong, Irish). A number of matters have involved the state as respondent and thus could be considered administrative in nature. However, a recent large-scale product liability matter is entirely private and thus can be considered an arbitral procedure. ibid. See also "Go-Ahead for Alternative Dispute System Over Defective Implants: Move Aimed at Freeing Up High Court List and Ensuring Cases Against DePuy Decided Quickly," *Irish Times* (16 December 2015), available at <www.irishtimes.com/news/crime-and-law/courts/high-court/go-ahead-for-alternative-dispute-system-over-defective-implants-1.2468833>.

5 Strong, *Class, Mass, and Collective Arbitration* (n 1) 16-17, 74-38. Investment arbitration has also seen a number of large multiparty proceedings that are somewhat akin to mass arbitration. Strong, SI, "Heir of *Abaclat*? Mass and Multiparty Proceedings: *Ambiente Ufficio SpA v Argentine Republic*," *ICSID Review-Foreign Investment Law Journal*, 29, 2014, 149; Strong, SI, "Consent in Multiparty Arbitration – The Most Recent Installment," (11 December 2014), <http://kluwerarbitrationblog.com>.

6 A number of US Supreme Court cases are considered central to this analysis. *Keating v Superior Court*, 645 P2d 1192 (Cal 1982), rev'd on other grounds sub nom *Southland Corp v Keating*, 465 US 1 (1984); *Green Tree Financial Corp v Bazzle*, 539 US 444 (2003); *Stolt-Nielsen SA v AnimalFeeds Intl Corp*, 559 US 662 (2010); *AT&T Mobility LLC v Concepcion*, 563 US 333 (2011); *Oxford Health Plans LLC v Sutter*, 133 SCt 2064 (2013); *American Express Co v Italian Colors Restaurant*, 133 SCt 2304 (2013).

7 Strong, *Class, Mass, and Collective Arbitration* (n 1) 2-3.

8 See Directorate General for Internal Policies, *Overview of Existing Collective Redress Schemes in EU Member States*, IP/A/IMCO/NT/2011-16, 5 (July 2011) (noting 16 of the then-27 Member States of the European Union had some form of collective redress, with more Member States contemplating development of large-scale judicial relief); Strong, *Class, Mass, and Collective Arbitration* (n 1) 282-83, 304-24.

9 *AT&T Mobility LLC v Concepcion*, 563 US 333 (2011); *American Express Co v Italian Colors Restaurant*, 133 SCt 2304 (2013). At this point, it is unclear whether and to what extent waivers of class claims extend to collective claims. Furthermore, there are significant policy issues associated with the ability of private parties to eliminate one of the primary regulatory mechanisms used in the US legal system. Strong, *Class, Mass, and Collective Arbitration* (n 1) 205-27 (discussing the role of private litigants as 'private attorneys general' in US law). Although the US law concerning waivers is problematic for parties in US class arbitrations, the US Supreme Court has indicated that class arbitration may proceed in cases where the arbitration agreement is silent or ambiguous as to class proceedings and that the arbitral tribunal is competent to decide that issue. *Stolt-Nielsen SA v AnimalFeeds Intl Corp*, 559 US 662 (2010); *Oxford Health Plans LLC v Sutter*, 133 SCt 2064 (2013); Strong, *Class, Mass, and Collective Arbitration* (n 1) 183-88. This point is occasionally misunderstood by commentators who mistakenly read *Stolt-Nielsen* as requiring explicit consent to class arbitration. ibid 183-84, 187 (noting *Stolt-Nielsen* allows implicit consent).

10 Strong, *Class, Mass, and Collective Arbitration* (n 1) 37 (discussing *Abaclat v Argentine Republic*, ICISD Case No ARB/07/5 (involving more than 60,000 claimants), *Ambiente Ufficio v Argentine Republic*, ICSID Case No ARB/08/9

(involving 90 claimants) and *Alemanni v Argentine Republic*, ICSID Case No ARB/07/8 (involving 74 claimants)); (n 5). Although large-scale investment arbitration begin with a trio of cases involving Argentina, a new series of disputes appears to have arisen involving Cyprus. Marfin Investment Group Holdings, SA v Republic of Cyprus, ICSID Case No ARB/13/27 (involving eighteen claimants); Adamakopoulos v Republic of Cyprus, ICSID Case No ARB/15/49 (involving 676 individual and institutional Greek investors with 434 claims); *see also* Stelios Orphanides, 'Greek bailed-in investors and bondholders seek €120m in damages with ICSID appeal' Cyprus Business Mail (29 September 2015), **http://cyprusbusinessmail.com/?p=15139** (discussing a newly filed ICSID arbitration involving 676 claimants).

11 This question appears to be put to rest by developments in Ireland. See Strong, Irish (n 4).

12 The author has considered this issue to some extent previously. Strong, SI, "Class Arbitration Outside the United States: Reading the Tea Leaves," in Hanotiau, Bernard, and Schwartz, Eric A (eds), *Dossier VII: Arbitration and Multiparty Contracts* (ICC Institute of World Business Law 2010) 183, 194-206 (hereinafter Strong, Tea Leaves).

13 Strong, SI, "Regulatory Litigation in the European Union: Does the US Class Action Have a New Analogue?" *Notre Dame Law Review*, 88, 2012, 899 (hereinafter Strong, Regulatory Litigation); Hensler, Deborah R, "The Globalization of Class Actions: An Overview," in Hensler, Deborah, Hodges, Christopher and Tulibacka, Magdalena (eds), *The Globalization of Class Actions,* 622 *The Annals of the American Academy of Political and Social Science* (2009) 7.

14 Some authorities believe that consent to a large-scale proceeding can be implicit and arise as a result of the initial decision to arbitrate. Strong, *Class, Mass, and Collective Arbitration* (n 1) 172-80, 183-205. Other authorities take the view that parties must explicitly consent to a particular form of large-scale arbitration. ibid. It is impossible to resolve this particular debate within the context of the current discussion.

15 ibid 284-304 (discussing the relative merits of large-scale arbitration and large-scale litigation).

16 ibid 82 (discussing the preliminary award in *Abaclat v Argentine Republic*, which noted that ICSID would be unable to administer 60,000 individual claims simultaneously).

17 For example, Argentina has expressed concerns about inconsistent awards in investment arbitration on various occasions, which could be seen as undercutting its objection to mass proceedings. ibid 274.

18 Some concerns could arise if claimants who have experienced identical injuries are treated differently as a result of differences in the underlying law. ibid 287.

19 Empirical studies show that most class suits are not as frivolous as respondents believe. ibid 8, 67 (citing studies).

20 ibid 207, 343 n395.

21 Although the scope of disclosure in US-style class arbitration might be slightly less than the scope of discovery in US class actions, it is unlikely that an arbitral tribunal would prohibit the exchange of information in a class arbitration.

22 ibid 249, 295.

23 The conventional wisdom is that most large-scale actions settle prior to final resolution in court or in arbitration, since adjudicative mechanisms are both costly and risky. ibid 68 (discussing class arbitrations), 234 (discussing judicial class actions). See also Hensler (n 12) 19-20.

24 While some rules on large-scale arbitration provide for limited types of public disclosure (for example, class proceedings administered by the American Arbitration Association, collective proceedings administered by the Deutsche Institution für Schiedsgerichtsbarkeit (DIS) and mass proceedings administered by the International Centre for Settlement of Investment Disputes (ICSID) will be subject to a modified rule of confidentiality), other procedures do not (for example, class arbitrations administered by JAMS). Strong, *Class, Mass, and Collective Arbitration* (n 1) 64-66.

25 The WCAM is available on an opt-out basis for parties to both domestic and cross-border disputes. See *Wet collectieve afwikkeling van massaschades* (WCAM), Law of 23 June 2005, Stb 340; Tzankova, Ianika, and Lunsingh Scheurleer, Daan, "The Netherlands," in Hensler, Deborah, Hodges, Christopher, and Tulibacka, Magdalena (eds), *The Globalization of Class Actions, 622 The Annals of the American Academy of Political and Social Science* (2009) 149, 153-55. Notably, the WCAM does not require the assistance of a third party neutral. Instead, the parties may simply negotiate a settlement on their own.

26 A new international instrument is currently under discussion. Strong, SI, "Use and Perception of International Commercial Mediation and Conciliation: An Empirical Study" (forthcoming 2016) (hereinafter Strong, Empirical) (discussing efforts by the United Nations Commission on International Trade Law (UNCITRAL) to create a legal enforcement regime for mediated settlements which are currently quite difficult to enforce internationally).

27 Convention on the Recognition and Enforcement of Foreign Arbitral Awards, 10 June 1958, 330 UNTS 38 (hereinafter New York Convention); Strong, SI, "Beyond International Commercial Arbitration? The Promise of International Commercial Mediation," *Washington University Journal of Law & Policy*, 45, 2014, 11, 36 (hereinafter Strong, Mediation).

28 Newmark, Christopher and Hill, Richard, "Can A Mediated Settlement become an Enforceable Arbitration Award?" *Arbitration International*, 16, 2000, 81, 81-87; Strong, Mediation (n 27) 36. See also Strong, *Class, Mass, and Collective Arbitration* (n 1) 315-16.

29 Hensler (n 12) 25.

30 Strong, Spanish Statute (n 3) 501, 508-10 (discussing provisions requiring notice to be posted in the Official Journal).

31 Strong, *Class, Mass, and Collective Arbitration* (n 1) 94-96 (indicating that notice is generated as a result of information given by existing parties and involving 'Concerned Others').

32 US-style class actions tend to proceed on an opt-out basis, while various forms of collective and mass arbitration tend to proceed on an opt-in basis. ibid 7, 18-19, 78. However, it is unclear whether and to what extent the Spanish statute on collective consumer arbitration allows claimants to avoid group determination of their rights if the respondent chooses to proceed collectively. Strong, Spanish Statute (n 3) 504-05. That approach could be problematic from a constitutional or human rights perspective. ibid 505-06.

33 Strong, *Class, Mass, and Collective Arbitration* (n 1) 134.

34 Strong, SI, "Discovery Under 28 U.S.C. §1782: Distinguishing International Commercial Arbitration and International Investment Arbitration," *Stanford Journal of Complex Litigation*, 1, 2013, 295, 350-67 (discussing state interests in both private (contract-based) and public (treaty-based) arbitration).

35 In 2009, the German Federal Court of Justice (Bundesgerichtshof or BGH) created the possibility of large-scale arbitration in certain types of corporate disputes after the legislature failed to act. Strong, *Class, Mass, and Collective Arbitration* (n 1) 86.

36 In 2003, the US Supreme Court provided significant impetus to class arbitration with its decision in *Green Tree Financial Corp v Bazzle*, 539 US 444 (2003), although large-scale arbitration had existed in the United States for at least twenty years before that. Strong, *Class, Mass, and Collective Arbitration* (n 1) 7-12 (discussing *Bazzle* in addition to *Keating v Superior Court*, 645 P2d 1192 (Cal 1982), rev'd on other grounds sub nom *Southland Corp v Keating*, 465 US 1 (1984) and various state law and other developments). However, the Court reversed its support for class arbitration in 2009 and 2010 with a series of decisions curtailing class arbitration in some situations. *Stolt-Nielsen SA v AnimalFeeds Intl Corp*, 559 US 662 (2010); *AT&T Mobility LLC v Concepcion*, 563 US 333 (2011); *Oxford Health Plans LLC v Sutter*, 133 SCt 2064 (2013); *American Express Co v Italian Colors Restaurant*, 133 SCt 2304 (2013). See also (n 9) (discussing waiver and contractual silence). Although class arbitration still exists in the United States, it is nowhere near as prevalent as it was between 2003 and 2010. Strong, *Class, Mass, and Collective Arbitration* (n 1) 12.

37 Strong, Spanish Statute (n 3) 208-10 (translating Ley 231/2008).

38 Although Ireland has enacted a number of statutes requiring quasi-arbitral proceedings in situations where large-scale claims have been brought against the state, such statutes do not appear appropriate or possible in purely private actions. Strong, Irish (n 4).

39 Born, Gary B, *International Commercial Arbitration* (Kluwer Law International 2014) 1518 n593; Strong, *Class, Mass, and Collective Arbitration* (n 1) 304. See also Strong, Tea Leaves (n 12) 194-206. Indeed, this appears to be the case in Ireland, where a number of large-scale arbitrations or quasi-arbitrations appear to proceed on a documents-only basis, even though most if not all judicial proceedings contemplate an oral hearing.

40 *Mitsubishi Motors Corp v Soler Chrysler-Plymouth, Inc*, 473 US 614, 629 (1985).

41 Strong, *Class, Mass, and Collective Arbitration* (n 1) 2, 228-81.

42 ibid 235-41 (discussing various problems associated with transnational regulation, including the possibility of regulatory and procedural 'mismatches').

43 *Mitsubishi Motors Corp v Soler Chrysler-Plymouth, Inc*, 473 US 614, 638 (1985); Born (n 39) 980-81.

44 Of course, that 'support' could be exhibited at two different stages — when parties seek to enforce an arbitration agreement and when they seek to enforce an arbitration award.

45 Thus, for example, the Spanish statute on collective consumer arbitration may limit the ability of claimants to decide when, where, how and whether to assert a legal claim. Strong, Spanish Statute (n 3) 505-06.

46 For example, counsel for the plaintiff class may be tempted to collude with the defendant to obtain a fast and easy settlement that benefits the lawyers (who are often retained on a contingent fee basis) but that is not really in the best interest of the injured plaintiffs.

47 For example, in US-style class arbitrations, claimants can often opt out of actions. Furthermore, an arbitrator is supposed to review any settlement agreement so as to reduce the chance of collusion. Strong, *Class, Mass, and Collective Arbitration* (n 1) 322-23.

48 For example, concerns about collusion would likely not exist in cases where lawyers were not paid based on a percentage of the final award.

49 For example, states may not act in areas that are entirely private. Dorsett Niles, John, Tribble, Lauren E and Wimsatt, Jennifer N, "Making Sense of State Action," *Santa Clara Law Review*, 51, 2011, 885, 890; Strong, Irish (n 4).

50 Strong, Spanish Statute (n 3) 508-10 (translating Ley 231/2008).

51 Strong, *Class, Mass, and Collective Arbitration* (n 1) 15, 244-45. See also Strong, SI, "Resolving Mass Legal Disputes Through Class Arbitration: The United States and Canada Compared," *North Carolina Journal of International Law & Commercial Regulation*, 37, 2012, 921 (discussing Supreme Court and provincial cases in Canada). To date, one Canadian province, Manitoba, has considered this issue explicitly. Manitoba Law Reform Commission, Report 115, Mandatory Arbitration Clauses and Consumer Class Proceedings 3-4, 22-23 (April 2008). See also *MacKinnon v National Money Mart Co*, 2009 BCCA 103, ¶14 (calling for legislative consideration of class arbitration in British Columbia).

52 Strong, Irish (n 4).

53 Canadian courts have declined the opportunity to adopt large-scale arbitration as a common law device and have instead suggested that such issues are more properly subject to legislative action. Strong, *Class, Mass, and Collective Arbitration* (n 1) 15, 244-45.

54 The earliest type of class arbitration was developed in US state courts beginning in the 1980s. ibid 7-12 (discussing the effect of *Keating v Superior Court*, 645 P2d 1192 (Cal 1982), rev'd on other grounds sub nom *Southland Corp v Keating*, 465 US 1 (1984), as well as state law and other developments). The procedure evolved over the years into a more sophisticated system, particularly after the advent in 2003 of various institutional rules on class arbitration. ibid (discussing the effect of *Green Tree Financial Corp v Bazzle,* 539 US 444 (2003)).

55 Strong, *Class, Mass, and Collective Arbitration* (n 1) 84-85.

56 ibid 14-15.

57 Bundesgerichtshof 6 April 2009, II ZR 255/08 (Germany), digest by Kriendler for Institute for Transnational Arbitration (ITA), available at **www.kluwerarbitration.com.** See also Borris, Christian, "Arbitrability of Corporate Law Disputes in Germany," in Klaassen, CJM, and others (eds), *Onderneming en ADR* (Wolters Kluwer 2011) 55, 59-64. The DIS completed the process by adopting arbitral rules that complied with the BGH's requirements for those types of disputes. Strong, *Class, Mass, and Collective Arbitration* (n 1) 86. While the current DIS rules refer only to disputes involving closely held corporations, the mechanism would appear equally appropriate in cases involving larger companies or multinational entities. ibid.

58 Strong, *Class, Mass, and Collective Arbitration* (n 1) 86.

59 Strong, Tea Leaves (n 12) 197-205.

60 Mulheron, Rachael, *The Class Action in Common Law Legal Systems: A Comparative Perspective* (Hart Publishing 2004). The United Kingdom has resisted large-scale litigation and has adopted a mechanism (the Group Litigation Order or GLO) that reflects aggregate as opposed to representative relief. Civil Procedure Rules (England), Rules 19.10 to 19.15; Practice Direction 19B — Group Litigation.

61 Gidi, Antonio, "Class Actions in Brazil — A Model for Civil Law Countries," *American Journal of Comparative Law,* 51, 2003, 311.

62 Directorate General for Internal Policies (n 8) 5.

63 Strong, Regulatory Litigation (n 12) 904-06 (discussing various EU initiatives). The EU is particularly concerned about large-scale disputes involving consumers and competition law.

64 Some examples of 'proper procedures' can be found in the mass and collective context.

65 ibid 907, 911 960-64 (noting European reliance on compensatory relief rather than regulatory or deterrent effects).

66 ibid 945-46 (discussing decreasing public budgets to deal with regulatory non-compliance).

67 Strong, *Class, Mass, and Collective Arbitration* (n 1) 67-68, 99-100 (discussing AAA and DIS approach to fees and costs in large-scale arbitration).

68 Strong, SI, "Class and Collective Relief in the Cross-Border Context: A Possible Role for the Permanent Court of Arbitration," *The Hague Yearbook of International Law 2010*, 23, 2011, 113, 124-33.

69 (n 23).

70 (n 25). At the very least, such efforts will be expensive and time-consuming. See also Strong, Mediation (n 27) 26-28, 36; Strong, Empirical (n 26).

71 Strong, Mediation (n 27) 36 (noting that mediated settlement agreements may be considered a type of arbitral award for purposes of the New York Convention, although that approach is disputed). Steps are being taken to increase the international enforceability of mediated settlements. Strong, Empirical (n 26).

72 While steps are being taken by the international community to eliminate the disparity between matters that are subject to an arbitration agreement and those that are not, it is unknown when the international community will act. See Report of Working Group II (Arbitration and Conciliation) on the work of its sixty-third session (Vienna, 7-11 September 2015), UN Doc A/CN.9/861 (17 September 2015) (noting work on an international instrument concerning international settlement agreements arising out of mediation); Strong, Empirical (n 26).

73 Strong, *Class, Mass, and Collective Arbitration* (n 1) 18-19.

74 This has been the case in both Germany and the United States. ibid 40-74, 86-101.

75 There is a considerable body of literature concerning default rules. Although interesting, this discussion is outside the scope of the current chapter. See eg Ayres, Ian, "Valuing Modern Contract Scholarship," *Yale Law Journal*, 112, 2001 881; Ayres, Ian and Gernter, Robert, "Filling Gaps in Incomplete Contracts: An Economic Theory of Default Rules," *Yale Law Journal*, 99, 1989, 87; Ayres, Ian and Gernter, Robert, "Majoritarian vs. Minoritarian Defaults," *Stanford Law Review*, 51, 1999 1591; Ayres, Ian and Gernter, Robert, "Strategic Contractual Inefficiency and the Optimal Choice of Legal Rules," *Yale Law Journal*, 101, 1992, 729; Johnson, Jason Scott, "Strategic Bargaining and the Economic Theory of Contract Default Rules," *Yale Law Journa*l, 100, 1990, 615; Posner, Eric A, "Economic Analysis of Contract Law After Three Decades: Success or Failure?" *Yale Law Journal*, 112, 2003, 829. However, it is clear that the state's choice of a default rule will affect the bargaining positions of the parties. Gidi (n 61) 338; Rau, Alan Scott and Sherman, Edward F, "Tradition and Innovation in International Arbitration Procedure," *Texas International Law Journal*, 30, 1995, 89, 117 n152.

76 Furthermore, having a law, of itself, does not appear to be sufficient to have encouraged parties to use the procedure. See Strong, Spanish Statute (n 3) 496-97.

77 Perry, Sebastian," BITS, BATS and Buts," *Global Arbitration Review* (28 January 2013). See also Draft Model Bilateral Arbitration Treaty, https://**www.wilmerhale.com/uploadedFiles/Shared_Content/Editorial/News/Documents/Draft-Model-BAT.pdf;** Gary Born, BITS, BATS, and Buts: Reflections on International Dispute

Resolution (speech at the University of Pennsylvania) https://www.wilmerhale.com/uploadedFiles/Shared_Content/Editorial/News/Documents/BITs-BATs-and-Buts.pdf.

78 Rau and Sherman (n 75) 117 n152 (noting parties may be 'reluctant to opt out even of rules that are inefficient for them' if the transaction costs to alter the default rule are too high or onerous).

79 Any provision that reads 'unless the parties agree otherwise' constitutes a default rule.

80 For example, most national arbitration laws indicate that the court at the seat will assist with the selection of the arbitrator(s) unless the parties agree otherwise. See eg 9 USC s 5; Arbitration Act 1996 s 16.

81 For example, the Inter-American Treaty on Recognition and Enforcement of Foreign Arbitral Awards (Panama Convention) contains a set of procedural rules that applies unless the parties agree otherwise. Inter-American Convention on International Commercial Arbitration, 30 January 1975, art 3, OASTS No 42, 14 ILM. 336 (1975).

82 To do so, the statute would have to be amended to require parties to use the collective procedure in question rather than to simply permit them to do so.

83 US Federal Rules of Civil Procedure 4(d)(3), 12.

84 Born (n 39) 232.

85 ibid 73; Strong, Mediation (n 27) 12 (noting mediation and conciliation were the preferred means of resolving international commercial disputes prior to World War II).

86 New York Convention (n 27).

87 UNCITRAL, UNCITRAL Model Law on International Commercial Arbitration, 18th Sess, Annex 1, UN Doc A/40/17 (21 June 1985), revised by UNCITRAL, Revised Articles of the UNCITRAL Model Law on International Commercial Arbitration, 39th Sess, Annex, UN Doc A/61/17 (7 July 2006).

88 Strong, *Class, Mass, and Collective Arbitration* (n 1) 163 (quoting Gary Born), 243-47 (discussing the concept of 'procedural non-arbitrability').

89 ibid 316-18, 322.

90 ibid 46-57 (discussing certain partial final awards built into the AAA and JAMS class arbitration regimes).

91 Investment tribunals often render preliminary awards on admissibility and jurisdiction.

92 Of course, some countries do not allow punitive damages to be recovered because of their deterrent or criminal law function. Born (n 39) 3077-82.

93 For example, use of an opt-in rather than opt-out system tends to decrease the number of claimants, since people must take an affirmative step to become involved in a particular dispute. However, respondents still may experience some concerns about how many claimants might join into an action if the respondents are required to give wide notice of the pending proceeding, as is the case under the Spanish statute. Strong, Spanish Statute (n 3) 501-03.

94 In some jurisdictions, most notably the United States, punitive or treble damages are used as an incentive to plaintiffs and plaintiffs' counsel to bring cases that operate for the public good. Strong, *Class, Mass, and Collective Arbitration* (n 1) 259-60.

95 ibid 323, 353. See also Shannon, Victoria A, "Harmonizing Third-Party Litigation Funding Regulation," *Cardozo Law Review*, 36, 2015, 861, 865.

96 The economics and incentives associated with domestic competition or antitrust law disputes have been well-documented, as have the economics and incentives of investment arbitration. Strong, *Class, Mass, and Collective Arbitration* (n 1) 113, 343.

97 ibid 163 (quoting Gary Born as stating 'it is difficult to see what . . . non-arbitrability objections could be raised to class arbitration').

98 This rule already exists in some national courts. Civil Procedure Rules (England), Rule 31.22 (limiting subsequent use of documents or information produced in litigation).

99 See eg AAA, Consumer Arbitration Rules, 33-36 <**www.adr.org**>.

100 Strong, *Class, Mass, and Collective Arbitration* (n 1) 205-27.

101 Strong, Spanish Statute (n 3) 496-97.

102 Strong, *Class, Mass, and Collective Arbitration* (n 1) 19 (discussing how the collective arbitration rules apply only to closely held corporations). Although this procedure is relatively new, it has already enjoyed some success. ibid.

103 Civil Procedure Rules (England), Part 36; Practice Direction 36A — Offers to Settle.

104 The rules vary slightly depending on who made the offer and what type of dispute is at issue, but the basic principle holds true. Civil Procedure Rules (England), Part 36.

105 (n 90).

106 Strong, Regulatory Litigation (n 12) 960-61, 966-67 (discussing problems with European collective redress systems).

107 ibid (noting concerns regarding representative relief, broad discovery, punitive damages and contingent fees). Commentators have noted that many jurisdictions are hampered in their efforts to create a workable system of collective redress by the unavailability of contingent fees or third-party funding and the imposition of the loser-pays rule under national law. ibid.

108 ibid.

109 (n 68) (discussing jurisdiction, conflict of laws, procedure and enforcement).

110 At one time, ODR appeared to be on the fast track to standardization. Eidenmuller, Horst and Engel, Martin, "Against False Settlement: Designing Efficient Consumer Rights Enforcement Systems in Europe," *Ohio State Journal on Dispute Resolution*, 29, 2014, 261, 275-76 (discussing ODR initiatives from the EU and UNCITRAL). However, efforts at UNCITRAL have been delayed and are now moving forward in a much more fractured form. ibid. See also Annotated Provisional Agenda, UNCITRAL Working Group III (Online Dispute Resolution), at 2-4, UN Doc A/CN.9/WG.III/SP.135 (28 September 2015) (noting nearly fifteen-year history of the debate about ODR at UNCITRAL).

111 Billiet, Philippe, *Class Arbitration in the European Union* (Maklu Publishers 2013).

112 Strong, *Class, Mass, and Collective Arbitration* (n 1) 27-104. Inspiration might also come from procedures used by mass claims tribunals, although those processes typically do not attempt to resolve all disputes at a single time, in a single forum. ibid 330-32.

113 For example, the DIS Supplementary Rules for Corporate Law Disputes would be very useful as a means of resolving large-scale disputes involving trusts. Strong, SI, "Mandatory Arbitration of Internal Trust Disputes: Improving Arbitrability and Enforceability Through Proper Procedural Choices," *Arbitration International*, 28, 2012, 591, 637-49.

114 This was the role that the German BGH took. Strong, *Class, Mass, and Collective Arbitration* (n 1) 18-19, 86. Courts in the United States have been less forthcoming about the procedural minimums that must be met, although that is likely because class arbitration closely resembled judicial class actions, which had already been determined to be procedurally fair. ibid 38-40, 43.

115 This was the approach used in Spain and, to a lesser extent, the United States. In Spain, the legislature created a specific procedural statute outlining every nuance of the procedure. In the United States, the legislature approved the rules of court (ie the Federal Rules of Civil Procedure) that outline judicial class action procedures. ibid 276. Although the legislature did not explicitly extend those rules to arbitration, legislative intent was to some extent reflected in US class arbitration procedure, since common law and rules-based class arbitration essentially mirror US class action procedure. ibid 38-40, 43, 276.

116 ibid 12.

117 ibid 240, 304, 332-33.

118 ibid.

119 ibid 331 (discussing the resolution of certain Holocaust-related claims).

120 For example, the tribunal in *Abaclat* considered adopting some of the evidentiary procedures used by mass claims commissions. ibid 332.

121 (n 10) (discussing mass and multiparty claims involving Argentina and Cyprus).

122 US 444 (2003).

Chapter 12

Will Canada Be the Next Frontier in Class Arbitration?

Not Likely

Pierre J. Dalphond*

1 INTRODUCTION

Arbitration is a widely accepted alternative to domestic courts in commercial disputes, domestic and international. It is also the forum for disputes involving a commercial entity and a state or an entity of a state in international trade.

In Canada, since the 1980s, courts recognize that parties' autonomy should prevail, and widely accept the use of a private dispute prevention and resolution process to solve commercial disputes, especially arbitration. Even governments in Canada embrace arbitration; for example, all federal major public work contracts include an arbitration agreement.

Eager to increase access to justice, governments are now favouring private dispute prevention and resolution processes to solve almost all kind of civil disputes.[1] As my panel colleague Elie Kleiman states in his paper: "Out-of-court resolution of disputes can serve as a complement to judicial proceedings as it would allow low-value disputes that would not have been otherwise submitted to a court to proceed and be resolved."[2]

In some jurisdictions, consideration or use of alternative dispute resolution processes (ADR) are even a condition precedent to court litigation. The most recent example is the new Code of Civil Procedure of Quebec that states in its article 1 that "parties must consider private prevention and resolution processes before referring their dispute to the courts."[3] Commenting this provision, the Minister of Justice of Québec said that "although it is not binding as to render inadmissible the lawsuit that would not have been preceded by an attempt to settle, the provision should, because of its mandatory nature, cause a significant change in the role of lawyers who should now discuss with their clients the range of possibilities for conflict resolution."[4]

As elsewhere, the two main ADR contemplated by this new code are mediation and arbitration. It is fair to say that arbitration is now a method of dispute adjudication welcomed in almost all areas of the law as a matter of public policy.

Class action is a frequently used court procedure in Canada. It represents a substantial part of the case load in the Courts, especially in the largest provinces, Ontario, Quebec and British Columbia. Since it consumes a large

* Senior Counsel, Litigation and ADR, Stikeman Elliott, Montréal, Canada, Certified Mediator and Arbitrator, Visiting Professor at Université de Montréal (teaching domestic and international arbitration), former Senior Judge, Quebec Court of Appeal.

portion of the scarce judicial resources, one could think that the governments should push for private class arbitration to remove some of the strain on the judicial system.

Though this could be seen as the next logical thing to do, so far neither the Canadian legislatures nor the courts have considered in what circumstances arbitration could be considered as an alternative to class action to determine a class claim or how they could be combined to achieve more access to justice or to improve the efficiency of the court system.

I will discuss below public policies, legal impediments and commercial reasons that appear to be preventing the emergence of class arbitration in Canada.

2 CLASS ACTIONS IN CANADA

Canada is a federal state. Civil rights and civil procedure are matters reserved for the provinces (equivalent to states in the US and Australia). Contrary to the US Congress, the Canadian Federal Parliament has no significant role to play in connection with court proceedings, mediation and arbitration. Thus my comments addressed the situation according to provincial laws.

Class and group actions are two distinct procedures not to be confused. In Canada, a class action is a procedure pursuant to which a person is authorized to act on behalf of a group defined by the court and composed essentially of absentees. A group action is essentially a consolidation of individual claims in which each claimant is identified and has consented to the proceedings.

Class action is no longer a new proceeding in Canada.[5] It is widely known and used. Each province except one has enacted a comprehensive class action act. There are also federal rules of civil procedure authorizing class actions before the Federal Court (these are rarely used considering the limited jurisdiction of the Canadian Federal Court compared to the US Federal Courts).

For class action related to publicly traded securities, a model act was negotiated by the 10 provincial regulators and then enacted by each province. It provides for specific redress and procedures and raises the threshold to get an authorization to proceed, called a certification.

In Canada, like in the US, class action is defined as a procedural right, not as a substantive right. The same is true for arbitration.

The driving principle behind class actions is that they provide access to justice in situations where no redress would be sought if left to individual claimants. In the seminal case *Western Canadian Shopping Centres Inc. v Dutton* [2001] SCC 46, the Canadian Supreme Court held:

> Class actions offer three important advantages over a multiplicity of individual suits. First, by aggregating similar individual actions, class actions serve judicial economy by avoiding unnecessary duplication in fact-finding and legal analysis. The efficiencies thus generated free judicial resources that can be directed at resolving other conflicts, and can also reduce the costs of litigation both for plaintiffs (who can share litigation costs) and for defendants (who need litigate the disputed issue only once, rather than numerous times) (...)

> Second, by allowing fixed litigation costs to be divided over a large number of plaintiffs, class actions improve access to justice by making economical the prosecution of claims that would otherwise be too costly to prosecute individually. Without class actions, the doors of justice remain closed to some plaintiffs, however strong their legal claims. Sharing costs ensures that injuries are not left unremedied(...)
>
> Third, class actions serve efficiency and justice by ensuring that actual and potential wrongdoers do not ignore their obligations to the public. Without class actions, those who cause widespread but individually minimal harm might not take into account the full costs of their conduct, because for any one plaintiff the expense of bringing suit would far exceed the likely recovery. Cost-sharing decreases the expense of pursuing legal recourse and accordingly deters potential defendants who might otherwise assume that minor wrongs would not result in litigation(...)

This does not mean that class actions are confined to cases where each member of the class is awarded a small amount. In fact, it is also used to claim substantial compensatory damages in cases where plaintiffs will unlikely be able to finance the high costs associated with an individual proceedings (for examples, the breast implant[6], the weight control pills[7] and the tobacco smoking related cancers cases[8]).

The Canadian class action system is essentially an opting-out model and the two major forum for class actions, Quebec and Ontario, do certify Canadian and international classes, while in British Columbia, non-residents have to opt-in to become members of the class.

Finally, contrary to the US, class actions in Canada are decided by a judge alone without any civil jury.

The current hot issues are related to proper notices to opt out, collective recovery[9] versus individual claims, information about the claim process once a judgment rendered in favor of the class (low take-up rate), cypress orders (relating to the distribution of huge unclaimed amounts when collective recovery was ordered instead of individual claims), punitive damages, class lawyers' fees and third-party financing.

Some of these issues are accentuated when you have a national or international class and may result in a refusal to recognize or enforce the settlement/judgment in other jurisdictions exposing the defendant to a new class action. Thus lawyers file similar class actions in many provinces. Subsequently, all but one of them are suspended until a settlement is reached or a judgment is rendered in the chosen province. This settlement or judgment is afterwards used to terminate the others stayed class actions trough settlements.

Most of these problems could be solved if the provinces were to agree on uniform procedures for notices and an enforcement process. But despite invitations to do so from the Supreme Court of Canada and the bar, the provinces have not yet embarked on such a project.

Notwithstanding the potential improvements suggested, the class action procedure in Canada is widely considered a success.

This success results from many factors: an active specialized bar; comprehensive set of rules in each province; relatively low threshold to get certification;[10] limited requirements on who can act as a representative and initiate the proceedings; courts' familiarity with the process; no restriction on remedies that can be sought, including injunctive reliefs, compensatory damages and punitive damages; no limit on parties that can be sued or made part to the process including local, provincial or federal governments; public acceptance of class proceedings as an effective mean to redress tort, including those caused by the governments and its agents, and large contractual breaches; availability of public and third party financing; large rewards for class lawyers if they win;[11] etc.

Based on my experience in class actions, the two most important factors that explain its success are:

1) The authorization to proceed is given by the courts on behalf of a group of absentees. In fact, the representative has only to establish the existence of class and the difficulty for its members to act together as a group of joint plaintiffs. The system does not require the members of the class to express consent to the proceeding or to join the class. In jurisdictions where this is not the case, very few class actions are initiated (see, for example, Italy);

2) The binding nature of the final judgment or judicially approved settlement on all the members of the class, except those who have opted out. This is a factor that often brings defendants to agree to settle and get judicial amnesty.

Because the representative is entitled to act on behalf of absentees, Court supervision is extensive to make sure that their interests are adequately protected throughout the process.

In addition, public notices, public records and access to the judge are critical to the due process of the class action proceedings for the class members, including the right to opt out or to oppose a proposed settlement. Thus the importance of adequate publicity and transparency at all critical steps to ensure the opposability of the judgment or settlement to all members of the class.

Finally, a defendant that faces a mass claim wants the option to appeal to a higher court should the class action be granted for millions of dollars. In each province, the final judgment in the class proceedings can be appealed as of right to the provincial court of appeal and on leave, to the Supreme Court of Canada. Errors of law and palpable and overriding errors of fact committed by the trial judge can be corrected.

Higher courts supervision provides the parties additional comfort in the class action process. Lawyers representing classes and defendants are almost unanimously resisting any attempt to reduce the appeal options during and after the class action certification.

3 CONTRASTING FEATURES OF ARBITRATION

Nine of the 10 provinces have adopted arbitration acts dealing separately with domestic and international arbitrations, generally modelled on the UNCITRAL Model Law for international commercial arbitration.[12]

The National Assembly of Quebec and the Canadian Federal Parliament have adopted one legislation covering both domestic and international arbitration, based on the Model Law.

Incidentally, a case involving parties in two different provinces is considered an international arbitration under the principles of private international law in Quebec, but not in the other provinces.

In Canada, as in all countries that have applied the Model Law, arbitration is based solely on consent. It follows that a party cannot be bound by an arbitral award unless it specifically agreed to the arbitration process to solve the relevant dispute. In other words, opting-in to the arbitration process is essential.

Arbitration acts recognize parties' autonomy to the point of choosing their arbitrators and the rules governing the resolution of their dispute to the exclusion of state courts. As a result, state courts cannot exercise supervision on a large scale.

One of the many reasons why commercial parties prefer arbitration to court proceedings is the confidentiality surrounding the process. It is often said that arbitration comes with a presumption of privacy and confidentiality.[13]

Recognizing this, the new Quebec Code of Civil Procedure states that parties that opt for a private dispute resolution process and the third party assisting them undertake to preserve the confidentiality of anything said, written or done during the process, subject to any agreement between them stipulating otherwise. Of course, the arbitrator can express his reasoning in the award and enforcement or annulment procedures before a state court will require making public parts of the arbitration process.

Another often quoted reason for choosing arbitration is the finality of the process, with no time and money spent on appeals. However, in the nine common law provinces, following English law on arbitration, a limited right of appeal exists in domestic arbitration, but not in international arbitration where the sole procedure available is an annulment on the grounds listed in the Model Law. In Quebec, the sole recourse is annulment on the grounds listed in the Model Law.

4 SPECIFIC FEATURES OF CLASS ARBITRATION

Class-action arbitration, as it exists in the US, differs substantially from bilateral arbitration.

First, like some group arbitrations, it involves a large number of claimants, but mostly absentees. The representative does not have to identify all the members of the class and does not have to seek a mandate or proxy to act on other behalf. All that is required is the publication of adequate notices to a large audience.

This is a striking advantage compare to group arbitration. As an example, in the arbitration proceeding stemming from the global financial crisis and the 2013 bailout of Cyprus, it took more than a year to identify a group of about 700 Greek investors willing to file claims against the Republic of Cyprus.[14]

Second, you need special rules to define the class, to determine the legal representative and to provide for the payment of the applicable administrative fees and the arbitrator's remuneration and costs.

Third, the appointment of arbitrators may become as problematic as in multi-party arbitration proceedings or, at least, be more complex than in a bilateral arbitration.

Fourth, the process will inevitably imply the loss of the presumption of privacy and confidentiality. On this topic, Professor Strong writes: "[...] (indeed some arbitral institutions have already identified the various ways in which information about class, mass or collective proceedings should be made public), but the amount of publicity nevertheless appears to be more limited than in many types of litigation."[15]

Finally, for the defendant, the potential financial exposure is magnified compared to a bilateral arbitration.

These differences are so significant that a general consent to arbitration does not suffice to give competence to the arbitration tribunal on a class claim, as the US Supreme Court held in *Stolt-Nielsen*:

> (...) class-action arbitration changes the nature of arbitration to such a degree that it cannot be presumed the parties consented to it by simply agreeing to submit their dispute to an arbitrator.[16]

It follows that a class-action arbitration cannot be imposed on a defendant that has not specifically agreed to it.

However, these differences with traditional two-party arbitration do not mean that class proceedings cannot be managed by arbitral institutions. However, they require substantial amendments to the rules applicable to bilateral arbitration.

In 2003, the American Arbitration Association (AAA) enacted rules on class arbitration inspired from the American case law.

Regarding confidentiality, they currently provide:

> 9. Confidentiality; Class Arbitration Docket
>
> (a) The presumption of privacy and confidentiality in arbitration proceedings shall not apply in class arbitrations. All class arbitration hearings and filings may be made public, subject to the authority of the arbitrator to provide otherwise in special circumstances. However, in no event shall class members, or their individual counsel, if any, be excluded from the arbitration hearings.
>
> (b) The AAA shall maintain on its Web site a Class Arbitration Docket of arbitrations filed as class arbitrations. The Class Arbitration Docket will provide certain information about the arbitration to the extent known to the AAA, including:
>
> (1) a copy of the demand for arbitration;
>
> (2) the identities of the parties;
>
> (3) the names and contact information of counsel for each party;
>
> (4) a list of awards made in the arbitration by the arbitrator; and
>
> (5) the date, time and place of any scheduled hearings.

Clearly, these rules attempt to make the process open and transparent.

Other rules provide for the appointment of the arbitrator by the AAA from a national roster of class arbitrators, the construction of the arbitration clause and the certification of the class. With regard to public notices, a critical element to the *res judicata* and to the enforcement of the award, Rule 6(a) states that class members shall be "provided the best Notice of Class Determination practicable under the circumstances."

According to the AAA Docket, there are now about 120 active cases pending before ICDR/AAA, most initiated between 2012 and now with the oldest one going back to 2002. None is described as an international class arbitration and 69 are employment related.

In contrast, each year, in the US Federal Courts, about 6,000 new class actions are introduced, excluding those filed before state courts. Thus, it seems that class action arbitration does not represent a substantial part of the class redress in the US.

In summary, class action arbitration is possible but it does require major adjustments to the usual arbitration rules, especially in connection with the appointment of arbitrators, the setting aside of confidentiality generally associated to the arbitration process and the sending of public notices.

It also requires a judiciary willing to support it, namely in enforcing class awards and refraining from using due process as an extensive concept to annul its procedural orders.

5 WILL CANADA BE THE NEXT FRONTIER?

In my view, this is not going to happen for various reasons.

I. Public Policy Reasons

There is clearly no momentum for class arbitration in consumer cases in Canada for public policy reasons.

On one hand, class action is widely seen as a mechanism to provide consumers with an effective tool to seek redress and have access to justice. It is free for the claimants since the representative's counsel finances it or finds third party's financing, and the process is effortless since said counsel drives it. For the governments it is an important means to strike a balance between consumers and large businesses, thus solving an important public policy concern at relatively low costs.[17]

Since the process involves absentees, the governments are concerned about adequate protection of their interests. This public policy concern is considered best addressed by Canadian superior courts made of judges appointed for life.[18]

Arbitration, on the other hand, is perceived as a private process managed by individuals and institutions that thrive on it. Moreover, arbitrators are lawyers often also acting as counsel in other cases and perceived as having an interest at stake in the process.

Arbitration is welcome in commercial disputes involving two commercial businesses freely consenting to it. However, there seems to exist among consumer groups and some lobbyists, a lack of trust towards private arbitration of consumer disputes pursuant to an arbitration agreement that is a part of a contract of adhesion imposed upon the consumers.[19]

The perceived economic imbalance between the parties and the fear of a lack of real consent to arbitration are the source of distrust toward the private arbitration clauses provided in consumers' contracts. Consumers' reluctance is observed even in the United States where, according to a study, "the AAA may be more amenable to consumer plaintiffs than other venues" partly because "the AAA has adopted Consumer Due Process Protocols which strive for fundamental fairness."[20]

This distrust cannot be better illustrated than by the quick responses of the provincial governments to the landmark decision of the Supreme Court of Canada in the *Dell Computer* case,[21] where the highest court of Canada concluded that a Quebec consumer who bought a computer from Dell on the internet was bound to submit its dispute to an arbitral institution situated in Minneapolis, Minnesota, where forms in French were not available.

Concurrently, the two largest provinces of Canada, Ontario and Quebec, amended their *Consumer Protection Act* (CPA) to declare void and of no effect, a clause in a consumer contract providing for arbitration.

In Alberta, the CPA was amended to provide that such a clause must be approved by the government before becoming effective; to this day, none was ever approved.

In British Columbia, further to a judgment of the Supreme Court of Canada rendered after Dell,[22] some provisions of the CPA have been interpreted as excluding arbitration in connection with certain redresses. So arbitration cannot offer access to all the possible remedies and it is therefore less attractive than class action.

In fact, there seem to exist a reluctance to have policy considerations decided by private arbitrators. Since CPA are essentially social legislation complementing policy consideration, arbitration is not perceived as an adequate process. This distrust for arbitration to deal with social issues is further illustrated by the reluctance in Europe and in the US Congress to leave investor-state disputes to private arbitrators, especially if there is no appeal option.[23]

However, arbitration could be made the exclusive procedure available in commercial and corporate litigation. Nothing legally then prevents parties from agreeing to arbitration, including specifically a class-action arbitration in cases involving a group of clients or shareholders.

II. Commercial Reasons

It remains that in Canada, following an American trend, an arbitration clause is often used in a contract for the sale of products/services to prevent clients (subject to restrictions found in the relevant CPA) from initiating a class action or from being part of one.

In the US, an empirical study conducted by the Consumer Financial Protection Bureau (CFPB), released in March 2015, found that a majority of agreements regarding credit card loans, prepaid cards, payday loans, wireless third-party billing and checking accounts has an arbitration clause.[24] The CFPB study further reported that nearly all the American arbitration clauses studied included provisions stating that arbitration may not proceed on a class basis.

On this point, two professors from University of California, who conducted an empirical study on approximately 5000 AAA consumer arbitrations, mention that: "the arbitration has displace litigation as the primary method by which consumers resolve disputes against companies." Commenting the study, Kaplinsky and Levin wrote: "Not only are these extreme assertions not supported by any facts or figures, but they contradict the study's own statement that only a 'handful of matters ... trickle into the arbitration forum.' [...] The CFPB [Consumer Financial Protection Bureau] found that arbitration was a factor in only 8% of the 562 class actions studied."[25]

In other words, the impact of arbitration clauses on class actions in the US remains a hot issue!

Following this pattern, many Canadians non-consumer contracts have an arbitration clause and some even include a specific waiver of the right to be part of a class action (though according to Canadian case law it is not necessary if there is a valid arbitration clause covering every and all potential disputes).

In contracts of adhesion, the expectation of the business providing the services/products is that for a relatively small amount of monetary relief, very few, if any, clients, especially commercial clients, will bother to send an arbitration notice and engage the expenditure of time or money for initiating an individual arbitration proceeding. Arbitration clause then become a shield against individual claims and class actions.

In such cases, it is not obvious why these services/products providers will agree to displace before an arbitration panel a class redress that they wish to avoid before a court. Moreover, why would they agree to a class redress without a possibility of an appeal. In fact, some businesses will rather have an arbitration clause with a waiver of class arbitration in their contracts.

III No Appetite from The Court to Favor It

Failing the enactment of legislative provisions regarding class arbitration, the only way to provide parameters to class arbitration might be through the courts, in cases where there is no CPA provision preventing arbitration.

A court could, in a case where the non-consumer party bound by an arbitration clause asks to act on behalf of a class for compelling reasons, be called to consider the California Supreme Court approach in *Keating v Superior Court*[26] and of state courts in certain other US states.

Under this approach, the state courts authorize class procedures and notices, and approve settlements/awards, while arbitration tribunals decide the merit of the dispute and determine the remedies.

This would require a very creative bench and it would result in a rather complex solution with no governing rules except those made from time to time by the court.

It seems more likely that judges would try to find a way to invalidate the arbitration clause and to authorize a plain class action if the plaintiff qualifies to introduce one.

Professor Strong is of the view that "[...] [T]he situation does not require an all-in or all-out solution. Jurisdictions that are still undecided about the propriety of large-scale arbitration can adopt an intermediate step similar to that taken in Germany in cases involving corporate disputes." Indeed, the Federal Court of Justice of Germany (BGH) did not encourage or discourage collective arbitration but declared the dispute arbitrable and determined some basic procedural protections if ever the parties decided to move into arbitration proceeding.[27]

IV Practical Reasons

Finally, the arbitration provisions of all the relevant provincial legislation do not contemplate class arbitration. So the parties would have to provide in the arbitration clause the rules to be applied or agree to be governed by the rules of an organization providing for class arbitration (for example the rules of the AAA or JAMS).

Needless to say, the effectiveness of an arbitration award rendered further to a class arbitration to prevent an absent party to initiate an individual claim on the ground of *res judicata* would be challenged. Incidentally, it is not rare in Canada in national class actions heard in another province. This would be particularly true if the class arbitration was held outside Canada and the award was opposed to a Canadian resident.

In conclusion, the combination of these policy, commercial and practical reasons makes it unlikely that Canada will be the next frontier in class arbitration.

6 GROUP ACTIONS IN ARBITRATION

Despite the fact that Canada does not appear to be ready for class arbitration, nothing legally prevents group arbitration through a consolidation of pending cases or a joint demand in arbitration signed by a large group of plaintiffs when the parties agree.

However, consolidation without consent is a violation of party autonomy, of party's right to appoint its own arbitrator or to agree to a procedure for such appointment and of the right to confidentiality related to the privity of the contract.

In most provinces of Canada but not in Quebec, a consolidation requires in addition an authorization by a court.[28] Failing an agreement between the litigant parties, most courts will refuse to order a consolidation. Efficiency does not trump consent.

In fact, group arbitration is a procedural issue that should be addressed by the parties in the arbitration clause or by the rules of the selected arbitral institution (subject to limits imposed by the relevant domestic law).

It remains that group arbitration, when agreed or ordered under the rules applicable to the arbitration, does not alter the nature of the arbitration process which rests on consent or its features, such as confidentiality and the ability of each party to actively participate in the process, including the appointment of the members of the arbitral tribunal (or challenging an arbitrator proposed by the arbitral institution).

A potentially interesting field for group arbitration is shareholders' claims. Some publicly traded companies are now considering including in their bylaws that a shareholder raising a claim against the company should turn to arbitration to the exclusion of any court. Then you could argue that every shareholder, when acquiring shares in the capital stock of the company, is agreeing to arbitration in the event of a future dispute.

Assuming this is considered a sufficient consent to arbitration and that group arbitration is not excluded specifically, large institutional investors could initiate an impressive group arbitration. In the case of publicly traded shares this option would be, of course, subject to limitations provided in the relevant securities acts.

7 CONCLUSION

There is a future for group arbitration in Canada, but not for class arbitration. On the latter, the situation in Canada seems to be closer to Europe than to the US, despite the fact that class actions US style are widespread north of the US borders.

NOTES

1 Incidentally, it may reduce state expenses, a factor that governments appreciate.

2 Elie Kleiman, "*The Future of Class, Collective and Mass Arbitrations in Europe, A European approach to collective redress*" (2016), Dossier of the Institute [forthcoming in 2016].

3 *Code of Civil Procedure*, RLRQ, 2015, c C-25.01, s 1.

4 Stéphanie Vallée, Minister of Justice, Legislative Comment on Code of Civil Procedure, RLRQ, 2015, c C-25.01, s 1. Annotated Code of Civil Procedure (2015) (CAIJ) Translated from French : « Bien qu'elle ne soit pas contraignante au point de rendre irrecevable l'action en justice qui n'aurait pas été précédée d'une tentative de règlement, la disposition devrait, en raison de son caractère impératif, entraîner un changement important dans le rôle des juristes qui devraient désormais présenter à leurs clients un ensemble de possibilités pour la résolution des conflits.»

5 The source of modern class actions goes back to a 1966 amendment to rule 23 of the US Federal Rules of Civil Procedure, the rule governing the conduct of class actions in the US Federal Courts. The first class action act in Canada was enacted in Quebec in 1978. Ontario followed in 1992.

6 *Doyer c. Dow Corning Corporation*, 2008 QCCS 5746 (Quebec Superior Court)

7 *Hotte c. Servier Canada Inc.*, [2002] RJQ 230 (Quebec Superior Court)

8 *Létourneau c. JTI-MacDonald Corp.*, 2015 QCCS 2382(Quebec Superior Court awarding US$15 billion).

9 Collective recovery means that the judgment orders the defendants to pay an amount corresponding to the value of the claims of all the members of the class, independently of the number of claimants that may then complete the steps to collect their shares.

10 Certification is a judicial authorization to proceed with the class action, granting status to plaintiff to act on behalf of the class and ordering the publication of certain notices.

11 Fees are paid to lawyers before distribution to class members and subject to court scrutiny. Very few guiding principles so far, court's approval being largely done on a case by case basis.

12 *UNCITRAL Model Law for international arbitration*, 1985 With amendments as adopted in 2006, UN doc A/40/17.

13 For example, see the US Supreme Court in *Stolt-Nielsen S.A. v Animal Feeds International Corp.*, 130 S. Ct. 1758, [*Stolt-Nielsen*] at 1776.

14 Allan Ripp and Elise Martin, "Greek Investors Bring Legal Action against Republic of Cyprus, Alleging Deposits and Bonds Were Wrongly Confiscated Following Bailout of 2013", Online: (2015) PR Newswire at 5 < **http://www.prnewswire.com/news-releases/**>

15 Strong, SI, "*Incentives for Large-Scale Arbitration: How Policymakers Can Influence Party Behaviour*" (2016), Dossier of the Institute [forthcoming in 2016] p 5 [Strong, SI: How Policymakers Can Influence Party Behaviour].

16 *Stolt-Nielsen, supra* note 11 at 1775.

17 Refer to "*Incentives for Large-Scale Arbitration: How Policymakers Can Influence Party Behaviour"* (precited), from Professor Strong to know more about States' incentives and disincentives to large-scale arbitration.

18 In fact, they must retire at 75.

19 For an example, see : David Horton and Andrea Cann Chandrasekher, *After the Revolution: An Empirical Study of Consumer Arbitration*, Georgetown Law Journal, vol. 104, 2015.

20 Id, at para 5

21 *Dell Computer Corp. v Union des consommateurs*, [2007] 2 S.C.R. 531.

22 *Seidel v.Telus Communications Inc.*, 2011 SCC 15.

23 On this very issue, see also Elie Kleiman's text, under the heading "Private interests and policy issues at a crossroads."

24 US, Consumer Financial Protection Bureau, Arbitration Study (Report to Congress, pursuant to Dodd-Frank Wall Street Reform and Consumer Protection Act § 1028(a), 2015)

25 Alan S. Kaplinsky and Mark J. Levin, "New empirical study of AAA arbitrations is a study in contradictions", Online: (2015) CFPB Monitor at para 3 < https://**www.cfpbmonitor.com/**>.

26 *Keating v Superior Court*, 645 P. 2d 1192.

27 *S.I. Strong: How Policymakers Can Influence Party Behaviour*, *supra* note 13 at p 13

28 See for example, section 27(2) of the *International Arbitration Act* of British Columbia.

Chapter 13

The Future of Class, Collective and Mass Arbitrations in Europe

A European Approach to Collective Redress

Elie Kleiman*

INTRODUCTION

Is European class arbitration an oxymoron? For the past 50 years, international arbitration has been mainly associated with international commerce and international investment. It has evolved into an extremely sophisticated dispute resolution system, that has proved quite fitting for the purposes of resolving the most complex high-stakes disputes between large multinationals. It would be fair to say that, for most arbitration practitioners at least, the resolution of mass disputes arising from abuses of uneven bargaining power and the need to protect weaker parties aggrieved by unfair commercial dealings, have not been an area of focus. But it would be equally unfair to suggest that consumer protection or "B2C" arbitration has not been a matter of academic studies.[1] The future of class arbitration in Europe, however, is largely uncertain and will depend on many factors including whatever room will be left to party autonomy in a domain of the law where European lawmakers have not hesitated to regulate. One cannot help but notice the proliferation of European generated legislation regarding dispute resolution. It cannot be disputed that the administration of justice before State courts is a matter of sovereignty and as such should be regulated. Understandably, the European Union (the "EU" or the "Union") also claims to regulate and supervise matters that involve the protection of weaker parties, which lies at the very heart of the domain of class actions.

Over the past few years, the EU has adopted a global framework for collective redress and alternative dispute resolution ("ADR") in several sectors. While more than half of the EU Member States have implemented national collective redress systems, their individual features and scope differ greatly.[2] For the last few decades, the introduction of collective redress mechanisms has been a matter that divided not only the legal community, but also civil societies of countries in which this issue has been raised. The EU has supported the introduction of collective redress mechanisms in its Member States while insisting on its opposition to the US class actions' system.[3] The Commission noted that: [4]

> "[t]he primary difference of opinion concerning the benefits that could flow from introducing new mechanisms of collective redress is between citizens/consumers and business: consumers are generally in favour of introducing new mechanisms, while businesses are generally against. Academics are generally in favour. Lawyers are divided on this issue, although those who are sceptical or opposed outnumber those in favour."

* Partner, Freshfields Bruckhaus Deringer LLP — the author expresses his gratitude to Ms. Hanna Maalèj, an associate at Freshfields Bruckhaus Deringer LLP, for her assistance.

The proliferation, however, of EU law in the field of alternative dispute resolution, a domain that has traditionally been thought to be inherently contractual in nature, is more difficult for the business law practitioner to understand. The abundance of EU-led initiatives and ensuing increase of regulation in the field of dispute resolution, has become a cause for concern in the arbitration community.[5] One may indeed query whether encouraging uniformity and integration in matters of alternative dispute resolution should be a priority for EU lawmakers. By looking at recent developments and trends in EU circles, one can begin to predict the future of class arbitration and whether it will have any meaningful role in an increasingly regulated world. The European approach to settlement of disputes suggests — in sometimes not so subliminal terms — that arbitration may not be an adequate forum for the resolution of disputes that inherently address public policy issues. Class arbitration is one such method brought into question.

This paper will attempt to discuss this topic and offer some — very speculative — suggestions in this regard. It may indeed be possible to suggest that arbitration may and should offer a safe and reliable means of recourse for the protection of weaker parties, and indeed the preservation of the general interest, while also ensuring fair process for all concerned.

In its assessment of the collective redress procedures available in its Member States, the EU distinguishes between injunctive relief and compensatory relief: the aim of injunctive relief is to grant to harmed parties the possibility of seeking an order to stop illegal business practices. Existing EU legislation and international agreements require that Member States have such procedures in place in certain sectors, such as the consumer and environmental protection sectors. As a consequence, all Member States have provisions that provide collective injunctive relief. The aim of compensatory relief is to award damages to victims harmed by illegal business practices. Procedures for the collective claim of compensatory relief in certain sectors have been introduced in the majority of Member States and vary widely throughout the EU.[6] This paper will therefore only focus on collective compensatory relief as arbitration is best suited to this form of relief.

This paper will address the current issues relating to the development of class arbitration in Europe. Section I describes the regulated framework for collective redress mechanisms in the EU; Section II addresses the challenges and obstacles to the development of class arbitration in Europe; and Section III discusses the new challenges that the arbitration field will face due to the increasing prevalence of class arbitrations.

1 A REGULATED FRAMEWORK FOR COLLECTIVE REDRESS PROCEDURES IN EUROPE

A. Implementation of Collective Redress Mechanisms in EU Member States

In its Recommendation of 11 June 2013, the Commission stated that "[a]ll Member States should have collective redress mechanisms at national level for both injunctive and compensatory relief" by 26 July 2015.[7]

By 2011, 16 EU Member States had already implemented collective redress mechanisms.[8] There are significant differences in the approaches taken by

Member States towards collective redress schemes: every national system of compensatory redress is unique.[9]

A collective action is defined as "a procedural device allowing plaintiffs to sue not only for injury done to themselves but on behalf of other persons similarly situated for injury done to them."[10]

Collective redress procedures, even those already in existence, are not set in stone. For example, several EU Member States created or amended their collective redress procedures very recently: (i) in Belgium, a representative-based collective actions regime was introduced to the Economic Law Code on 28 February 2014; (ii) in France, the *Loi Hamon* introduced class actions for competition and consumer law on 1 October 2014 and the French Parliament is also discussing a further class action regime for healthcare-related physical injuries; and (iii) in the United Kingdom, a limited opt-out regime for antitrust claims has been available since 1 October 2015 under the Consumers Rights Act 2015.

Group actions are the most common form of collective redress mechanisms in the EU and are divided into (i) group actions in which individual actions are grouped into one procedure, (ii) actions brought by groups of victims and (iii) group actions brought by an ombudsman, consumer organization or leading plaintiff.[11]

The most significant issues with regard to national collective redress schemes are scope of application, types of remedies available, implementation of an opt-in or opt-out mechanism and funding.[12]

Most national systems allow compensatory redress for consumers and only a few allow general standing. National laws also diverge on the question of who should receive the benefits of the remedies: the public purse, associations (e.g. consumer associations) or victims. With regard to the effects of the decisions rendered in collective redress procedures, most Member States have implemented an opt-in mechanism, pursuant to which the decisions only bind those who have expressly consented to the proceedings. A few Member-States,[13] however, have adopted an opt-out mechanism, allowing for the decision to become binding for all members of the group unless they have expressly stated otherwise.[14]

Funding is another main area of concern. The US class action system, which allows contingency fees and is therefore seen as facilitating the commencement of large-scale class actions whose only aim is to force settlement with the corporate defendant through mass media coverage, has attracted criticism in the EU and international legal community on the basis that it encourages claims which are cynical and sometimes meritless. Funding is therefore considered a central issue when discussing the features of collective redress procedures in Europe and one of the European institutions' main objectives is to avoid abusive actions.[15] Conditional and contingency fees are not banned in all EU Member States but, in some of the jurisdictions in which they are allowed, these fees are subject to court scrutiny. The possibility of having recourse to third party funding is unregulated in a majority of EU Member States.[16]

B. Lack of Efficiency in Existing Procedures and Calls for Harmonization at the EU Level

A 2008 study on collective redress mechanisms in the EU Member States conducted by the European Commission concluded that these procedures have proved to not be fully effective.[17] This study focused on the collective redress judicial procedures that had been implemented thus far in 13 Member States. Although this study did not take into account the latest developments in the field and had a limited scope (it only dealt with consumer protection), its conclusions can certainly still be considered relevant and can be extrapolated to apply to collective redress mechanisms in Europe as a whole.

The evaluation of the effectiveness of the then available collective redress mechanisms focused on: (i) the degree to which they fulfil the objectives of the implementing national laws; (ii) the incentives provided by the mechanisms; (iii) their accessibility; and (iv) the way collective actions are financed.

On these four issues, the study concludes that:

1. the majority of the collective mechanisms do not fulfil the objectives attached to them by national legislation and the direct benefit to consumers is often limited;[18]
2. the existing collective redress mechanisms neither seem to ensure a change in the behaviour of potential defendants nor constitute a significant deterrent to them, yet at the same time these mechanisms do seem to discourage unmeritorious claims as a result of the application in most Member States of the 'loser pays' principle;[19]
3. group actions that are pursued by representatives are usually relatively easy to join although low-value cases may pose joinder problems for consumers; and
4. the financing of collective actions is a very significant obstacle for their use since the budgets of all potential intermediaries are limited and the risk of severe loss is high due to the 'loser pays' principle.[20]

The study notes, however, that "collective redress mechanisms have an added value to consumers' access to justice in all Member States where they exist, even in those where individual litigation and ADR is easily accessible."[21] From a critical point of view, it could be inferred from this statement that consumer protection in EU Member States must be very low if mechanisms that are not deemed efficient are nevertheless considered a means of improving EU consumers' access to justice. In any event, there is no doubt that should the effectiveness of the collective redress procedures improve, consumers' effective access to justice will be guaranteed. This is precisely the goal that EU institutions are working towards.

The work of EU institutions on collective redress has resulted in a vast number of publications, including a Green Paper (2009), several Consultation Papers (2009, 2011), a Resolution of the European Parliament (2012) and, lastly, a Recommendation of the European Commission (2013) whose first recital recalls that "the Union has set itself the objective of maintaining and developing an area of freedom, security of justice, inter alia, by facilitating access to justice, as well as the objective of ensuring a high level of consumer protection."[22]

The Recommendation — although not binding — encourages Member States to implement collective redress mechanisms which should be available in different areas where EU law grants rights to citizens and companies, including consumer protection, competition law, environmental protection, protection of personal data, financial services legislation and investor protection.[23] Member States should ensure that the procedures are "fair, equitable, timely and not prohibitively expensive."[24]

The approach of the Commission on this topic is interestingly oriented towards a balance between two competing considerations: (i) an improved access to justice for EU citizens and (ii) the avoidance of abusive litigation. The EU's position revolves around a strong opposition to the US' class actions system.[25] As the European Commission stated: "the European approach to collective redress clearly rejects the US style system of 'class actions'."[26]

To this end, the Commission has set forth several "European principles on collective redress" which illustrate its rejection of the US class actions system. The Commission recommends:

- the implementation of opt-in systems of collective redress, while the opt-out systems should remain the exception and should be duly justified by reasons of sound administration of justice; and
- the implementation of "procedural safeguards aimed at protecting the procedural rights of the parties and avoiding incentives to abuse the collective redress systems", e.g. the avoidance of contingency fees and punitive damages.[27]

The Commission is particularly careful with regards to funding as it is one of the issues that reflects the tensions between these two competing considerations: "while lack of funding should not limit access to justice, funding mechanisms available for collective actions should not create incentives for abusive litigation."[28] The Commission is particularly circumspect in relation to third-party financing and even considers that contingency and success fees constitute *de facto* third-party financing.[29]

C. Cross-Border Implications of Collective Redress Mechanisms and the Relevance of Class Arbitration

The 2008 study conducted by the European Commission indicated that of the 13 collective redress procedures available in EU Member States, around 10% of the collective redress cases involved cross-border litigation.[30] This study also pointed out that 40% of collected mass claims contained a cross-border element.[31]

This issue is critical for obvious reasons: while promoting the introduction of collective redress mechanisms in the Member States, the EU did not suggest, let alone implement adequate means of processing these collective claims at a transnational level. The existing hurdles to the administration of collective claims across the Union have been known for several years. In a briefing note, the European Parliament referred to similar difficulties encountered by the US system with regards to multi-state litigation and the potential resolution of these multi-state collective claims at the federal level.[32]

The Recommendation of the Commission nonetheless only contains two paragraphs on "cross-border cases."[33] As the Recommendation is a non-binding instrument, it could not provide the necessary regulations for the efficient and effective handling of cross-border mass claims.[34] The guidance provided in the Recommendation will thus necessarily be of a limited scope. These provisions only address the issue of legal standing of representative entities and do not provide any guidance on how to deal with the private international law issues that may arise should cross-border elements be involved.[35] These private international law issues include the determination of the competent courts to hear the case and the applicable procedural and substantive laws.

These points are all the more relevant if we consider that one of the natural domains of collective actions will arise from violations of EU law,[36] notably in the fields of consumer protection or competition law, that are highly likely to involve cross-border elements, e.g. the victims are citizens of different Member States and want to collectively sue a corporate defendant for infringement of EU regulations. To date, the European framework for collective redress lacks guidance and clear rules on how to resolve these issues.

None of the European private international law instruments provide specific rules for collective claims: neither the Brussels I Regulation (in its 2000 or 2012 version, together the "Brussels Regulations") nor the Rome I and II Regulations deal with the particular problems of proceedings related to collective redress. [37] These regulations would nonetheless be applicable by default pending the adoption of specific rules for collective redress procedures.

The first issue to arise would be the determination of the competent courts to hear the case. Applying the Brussels Regulations to collective redress procedures could lead to surreal solutions. For example:[38]

- the general provision states that courts of a Member State where the defendant is domiciled have jurisdiction to hear the case;
- in disputes concerning consumer contracts, consumers can also file a claim in the courts of the Member State where they are domiciled (if they are not represented by an ombudsman or consumer association);
- in matters relating to a contract, the courts of the place where the obligation is to be performed will also have jurisdiction; and
- if several defendants are being sued, the courts where any defendant is domiciled will have jurisdiction, provided that the claims are so closely connected that it is expedient to hear and determine them together to avoid the risk of irreconcilable judgments that may result from separate proceedings.

The conflicts between the above-mentioned rules would end up being unavoidable in cross-border collective redress procedures. Several courts, which would all have jurisdiction pursuant to the applicable Brussels Regulation, could be seized in different EU Member States. The complexity of cross-border collective litigation and the significant risks of inconsistent or varying determinations and adjudication in different jurisdictions have already been pointed out.[39]

The provisions of the Brussels Regulations regarding lis pendens and parallel proceedings would be of little help. These provisions address the problem of parallel proceedings and irreconcilable judgments by giving preference to the court where the proceedings were first initiated. Both Brussels Regulations require not only "the same cause of action" in all proceedings, but also the participation of "the same parties." [40] These provisions would therefore not apply to parallel proceedings initiated by different representative entities or by a group of individuals that could be different before each court seized.

The determination of the applicable procedural and substantive laws also raises similar issues and would involve conflicts between several EU rules that would be intended to apply to the mass claimants. Enforcement of any judicial decision rendered in the course of the collective action proceedings would also be difficult.

The private international law rules contained in the EU regulations are not designed to deal with the issues raised by cross-border collective redress procedures. Practitioners and scholars have called for a broad discussion on private international law issues relating to collective redress.[41]

If the collective redress procedures implemented in the Member States at the initiative of the EU institutions cannot deal with cross-border cases, the effective access to justice of the European citizens would be questionable. So long as special rules are not adopted at the EU level to deal will cross-border cases, the collective redress procedures cannot be deemed effective. Should we regard procedures which can lead to inconsistent decisions and be paralysed with unresolved issues when used in cross-border cases as meaningfully guaranteeing EU citizens' access to justice? The answer is certainly negative.

For now, the collective redress procedures that have been introduced in the legislations of a majority of the EU Member States are not suited for cross-border cases for all the above mentioned reasons.

Other means of resolving cross-border collective disputes therefore appear more suitable: these means have been mentioned by the Recommendation under the label "alternative dispute resolution and settlements."[42] The Recommendation states that:

> "[t]he Member States should ensure that judicial collective redress mechanisms are accompanied by appropriate means of collective alternative dispute resolution available to the parties before and throughout the litigation. Use of such means should depend on the consent of the parties involved in the case."

Applying the poorly adapted rules of the Brussels Regulations to the collective redress procedures leaves the parties in an area filled with uncertainty and unpredictability. The uncertain outcome of this preliminary and fundamental issue, that is the question of jurisdiction, could jeopardize and complicate the whole procedure. A more effective mechanism would, to the extent possible, provide certainty by minimising the difficulties and inconsistencies that may stem from the application of default jurisdictional rules. Recourse to arbitration could achieve this aim.

Pending solutions on the topical private international law issues, when collective cases involve a cross-border element, the resolution of these disputes through out-of-court procedures appears to be a satisfactory alternative to judicial procedures. Class arbitration is one ADR mechanism available for resolving cross-border collective disputes. The Recommendation has put a focus on consent of the parties: this is consistent with the approach used in arbitration ("consent remains the cornerstone of arbitration"[43]) and ADR in general.

The features of arbitration — its contractual nature, the flexibility of its procedure and its adaptability to cross-border cases — would help in dealing with cross-border collective cases. Among these features, the following would facilitate overcoming the hurdles of cross-border related issues before judicial courts:

- jurisdiction would be centralized before a sole arbitral tribunal upon consent of the members of the class (be they individuals or representative entities). Consent to jurisdiction of the arbitral tribunal could be achieved by means of pre- or post-arbitration agreement which respect the opt-in principle;
- the applicable procedural and substantive law would be determined by the parties to the dispute either before or after the commencement of the proceedings; and
- the enforcement of the arbitral award in multiple jurisdictions would be facilitated by the Convention on the Recognition and Enforcement of Foreign Arbitral Awards ("New York Convention"), thereby reducing the risks of contradictory decisions being enforced in different jurisdictions.

In such context, it might be appropriate to establish a requirement similar to that of the US class action system pursuant to which, before initiating class arbitration proceedings, it must be ascertained that resolution of the dispute through ADR "is superior to other available methods for the fair and efficient adjudication of the controversy."[44] As EU law currently stands (and pending the introduction of specific rules on the resolution of cross-border collective disputes), it can reasonably be inferred that ADR and class arbitration in particular would be considered superior to judicial resolution of cross-border collective cases.

2 CHALLENGES AND OBSTACLES TO THE DEVELOPMENT OF CLASS ARBITRATION IN EUROPE

A. Private Interests and Policy Issues at a Crossroads

The EU institutions' main concern with regard to collective redress is ensure effective enforcement of rights and to "facilitate access to justice."[45] The Recommendation of the European Commission on collective redress further states that "[i]t is a core task of public enforcement to prevent and punish the violations of rights granted under Union law. The possibility for private persons to pursue claims based on violations of such rights supplements public enforcement."[46] "Rights which cannot be enforced in practice are worthless."[47] The protection of weaker parties and consumers in particular is clearly considered a matter of policy and public interest.

The protection of private interests and the policy issues underlying the prosecution of infringement of the EU citizens' rights are closely intertwined. The boundaries between public policy and private enforcement of individual rights are permeable. As Professor Strong states: "[t]he failure to pursue individual claims injures more than individual claimants. [...] When that mechanism fails to operate as intended, society as a whole suffers."[48] The following statement of an American court could easily be said to hold true in respect of Europe: "[t]he realistic alternative to a class action is not 17 million individual suits, but zero individual suits, as only a lunatic or a fanatic sues for $30."[49]

Economic considerations are also driving the proposals to improve the enforcement of EU citizens' rights. For example, the European Commission noted that in 2010, one in five consumers in the EU encountered problems when buying goods or services in the European Single Market, leading to financial losses estimated at 0.4% of the EU's GDP. However, only a small fraction of consumers sought and secured effective redress.[50]

Collective redress, by means of judicial and out-of-court procedures, is seen as a means not only of facilitating EU citizens' access to justice but also to reinforce the Single Market. ADR and simplified procedures for the enforcement of the rights of the EU citizens are a major part of the EU's initiatives. The 2013 directive on ADR for consumer disputes states in its third recital that:

> "Fragmentation of the internal market is detrimental to competitiveness, growth and job creation within the Union. Eliminating direct and indirect obstacles to the proper functioning of the internal market and improving citizens' trust is essential for the completion of the internal market."[51]

To this end, the Directive favours recourse to ADR for consumer disputes. Out-of-court resolution of disputes can serve as a complement to judicial proceedings as it would allow low-value disputes that would not have been otherwise submitted to a court to proceed and be resolved. [52]

Whether arbitration will be able to address the needs of fair and effective collective claims resolution is not an abstract question. While no one doubts that international arbitration will continue to be the forum of choice for sophisticated dispute resolution of complex disputes arising out of high stakes transactions between large multinational corporations, one may wonder whether the same concept is flexible enough to discharge the social function that is attached to class actions. In consumer disputes, dispute resolution fulfils a corrective function: it is designed to restore the balance between the weaker party (e.g. the consumer or investor) and the dominant party that is accused of having infringed on the former's rights. A parallel can sensibly be drawn with investment disputes: a similar concern for the preservation of the public interest has been identified in that field, in which disputes engaging public policy issues have been subject to close scrutiny by governments, institutions, non-governmental organizations and the legal community. To some extent, class arbitration and investment arbitration may be seen as sharing common issues: they require transparency, efficiency and a reinforced sense of equality between the parties. In the absence of demonstrable evidence that these features are available, the perceived legitimacy of the system will remain in question. This is cause for concern in light of recent developments in the domain of investment protection, where EU oversensitivity to political reactions triggered by anti-arbitration activists opposed to the draft Transatlantic Trade and Investment Partnership, resulted in a proposal by the EU Commission to replace an investor-state dispute settlement process with dedicated permanent courts composed of state-appointed judges.[53]

Arbitration of disputes engaging public policy issues is evolving towards more regulation. While the distinctive features of arbitration are not put into question, it is possible to imagine that collective arbitration may morph into a hybrid mechanism based on (i) certain features of arbitration, mainly its contractual nature and (ii) regulatory supervision of those proceedings by state courts and/or arbitral institutions.

B. Consent

Consent may be an obstacle to the development of collective arbitration. Arbitration clauses contained in contracts entered into with consumers should preferably refer to class arbitration. Post-dispute arbitration agreements will likely enjoy a certain revival as they will be perceived as an effective means of remediating the absence or defectiveness of pre-dispute arbitration agreements.

1. Consent and National Laws of EU Member States

The various laws of EU Member States dealing with collective redress are not "particularly class-action friendly."[54] The insistence by the EU on the implementation of collective redress mechanisms will likely enhance the attractiveness and efficiency of these procedures. Class litigation, however, is often seen as a prerequisite to class arbitration, if only because consent issues arise.[55]

When compared with the rise of class arbitration in the United States, the evolution towards the widespread use of class arbitration in Europe will likely take a different path. In the US, the legislative instruments allowing for recourse through class-action litigation paved the way for class arbitration, although in an unexpected way: "class arbitration in the United States developed as the direct result of corporate defendants' own efforts." [56] It is indeed the inclusion of arbitration clauses in the contracts concluded by the corporate entities with their clients that led to the emergence of class arbitrations as "the only way that the parties' agreement to arbitrate could be given effect was to permit the claimants to proceed as a class." [57] The arbitration clause which had initially been designed as an "instrument of impunity"[58] for corporate actors turned into a means of ensuring collective redress through arbitration, with room being left for the arbitrators to decide on the most appropriate manner of enforcing the arbitration clause. Things are likely to be different in the EU. Remaining uncertainties on arbitrability of consumer disputes across the Union probably contribute to the underdevelopment of class arbitration-compatible clauses in business-to-consumer contracts.[59] Uncertainties that come from the coexistence of opt-in and opt-out legislation in Europe are probably the cause of other obstacles. The private international law issues arising with regard to cross-border collective actions before state courts may, however, induce corporations facing collective claims to invite prospective plaintiffs to turn to class arbitration as a means of resolving their disputes.

2. Consent and Arbitral Tribunals

Arbitration clauses in business-to-consumer contracts are relatively scarce in Europe. Even when contract contain arbitration clauses, they are standard clauses that do not expressly provide for class arbitration ("silent arbitration clauses"). The first and critical issue for arbitrators with regard to class arbitration is therefore the interpretation of such clauses. On this point of interpretation, the US approach, as set out in the *Green Tree v Bazzle* decision, is consistent with the prevailing view in Europe, i.e. that it is for the arbitrator to decide whether the silent arbitration clause authorizes or prohibits class arbitration.[60] The Court in *Green Tree v Bazzle* explained that this was not a question of whether the arbitration agreement was valid in the first place, but rather a question of the "kind of arbitration proceeding" that the parties had agreed to and was thus an issue of mere contractual interpretation for the arbitrator to decide.[61]

Favouring recourse to post-dispute arbitration agreements is also a means to develop class arbitration. The Spanish law that allowed collective consumer arbitration takes this position and provides the parties with the ability to establish collective arbitration through post-dispute arbitration agreements.[62] These post-dispute arbitration agreements would be an adequate and efficient way to overcome the obstacle of inarbitrability of consumer or employment disputes as the weaker party would consent to arbitration once the dispute has arisen.[63] This analysis would be consistent with the approach that has been adopted by the EU institutions thus far, and would mirror the Commission's Recommendation that "alternative dispute resolution procedures [...] should always be available alongside, or as a voluntary element of, judicial collective redress."[64] Unilateral option clauses for the benefit of consumers or employees have also been envisaged.

In the course of their analysis of the silent arbitration clause, arbitrators should also consider the relevance of the class arbitration procedure on a case-by-case basis. This is indeed one of the requirements in the US class-action system: the courts have to determine whether "a class action is superior to other available methods for the fair and efficient adjudication of the controversy."[65] This would also be in line with the Commission's Recommendation that "judicial collective redress mechanisms [should be] accompanied by appropriate means of collective [ADR] available to the parties before and throughout the litigation."[66]

3. Consent and State Courts

On all matters involving consent, state courts play a crucial role at the stage of applications for the annulment or refusal of recognition and enforcement of arbitral awards. In several jurisdictions, the parties to the dispute can also apply to state courts in the course of the arbitral proceedings.[67]

Looking at the Commission's "European principles on collective redress", one sees opposing positions on the two major obstacles that were identified for the enforcement of US class actions decisions, namely (i) the implementation of opt-in systems of collective redress and (ii) the implementation of "procedural safeguards aimed at protecting the procedural rights of the parties and avoiding incentives to abuse the collective redress systems", such as the avoidance of contingency fees and punitive damages.[68] Regarding the issue of consent in particular, these European principles can easily be applied to class arbitrations by favouring recourse to post-dispute arbitration agreements. It is also quite possible that combined litigation-arbitration systems may be put in place, where for example a state court could certify a class and decide on liability, whereas questions of quantum for example would be resolved through arbitration.

3 THE NEW CHALLENGES FACED BY ARBITRATION

A. Adaptability of Arbitration to Mass Claims: Same or Different?

The recent discussions on the need of collective redress procedures, especially in the EU, together with the EU institutions' commitment to this end leads to inevitable questions on the future of arbitration as a whole. Class arbitration is certainly a "novel form of arbitration"[69] — however, arbitration in and of itself remains unchanged.

The core features of arbitration will help overcome the above-mentioned obstacles and hurdles that will undoubtedly go along with the development of collective redress procedures. These core features are its contractual nature, emphasis on consent, neutrality, independence of arbitrators and effective award enforcement in almost every jurisdiction. The adequacy of arbitration to address mass claims, regardless of the amounts at stake (the mass claim will often be an aggregate of a significant number of low-value individual claims), leaves little doubt.

One remaining issue that falls to be addressed is that of arbitrability, for if not clarified it may impair the development of class arbitration. Arbitrability is "founded upon the protection of the general interest. This is as opposed to the requirement of valid consent, which is intended to protect the private interests of the parties to the arbitration agreements."[70] The uncertainties and legal obstacles to arbitrability in matters involving the imperative protection of the public interest will need to be clarified as a matter of law. It may be suggested that the case for arbitrability of matters involving economic redress is a rather straightforward one. The solution would be quite the opposite where bodily injury is at stake. It is, however, possible to suggest that even in these matters, for example in cases involving defective products or environment damage, there could be room for class arbitration in the quantification phase, after the liability phase arbitration was decided by a state court.

The debate on class arbitration is very much in line with the challenges of modernity: it is about finding new solutions to contemporary issues and also adapting arbitration as a whole to renewed stakes. In this regard, the Commission's Recommendation states that:

> "[t]he modern economy sometimes creates situations in which a large number of persons can be harmed by the same illegal practices relating to the violation of rights granted under Union law by one or more traders or other persons [...]. They may therefore have cause to seek the cessation of such practices or to claim damages."[71]

There will be no room for class arbitration in the EU if arbitration cannot provide solutions that ensure a balanced approach to the resolution of the kinds of disputes arising in the "modern economy." Class arbitration must be perceived as a trustworthy alternative.

B. Arbitral Institutions

To date, very few arbitral institutions have implemented specific rules for class arbitrations. The two renowned institutions that have implemented such rules are the American Arbitration Association ("AAA")[72] and the German Institution of Arbitration ("DIS"), the latter being limited in scope to corporate law disputes.[73]

Implementation of new rules dedicated to class arbitrations will likely flow from the development of class arbitrations in Europe. These rules should be adapted to the specificities of class arbitration. Both the AAA and the DIS rules address several topical issues of class arbitration. Among these issues is the appointment of arbitrators.

The issue of appointment of arbitrators is of utmost importance as it involves due process concerns. The appointment of arbitrators by mass claimants raises similar (and even more complex) issues to those raised by multi-party arbitrations involving several claimants or defendants.[74] To oppose the recognition of the award, any party to the arbitral proceedings could argue that it had been deprived of its right to participate in the appointment of the arbitrators and that, as a consequence, due process had been violated in the course of the constitution of the arbitral tribunal.[75] This issue would be even more important if we consider opt-out arbitration systems.

The AAA as well as the DIS Supplementary Rules almost exclusively provide default rules governing situations in which parties disagree as to the constitution of the arbitral tribunal. Where difficulties arise in this regard, both sets of rules provide for recourse to the arbitral institution in charge of the administration of the case:

- the AAA Supplementary Rules provide that if the parties cannot agree upon the number of arbitrators to be appointed, the dispute shall be heard by a sole arbitrator unless the institution, in its discretion, directs that three arbitrators be appointed;[76] and
- the DIS Supplementary Rules' approach appears to have taken into account the above-mentioned principle of equality that governs the appointment of the arbitrators. These Rules indeed provide that where either claimants or defendants do not reach an agreement on the appointment of the arbitrators within 30 days, the institution will nominate two arbitrators upon a request from either side.[77]

The underlying approach of both sets of rules is to resolve situations in which the parties cannot reach agreement on the nomination of their respective party-appointed arbitrators. In these circumstances, it is appropriate to derogate from the traditional approach to arbitral appointments: the arbitral institution should appoint the arbitrators.

In situations where mass claimants or defendants are involved, there is a high risk of difficulties in the course of the appointment process. In order to prevent these risks, we should consider extending the approach adopted by both institutions described above and implement a default rule pursuant to which the appointment of arbitrators would be part of the relevant arbitral institution's mandate. This proposal was suggested by Professor Jan Paulsson who wrote that "[u]nilateral appointments are not needed to constitute three-member tribunals. All three may be appointed by the neutral supervisory body."[78] This distinctive feature would be better suited to class arbitrations and would help avoid any challenges on the grounds of improper constitution of the tribunal in the course enforcement or annulment proceedings before judicial courts.

Institutional arbitration is also likely to play a key role in the development and legitimacy of class arbitration because handling very significant numbers of parties will quite probably prove a daunting task for any ad hoc tribunal, and quite certainly an uneconomical one while institutions should be able to benefit from economies of scale.

More fundamentally, it is suggested that arbitral institutions should endeavour to strengthen their cooperation with other stakeholders such as consumer protection organizations, federations of industries and the EU. A consensus-based approach may indeed permit to reach common ground on overarching principles that should be achieved through class arbitration mechanisms. For example, an agreement on the specifications that class arbitration rules should meet could ensure enhanced predictability and greater efficiency.

C. Online Dispute Resolution: The Future of Class Arbitration?

Along with its policy in favour of collective redress, the EU has also adopted a Directive[79] and a Regulation[80] that offer new mechanisms allowing EU citizens to enforce their rights through ADR and online dispute resolution ("ODR"). To date, the EU institutions have focused on consumer disputes. The rationale underlying both the development of (i) collective redress procedures and (ii) ADR and ODR procedures are very similar as they are both working towards promotion of the same objective: offering EU citizens enhanced access to justice. The new ADR and ODR systems also take into account economic considerations pertaining to the development of the European Single Market. It is the EU's position that developing a European area of free trade will not be possible without effective mechanisms for the enforcement of citizens' rights. The European Commission notes that: [81]

> "[i]t is estimated that if EU consumers can rely on well-functioning and transparent ADR for their disputes they could save around €22.5 billion a year, corresponding to 0.19% of EU GDP.
>
> This figure only includes direct financial savings, and does not account for less tangible factors which are also important for a well-functioning market, such as increased confidence, trust, customer relations and business reputation."

The most interesting feature of these instruments is certainly the EU-wide online dispute resolution platform for consumer disputes arising out of online transactions (the "ODR platform"), which will begin operating by January 2016. The ODR platform will constitute a "single entry point" and will link all national ADR entities. The ODR platform does not itself provide for the resolution of consumer disputes by ODR. Instead, it establishes a series of rules for the resolution of these disputes through national ADR entities.[82]

The ADR and ODR instruments expressly cover the resolution of cross-border disputes.[83] It can be inferred that as matters stand, and bearing in mind the private international law hurdles referred to above with regard to cross-border collective redress procedures,[84] the EU's position is that out-of-court procedures are the most appropriate method for the resolution of cross-border disputes. Class arbitration can and should play a central role in this respect.

Could this platform serve as a model for the development of the above-mentioned "novel form of arbitration"? [85] The implementation of ODR platforms that would not delegate the resolution of the disputes to national entities but would itself be in charge of the administration of the procedures could definitely be the next step forward. The emphasis that has been put by the EU institutions on the "simple, fast and low cost out-of-court solution to disputes between consumers and traders" could certainly be the basis for the implementation of an online arbitration platform. The reasons underlying the creation of these ODR tools are the same: offering small claims plaintiffs a chance to proceed through out-of-court procedures, regardless of whether the claims are individual or collective.

The future of class arbitration would likely imply "B2C arbitration agreements,"[86] be they pre- or post-dispute agreements. It follows from the above that consumer protection is currently the most suitable domain for the deployment of class arbitration.

4 CONCLUSION

Alternative dispute resolution crosses paths with the development (and future) of the EU as an area where freedom, security and justice should coexist. The EU instruments that have been implemented to deal with both individual and collective claims all aspire to fulfil this overarching objective. The implementation of new rules to govern judicial and alternative dispute resolution at the European level also tends to indicate that disputes engaging public policy issues are subject to greater scrutiny and supervision.

Despite class arbitration not being directly addressed by these instruments, it is necessary for the resolution of cross-border disputes. There is no doubt that the "triple benefits of flexibility, neutrality and enforceability"[87] that characterize arbitration are well suited to the resolution of collective disputes. Class arbitration can also provide stability, rationality and predictability in the resolution of collective disputes. In light of the current proliferation of relevant legislation, the future of class arbitration in Europe may require some legislative clarification (inter alia, on third-party funding and arbitrability of consumer related disputes). In an ever-expanding regulatory environment, however, this future will also largely depend upon how effectively the EU will be willing to interact and cooperate with all stakeholders, including arbitral institutions. This is not necessarily wishful thinking. Should this be achieved, European class arbitration is unlikely to be an oxymoron.

NOTES

1 Hanotiau Bernard, *Complex Arbitrations — Multiparty, Multicontract, Multi-issue and Class Actions*, Kluwer Law International, 2005; Fontmichel, Maximin (de), *Le faible et l'arbitrage*, Economica, 2013; Strong SI, a prolific author on that topic, *see inter alia*: *Class, Mass, and Collective Arbitration in National and International Law*, Oxford University Press, 2013; "Class arbitration outside the United States: Reading the Tea Leaves", Dossier of the ICC Institute of World Business Law: Multiparty Arbitration, 2010, p 183 *et seq*; "Does Class Arbitration 'Change the Nature' of Arbitration? Stolt-Nielsen, AT&T, and a Return to First Principles", *Harvard Negotiation Law Review*, Vol. 17, 2012, pp 201-271.

2 European Parliament, Directorate General for Internal Policies, Briefing note, "Overview of existing collective redress schemes in EU Member States", July 2011, p 13: 16 EU Member States had implemented collective redress mechanisms by this date.

3 European Commission, Memo/13/560, "Frequently Asked Questions: European Commission recommends collective redress principles to Member States", 11 June 2013, p 2.

4 Communication from the Commission to the European Parliament, the Council, the European Economic and Social Committee and the Committee of the Regions, "Towards a European Horizontal Framework for Collective Redress", COM(2013) 401/2, p 6.

5 Statement of Gabrielle Kaufmann-Kohler, "The Future — What Will Change ? Round Table Discussion" *in* Albert Jan van den Berg (ed), *Arbitration: The Next Fiflty Years*, ICCA Congress Series, Vol. 16, Kluwer Law International, 2012, p 197.

6 European Commission Staff Working Document, Public consultation, "Towards a Coherent European Approach to Collective Redress", Brussels, 4 February 2011, SEC(2011) 173 final, pp 3-4.

7 Commission Recommendation on common principles for injunctive and compensatory collective redress mechanisms in the Member States concerning violation of rights granted under Union Law, 11 June 2013, paras 1.2, 38.

8 European Parliament, Directorate General for Internal Policies, Briefing note, *supra* note 2, p 13: Austria, Bulgaria, Denmark, Finland, France, Germany, Greece, Hungary, Italy, Lithuania, the Netherlands, Poland, Portugal, Spain, Sweden and the United Kingdom (in England and Wales).

9 European Parliament, Directorate General for Internal Policies, Briefing note, *supra* note 2, p 38.

10 Hanotiau Bernard, *Complex Arbitrations — Multiparty, Multicontract, Multi-issue and Class Actions*, Kluwer Law International, 2005, para 560.

11 European Commission — DG SANCO, "Evaluation of the effectiveness and efficiency of collective redress mechanisms in the European Union", Final Report, Part I: Main Report, submitted by Civic Consulting (Lead) and Oxford Economics, 2008, pp 6-7.

12 European Parliament, Directorate General for Internal Policies, Briefing note, *supra* note 2, pp 39-41.

13 Portugal, Denmark, Netherlands and more recently the United Kingdom (England and Wales) have adopted an "opt-out" mechanism for some or all of their available collective redress procedures.

14 European Parliament, Directorate General for Internal Policies, Briefing note, *supra* note 2, pp 39-41.

15 European Commission, Memo/13/530, "Frequently Asked Questions: European Commission recommends collective redress principles to Member States", 11 June 2013, pp 1-2.

16 European Parliament, Directorate General for Internal Policies, Briefing note, *supra* note 2, p 41.

17 European Commission Evaluation (2008), *supra* note 11, p 9.

18 European Commission Evaluation (2008), *supra* note 11, p 9.

19 European Commission Evaluation (2008), *supra* note 11, pp 9-10.

20 European Commission Evaluation (2008), *supra* note 11, pp 10-11.

21 European Commission Evaluation (2008), *supra* note 11, p 13.

22 Commission Recommendation (2013), *supra* note 7, recital 1.

23 Commission Recommendation (2013), *supra* note 7, recital 7.

24 Commission Recommendation (2013), *supra* note 7, para 1.2.

25 European Commission, Memo/13/560, *supra* note 3, p 2.

26 European Commission, Memo/13/560, *supra* note 3, p 2.

27 European Commission, Memo/13/560, *supra* note 3, p 2.

28 Communication on European Horizontal Framework for Collective Redress, *supra* note 4, pp 15-16.

29 Communication on European Horizontal Framework for Collective Redress, *supra* note 4, p 15 and Commission Recommendation (2013), *supra* note 7, paras 29-32.

30 European Commission Evaluation (2008), *supra* note 11, p 44.

31 European Commission Evaluation (2008), *supra* note 11, p 33; note that the study indicated that this statistic was prepared on the basis of limited information.

32 European Parliament, Directorate General for Internal Policies, Briefing note, *supra* note 2, p 43.

33 Commission Recommendation (2013), *supra* note 7, paras 17-18.

34 European Law Institute, Statement on Collective Redress and Competition Damages Claims, 12 December 2014, p 36.

35 Commission Recommendation (2013), *supra* note 7, paras 17-18.

36 European Commission, Press Release, "Commission recommends Member States to have collective redress mechanisms in place to ensure effective access to justice", 11 June 2013.

37 European Law Institute, Statement on Collective Redress and Competition Damages Claims, 12 December 2014, p 36.

38 Brussels Regulation (EC) No 44/2001 and Brussels Regulation (EU) No 1215/2012.

39 European Parliament, Directorate General for Internal Policies, Briefing note, *supra* note 2, pp 42-44.

40 European Law Institute, Statement on Collective Redress and Competition Damages Claims, 12 December 2014, p 38.

41 European Law Institute, Statement on Collective Redress and Competition Damages Claims, 12 December 2014, p 36.

42 Commission Recommendation (2013), *supra* note 7, paras 25-28.

43 Park William W, Non-Signatories and International Contracts: An Arbitrator's Dilemma in *Multiple Party Actions in International Arbitration*, Oxford, 2009, para 1.03.

44 US Federal Rules of Civil Procedure, Article 23(3).

45 Commission Recommendation (2013), *supra* note 7, recital 1.

46 Commission Recommendation (2013), *supra* note 7, recital 6.

47 European Commission Staff Working Document, Public consultation, *Towards a Coherent European Approach to Collective Redress*, Brussels, 4 February 2011, SEC(2011)173 final, p 2.

48 Strong SI, "Class arbitration outside the United States: Reading the Tea Leaves", Dossier of the ICC Institute of World Business Law: Multiparty Arbitration, 2010, p 196.

49 *Carnegie v Household Int'l, Inc.*, 376 F. 3d 656, 661 (CA7 2004)

50 European Commission, Memo/13/193, "A step forward for EU consumers: Questions & answers on Alternative Dispute Resolution and Online Dispute Resolution", 12 March 2013, p 1.

51 Directive 2013/11/EU of the European Parliament and of the Council, on alternative dispute resolution for consumer disputes and amending Regulation (EC) No 2006/2004 and Directive 2009/22/EC, 21 May 2013, recital 3.

52 Bernheim-Devaux Sabine, "Litiges de consommation — Règlement extrajudiciaire et règlement en ligne", *La Semaine Juridique Entreprise et Affaires*, n° 27, 4 juillet 2013, 1402.

53 European Commission, Press release, "Commission proposes new Investment Court System for TTIP and other EU trade and investment negotiations", 16 September 2015.

54 Nater-Bass Gabrielle, Class-Action Arbitration: A new Challenge?, *ASA Bulletin*, Vol. 27, 2009, p 686.

55 Nater-Bass Gabrielle, Class-Action Arbitration: A new Challenge?, *ASA Bulletin*, Vol. 27, 2009, p 686.

56 Strong, SI, "Class arbitration outside the United States: Reading the Tea Leaves", Dossier of the ICC Institute of World Business Law: Multiparty Arbitration, 2010, p 196.

57 Strong, SI, "Class arbitration outside the United States: Reading the Tea Leaves", Dossier of the ICC Institute of World Business Law: Multiparty Arbitration, 2010, p 197.

58 Fontmichel Maximin (de), "Arbitrage et actions de groupe — les leçons Nord-Américaines", *Revue de l'Arbitrage*, Vol. 4, 2008, p 650.

59 Poudret Jean-François, Besson Sébastien, *Comparative Law of International Arbitration*, Sweet & Maxwell, 2007, p 333.

60 *Green Tree Fin. Corp. v Bazzle*, 539 US 444 (2003), 23 June 2003.

61 Nater-Bass Gabrielle, "Class-Action Arbitration: A new Challenge?", *ASA Bulletin*, Vol. 27, 2009, p 675.

62 Real Decretoley 231/2008 de 15 de febrero, por el que se regula el Sistema Arbitral de Consumo ; see Strong Sacie I, "Collective Consumer Arbitration in Spain: A Civil Law Response to US-Style Class Arbitration", *Journal of International Arbitration*, Vol. 30, 2013, p 497.

63 Consumer disputes are generally considered arbitrable: Poudret Jean-François, Besson Sébastien, *Comparative Law of International Arbitration*, Sweet & Maxwell, 2007, p 333.

64 Commission Recommendation (2013), *supra* note 7, recital 16.

65 US Federal Rules of Civil Procedure, Article 23(3).

66 Commission Recommendation (2013), *supra* note 7, para 26.

67 The French Arbitration Decree *e.g.* provides that should difficulties relating to the constitution of the arbitral tribunal arise, the "*juge d'appui*" could be seized to help resolve these difficulties.

68 European Commission, Memo/13/560, *supra* note 3, p 2.

69 Strong, SI, "Class arbitration outside the United States: Reading the Tea Leaves", Dossier of the ICC Institute of World Business Law: Multiparty Arbitration, 2010, p 197.

70 Gaillard Emmanuel, Savage John, *Fouchard/Gaillard/Goldman on International Commercial Arbitration*, Kluwer Law International, 1999, para 478.

71 Commission Recommendation (2013), *supra* note 7, recital 2.

72 American Arbitration Association's Supplementary Rules for Class Arbitration, effective on 3 October 2003.

73 DIS Supplementary Rules for Corporate Law Disputes, in force as from 15 September 2009; for a detailed commentary of these rules, see Strong Sacie I, "Collective Arbitration Under the DIS Supplementary Rules for Corporate Law Disputes: A European Form of Class Arbitration?", *ASA Bulletin*, Vol. 29, 2011, pp 45-65..

74 Nater-Bass Gabrielle, "Class-Action Arbitration: A new Challenge?", *ASA Bulletin*, Vol. 27, 2009, p 683.

75 The principle of equality pursuant to which each party has the same rights in the appointment of the arbitral tribunal has notably been established in France: Cour de cassation, 7 janvier 1992, Dutco, *Revue de l'Arbitrage*, Vol. 3, 1992, pp 470 *et seq*, note Pierre Bellet.

76 American Arbitration Association's Supplementary Rules for Class Arbitration, Article 2(b).

77 DIS Supplementary Rules for Corporate Law Disputes, Article 8.3.

78 Paulsson Jan, "Moral Hazard in International Dispute Resolution", Inaugural Lecture as Holder of the Michael R. Klein Distinguished Scholar Chair, University of Miami School of Law, 29 April 2010, p 8.

79 Directive 2013/11/EU of the European Parliament and of the Council on alternative dispute resolution for consumer disputes and amending Regulation (EC) No 2006/2004 and Directive 2009/22/EC ("Directive on consumer ADR"), 21 May 2013.

80 Regulation (EU) No 524/2013 of the European Parliament and of the Council of 21 May 2013 on online dispute resolution for consumer disputes and amending Regulation (EC) No 2006/2004 and Directive 2009/22/EC ("Regulation on consumer ODR"), 21 May 2013.

81 European Commission, Memo/13/193, *supra* note 50, p 3.

82 European Commission, Memo/13/193, *supra* note 50, p 2.

83 Directive on consumer ADR, recital 7 and Article 2 pursuant to which it "shall apply to procedures for the out-of-court resolution of domestic and cross-border disputes concerning contractual obligations stemming from sales contracts or service contracts between a trader established in the Union and a consumer resident in the Union"; pursuant to its Article 2, the Regulation on consumer ODR only deals with "online sales or service contracts between a consumer resident in the Union and a trader established in the Union."

84 See *supra*, section I.C.

85 Strong SI, "Class arbitration outside the United States: Reading the Tea Leaves", Dossier of the ICC Institute of World Business Law: Multiparty Arbitration, 2010, p 197.

86 Kaufmann-Kohler Gabrielle, Schultz Thomas, *Online Dispute Resolution — Challenges for Contemporary Justice*, Kluwer Law International, 2004, p 169.

87 Statement of Campbell McLachlan QC, "The Future — What Will Change ? Round Table Discussion" *in* Albert Jan van den Berg (ed), *Arbitration: The Next Fiflty Years*, ICCA Congress Series, Vol. 16, Kluwer Law International, 2012, p 193.

Concluding Remarks

Eric A. Schwartz, Co-editor*

At the ICC Institute's Annual Meeting in 2009, the Institute for the first time considered the subject of so-called "class arbitration," but on a limited basis in the context of its examination that year of the broader topic of multi-party arbitration. At the time, "class arbitration" had received the apparent blessing of a divided United States Supreme Court in the case of *Green Tree Financial Corp. v Bazzle*,[1] and this prompted widespread speculation about the possible expansion of class arbitration outside the boundaries of the United States.

But then, in 2010, in the case of *Stolt-Nielsen S.A. v AnimalFeeds International Corp.*,[2] the US Supreme Court dealt the first of a series of setbacks to the use of class arbitration. While the Supreme Court left parties free to agree to class arbitration, a majority of the Supreme Court concluded that "class action arbitration changes the nature of arbitration." Thus, class arbitrations would be allowed to proceed only where the parties agreed expressly to such a process. It was widely expected within the United States that class arbitration as a phenomenon would gradually wither away.

Nevertheless, Professor S.I. Strong, a speaker on this subject at the Institute's 2009 conference and again in 2015, commented, after the *Solt-Nielsen* decision was issued, that it was "by no means clear that the procedure [of class action arbitration or procedures like it] will either fade from use or remain limited to the United States."[3]

Writing six years ago, Professor Strong postulated that there were "at least three good reasons for thinking that the device [of class arbitration] will expand beyond US borders in one form or another in the not so distant future,"[4] even though the use of arbitration for the resolution of classes of claims or groups of claims of comparable size was then (and still is) virtually unknown outside the US.

First, she observed that the global legal community was "facing an unprecedented amount of interest in issues involving large-scale group injuries."

Second, she noted that class arbitration was "no longer limited to domestic US disputes," and she referred to different types of international class arbitrations that had already been brought, including, most notably, the international arbitration initiated by 195,000 Italian bondholders against Argentina in 2007.[5]

Third, as she further indicated "courts, commentators and legislatures in a variety of different jurisdictions have already begun to discuss the merits of allowing some form of class arbitration to develop within their borders."

* Partner, King & Spalding, United States and France; Former Vice-President and Secretary General, ICC International Court of Arbitration; Vice-Chair, ICC Institute of World Business Law

Six years later, the ICC Institute considered that it was timely to review these postulates, in the light not only of the experience gained in the United States and in international investment cases since the Institute's 2009 Annual Meeting, but also specific developments in relation to certain types of group actions in Spain and Germany.

SO WHAT HAVE WE LEARNED?

Broadly speaking, we have been left to conclude that, while the arbitration of "large-scale disputes" (of a class, group or other collective nature) garners mixed reviews and still has an uncertain future, it is unlikely to disappear. As we were told by the U.S. speakers, class arbitration has continued to thrive in the United States, notwithstanding an increasingly inhospitable legal environment and opposition from large corporations that have chosen arbitration as a dispute resolution mechanism for the very purpose of avoiding exposure in the U.S. courts to actions for class-wide relief. Meanwhile, interest outside the United States in various forms of collective recourse, albeit in limited, specific circumstances, has continued to develop, in the absence of existing judicial mechanisms such as those available in the United States. Thus, this conference and the discussions that transpired have generally been a testament to the prescience of Professor Strong six years ago.

From the discussions that occurred, it can reasonably further be concluded that the future of class and group arbitration is likely to be shaped by the answers to three broad questions.

First, are there certain categories of claims in respect of which collective redress is desirable? The answer to this question would appear to be uncontroversial: certainly, this is the case, in particular where no other mechanism exists for the cost-effective resolution of such claims or for their resolution with comparable efficiency. As one of the speakers noted in relation to the Argentine bond cases brought before ICSID, efficiency and access to justice militated in favor of trying to find a way to make a collective process work in those cases, failing which the claimants could be deprived of an effective mechanism for enforcing their substantive rights.

Second, where collective redress is desirable, does arbitration have a role to play in providing appropriate such redress? This requires the consideration of any possible advantages (or disadvantages) of arbitration in this regard, and, as to this, our conference provided no definitive answers. However, in a cross-border context, arbitration will, at a minimum, generally offer the advantages, as it does in respect of other matters, of (i) a neutral forum and (ii) the protections of treaties such as the New York and Washington Conventions, not to mention the usual procedural flexibility.

Third, where arbitration is perceived as preferable to judicial recourse, how can it be made to work fairly and effectively in a class or group claim setting? As we learned from our international investment arbitration panel, two concerns are fundamental in this regard: first, ensuring that the consent of all those participating or represented is obtained (either on an opt-in or opt-out basis) and second, ensuring that due process is respected. Lurking in the background of such proceedings there will always be a legitimate concern about their potential for procedural abuses, although the fairness and reasonability of the procedures adopted will need to be weighed against the benefit of broader access to justice that such proceedings are likely to confer.

In this regard, the experience of class arbitration in the United States and of mass or group claims in the international investment arbitration arena, together with new experiences in Germany, Spain or elsewhere, will continue to inform our views on this topic. As this conference has demonstrated, we still have much to learn from each other in respect of an area of arbitration practice that will continue to develop and evolve in the future.

NOTES

1 539 U.S. 444 (2003).

2 130 S. Ct. 1758 (2010).

3 Strong, SI, "Class Arbitration Outside the United States : Reading the Tea Leaves," *Multiparty Arbitration* , eds. Hanotiau and Schwartz (ICC 2010), 183.

4 *Id.*

5 *Beccara v Argentine Republic*, ICSID case no. ARB/07/5.

About the Authors

Philippe Billiet

Partner, Billiet & Co, Belgium; Director, AIA; Lecturer, Brussels VUB University

Philippe Billiet works as a lawyer for the Brussels law firm Billiet & Co, where he focuses on alternative dispute resolution and commercial law. He is frequently involved in matters with a diplomatic nature (involving sovereigns) and is member of the Advisory Board to the Brussels Diplomatic Academy (BDA). He lectures arbitration and mediation at the Brussels VUB University and at various training centres. He also holds a directorship mandate at the Association for International Arbitration.

As an arbitrator, Mr Billiet is registered with the Cour Belge d'Arbitrage pour le Sport (Belgium), CEDIRES (Belgium), the Raad voor Arbitrage (Belgium), the Institute of Arbitration (Belgium), the Vienna International Arbitral Centre (Austria), the Kuala Lumpur Regional Centre for Arbitration (Malaysia), the Commission de Litiges Voyages (Belgium), the Lagos Regional Centre for International Commercial Arbitration (Nigeria), the Commercial Arbitration Centre in Harare (Zimbabwe), the Chambre Régionale d'Arbitrage Aix-en-Provence (France) and the BANI Arbitration center (Indonesia).

As a mediator, he obtained EMTPJ cross border mediator certification, specializing in commercial matters. He speaks Dutch, French, German and English.

Christian Borris

Partner, Borris Hennecke Kneisel, Germany

Christian Borris has over 25 years of experience in the resolution of commercial disputes. After studying law at the Universities of Cologne and Miami/USA and qualifying for the office of a judge in the German state courts, he started his professional career in 1987 as Legal Assistant to Karl-Heinz Böckstiegel, then the President of the Iran-United States Claims Tribunal in The Hague (Netherlands).

In 1989, Mr Borris joined Deringer Tessin Herrmann & Sedemund in Cologne. When Deringer Tessin Herrmann & Sedemund merged with international law firm Freshfields in 2000 to form Freshfields Bruckhaus Deringer LLP, he became a partner in Freshfields Bruckhaus Deringer's Dispute Resolution practice group and International Arbitration Group, based in Cologne.

In 2014, Mr Borris founded an independent dispute resolution boutique Borris Hennecke Kneisel in Cologne. His practice encompasses the entire scope of international commercial disputes, with a particular focus on post-M&A, joint venture, corporate, and energy disputes, expert determination proceedings, as well as disputes in the areas of construction, investment protection, banking & finance, (re-)insurance, distribution, licensing and cross-border sales transactions.

He has acted as counsel and arbitrator in more than 110 arbitrations under a wide variety of institutional rules and in ad hoc arbitrations. He also represents clients in proceedings before the German state courts. He speaks German, English and French.

Luca Radicati di Brozolo

Partner, Arblit-Radicati di Brozolo Sabatini Benedettelli, Italy; Professor, Catholic University of Milan; Fountain Court Chambers, London; Member, LCIA Court

Professor Luca G. Radicati di Brozolo holds the chair of Private International Law at the Catholic University of Milan, where he also teaches international arbitration law and transnational commercial law.

His current practice focuses primarily on international arbitration as counsel, presiding, party-appointed and sole arbitrator and expert. He has significant experience in investor-State arbitration, having acted as counsel in several high-profile cases (including the ICSID cases *Saipem v Bangladesh* and *Ambiente Ufficio v Argentina* and *Giovanni Alpi v Argentina*) and in several UNICTRAL cases against the Czech Republic under the Energy Charter Treaty and several BITs). He also acts in court litigation and as an advisor, and appears as an expert, on matters of conflicts of laws and jurisdiction, and in the areas of law in which he practiced in the earlier part of his career as partner in two major Italian firms, European law and competition law, and particularly in private antitrust litigation.

He is the author of five books and over 150 scholarly articles on different topics on arbitration, public and private international law, European Union law and antitrust law, and is a co-editor of the leading Italian commentary of the law of arbitration.

He is a former member of the International Court of Arbitration of the ICC and former Vice-Chair of the IBA Arbitration Committee, a member and a former rapporteur of the Committee on International Commercial Arbitration of the International Law Association, a member of the American Law Institute, Consultative Group on the Restatement (Third), International Commercial Arbitration, co-chair of the Joint Working Group of the Competition and Arbitration Committees of the ICC Arbitration Commission on Antitrust Follow-on Actions and appointed to the ICSID Panel of Arbitrators by the Republic of Italy.

Laura Carballo

Associate Professor of Private International Law, University of Santiago de Compostela, Spain

Laura Carballo is Associate Professor at the University of Santiago de Compostela in Spain. She holds a Doctorate in Procedural Law Cum Laude, from the University of Santiago de Compostela, completed by another one in Private International Law Cum Laude from the University of Vigo.

Ms Carballo is an expert in international insolvency law as well as in international class and collective actions. Her areas of expertise are:

private international law, international litigation, international commercial arbitration, enforcement of foreign judgments, contract law and international bankruptcy law.

Ms Carballo was awarded a scholarship by the Alexander von Humboldt Foundation (2010-2012), carrying out a project on International Jurisdiction and Conflict of Laws in Maritime Labour and Employment Law, at the Max Planck Institute for Comparative and Private International Law in Hamburg.

James Carter

Senior Counsel, Wilmer Cutler Pickering Hale and Dorr LLP, New York, United States

James Carter is a Senior Counsel in the New York office of Wilmer Cutler Pickering Hale and Dorr LLP. He has more than 40 years of experience as arbitrator or counsel in more than 150 international commercial and investment arbitration cases.

Mr Carter previously was co-chair of the international arbitration and cross-border dispute resolution group at Dewey & LeBoeuf LLP. He was also co-chair of international arbitration, a position he held for more than 20 years, at Sullivan & Cromwell LLP. He has served as Chair of the Board of Directors of the American Arbitration Association, President of the American Society of International Law and a member of the London Court of International Arbitration.

Mr. Carter is Chair of the Board of the New York International Arbitration Center, a member of the Court of Arbitration for Sport and a graduate of Yale College and Yale Law School. He is the co-editor of International Commercial Arbitration in New York and the author of more than 50 articles and book chapters dealing with international disputes.

Pierre Dalphond

Senior Counsel, Stikeman Elliott, Montreal, Canada; Member, ICC Institute of World Business Law

Pierre Dalphond is a Senior Counsel with the Montréal office's Litigation Group, Certified Mediator, Arbitrator and a former trial and appeal judge. He provides legal and strategic advice, acts as a commercial mediator and arbitrator and teaches domestic and international arbitration law as an Invited Professor at Université de Montréal.

Before being named a judge, Mr Dalphond practised commercial law (investments in Canada, supply and construction contracts, private financing, joint ventures, mergers and acquisitions). He wrote over 1500 judgments and decisions as judge and arbitrator.

Mr Dalphond is on the arbitrators' lists of ICDR Canada/AAA, ICC Canada, Arbitration Place (Toronto) and the Montreal Bar. He is also a Vice-President of the Québec Society of Comparative Law, a director of the International Commission of Jurists-Canada, a faculty member of the Philippe Kirsch Institute (promoting international law) and a member of the ICC Institute of World Business Law, the LCIA North American Users' Council and the International Bar Association.

Yves Derains

Founding Partner, Derains & Gharavi, France; Former Secretary General, ICC International Court of Arbitration; Chairman, ICC Institute of World Business Law

Yves Derains, former Secretary General of the ICC International Court of Arbitration and Director of the Legal Department of the ICC, is member of the Paris Bar and a founding partner of the law firm Derains & Gharavi. He is specialized in international arbitration and is acting both as arbitrator and counsel of parties in arbitration proceedings.

Mr Derains is former Chairman of the Comité Français de l'Arbitrage and Chairman of the ICC Institute of World Business Law. He was Chairman of the Working Party on the Revision of the ICC Rules of Arbitration in 1998 and Co-Chairman of the ICC Task Force on the Reduction of Costs and Time in international arbitration.

He is a member of the French Committee on Private International Law since 1978. He is a member of the Governing Board of the International Council for Commercial Arbitration (ICCA) and member of various other organizations specialized in international arbitration and in international business law. He is Honorary Professor of the Law Faculties of San Ignacio de Loyola University, Universidad del Pacifico and the Universidad de Lima, Peru.

Mr Derains is also author of many publications on International Commercial Arbitration and on International Business Law, in particular: *Evaluation of damages in international arbitration*, ICC Institute of World Business Law, 2006; *A Guide to the ICC Rules of Arbitration* (Second edition, with E. Schwartz), Kluwer Law International, 2005.

Christopher R. Drahozal

John M. Rounds Professor of Law, University of Kansas School of Law, United States

Christopher R. Drahozal is the John M. Rounds Professor of Law and Associate Dean for Research and Faculty Development at the University of Kansas School of Law. He is an Associate Reporter for the Restatement of the U.S. Law on International Commercial Arbitration, is serving as a Special Advisor to the Consumer Financial Protection Bureau, and was the Chair of the Arbitration Task Force of the Searle Civil Justice Institute.

Mr Drahozal has written extensively on the law and economics of arbitration. He has authored a casebook on commercial arbitration published by Lexis Publishing (now in its third edition) and a co-edited a book on empirical research on international commercial arbitration published by Kluwer Law International. His articles have appeared in the Journal of Legal Studies, the Journal of Empirical Legal Studies, the Texas Law Review, the Vanderbilt Law Review, Law and Contemporary Problems, and the International Review of Law and Economics, among others. He has made presentations on arbitration law and practice throughout the United States, Canada, Europe, and Asia.

Bernard Hanotiau

Partner, Hanotiau & van den Berg, Belgium; Council Member, ICC Institute of World Business Law

Bernard Hanotiau is a member of the Brussels and Paris Bars and a Partner of Hanotiau & van den Berg. The firm has offices in Brussels and Singapore.

Mr Hanotiau is Professor Emeritus of the law school of Louvain University (Belgium). He is a member of the ICCA Governing Board and of the Council of the ICC Institute. He is a member of the Court of Arbitration of SIAC, of the Advisory Board of HKIAC and of the Governing Board of DIAC (Dubai) and a former Vice-President of the LCIA Court.

Since 1978, Mr Hanotiau has been actively involved in more than 400 international arbitration cases. In March 2011, he received the GAR "Arbitrator of the Year" award.

José Miguel Júdice

Founding Partner, PLMJ, Portugal; Member, ICC Institute of World Business Law

José Miguel Júdice is a Founding Partner of PLMJ (since 1980), a member of ICC International Court of Arbitration (since June 2009) and was Vice-President of ICC National Committee until 2012. He has acted for more than 35 years as arbitrator and counsel in national and international cases (ICC, ICSID, UNCITRAL, NAI, Brazil-Canadá, Cámara de Madrid, Portuguese arbitration centres and ad hoc), is a member of ICSID Roster of Arbitrators and Conciliators, of Permanent Court of Arbitration (The Hague) and other lists of Arbitration Centres in Brazil (7), Spain, Mozambique, Angola, Korea and Portugal.

Mr Júdice has developed PLMJ arbitration practice (since 2014 considered as one of the GAR 100) and has been instrumental to the development of arbitration in Portugal (Board of the Portuguese Arbitration Association, Co-author of the draft of the Portuguese Arbitration Law, President of the Lisbon Arbitration Centre of the CCIP, a member of ICC network, and Professor of Business Law and Dispute Resolution in two Lisbon Universities).

He has been Member of the High Council of the Judiciary, President of the Portuguese Bar Association and of its Human Rights Institute. He is a Portuguese citizen, graduated in Coimbra University, and speaks also French, English and Spanish.

Elie Kleiman

Partner, Freshfields Bruckhaus Deringer LLP, France

Elie Kleiman is a dispute resolution Partner of Freshfields based in Paris. He specializes in international arbitration and complex litigation. He regularly acts as Counsel in arbitral and court proceedings and also sits as arbitrator and mediator.

Mr Kleiman has significant trial experience and advises and represents clients in complex international disputes involving, in particular, corporate law, securities, M&A, joint ventures, banking, distribution, risk management and damage control. His wide sector knowledge notably covers energy, chemicals, pharmaceuticals and bio-technology, aeronautics, construction, financial institutions, telecoms and media. He is the author of numerous articles and is a frequent lecturer on international arbitration and complex litigation issues.

Mr Kleiman received law degrees from the University of Paris II and Paris X. He is admitted as an Avocat in France and as a Foreign Legal Consultant of the New York Bar. He is also the managing partner of Freshfields in Paris and among other roles is an Expert member of the Club des Juristes, the leading French legal think tank.

Carolyn Lamm

Partner, White & Case LLP, Washington, United States; Member, ICC Institute of World Business Law

Carolyn Lamm is a Partner of White & Case LLP based in Washington, DC and Co-Chair of International Arbitration Americas. She has served as a member of the Firm's Partnership Committee.

She regularly serves as lead counsel in high-stakes, cutting-edge cases, successfully resolving significant international arbitrations involving international corporates and sovereign clients. She also serves as lead counsel in arbitration-related litigation matters.

Her practice concentrates on international dispute resolution through international arbitration, litigation and international trade proceedings. She sits as an arbitrator in ICSID, ICDR and AAA arbitrations.

Ms Lamm was appointed by President Clinton to the US Panel and later by the Government of Uzbekistan to the Uzbek Panel of Arbitrators for ICSID arbitration.

She was a member of the American Arbitration Association Executive Committee and Board, and is currently a member of the ICCA Governing Board, a member of the Council of the American Law Institute. She is a founding member of the American Uzbekistan Chamber of Commerce and currently serves as Chairman of the Board.

Ms Lamm is a past President of both the District of Columbia Bar and the American Bar Association. She is currently serving as the American Bar Association's Representative to the International Bar Association. She has been recognized repeatedly for her professional expertise in international dispute resolution and leadership in the profession by numerous sources.

Eloïse Obadia

Partner, Derains & Gharavi, Washington D.C., United States; Former Senior Counsel and Team Leader, International Centre for Settlement of Investment Disputes (ICSID, World Bank Group)

Eloïse Obadia joined Derains & Gharavi in October 2013. She focuses her practice on international arbitration, including investor-state arbitration. She has represented private parties and governments in arbitration before ICSID and in UNCITRAL and *ad hoc* international arbitrations.

Prior to that, she was Team Leader at ICSID. She served as Secretary of tribunals, conciliation commissions and *ad hoc* committees in more than 60 proceedings brought under the ICSID Convention, Additional Facility Rules and UNCITRAL Rules. She also served as Coordinator in an Expert Determination under the Indus Waters Treaty.

Before joining ICSID, Ms Obadia was an associate at Curtis, Mallet-Prevost, Colt & Mosle, Paris where she participated in the representation of private-sector companies in international arbitrations and a sovereign State in an ICSID conciliation.

Ms Obadia is adjunct Associate Professor at American University, Washington College of Law where she teaches Investment Treaty Arbitration, and guest lecturer on International Economic Litigation Law, Master 2, International Economic Law, University of Panthéon–Assas.

She is admitted to the Paris and New York Bars and is registered as Special Legal Consultant in Washington, DC. She completed a Master of Laws at Duke University. She holds degrees from the University of Paris II Panthéon-Assas and the University of Paris-Dauphine. She speaks English, French, Italian and Spanish.

Geneviève Saumier

Peter M. Laing Professor of Law, Faculty of Law, McGill University, Canada

On faculty since 1996 and Associate Dean from 2005-08, Geneviève Saumier's research and teaching focus on dispute resolution, including arbitration, mediation and civil litigation in international and domestic law. Her articles on private international law and on consumer arbitration have been cited by the Supreme Court of Canada.

Ms Saumier holds degrees from McGill in Management and Law and obtained her PhD in private international law from the University of Cambridge.

An elected Member of the International Academy of Comparative Law and of the American Association of Private International Law, she is also a member of the board of the Quebec Consumer Protection Office.

Ms Saumier was a member of the Working Group for the Hague Principles on Choice of Law for International Commercial Contracts from 2010-14 and chaired the Drafting Committee at the intergovernmental Special Commission in 2012. She is currently co-rapporteur for the IACL's 2016 conference on enforcement of consumer protection.

Eric A. Schwartz

Partner, King & Spalding, United States and France; Former Vice-President and Secretary General, ICC International Court of Arbitration; Vice-Chair, ICC Institute of World Business Law

Eric Schwartz was educated at Dartmouth College (B.A.) and Yale University (J.D.) and is a member of the bars of both California and Paris. He is currently a Partner of King & Spalding in New York and Paris and formerly served as Secretary General (1992-1996) and as a member and Vice-President (2006-2015) of the ICC International Court of Arbitration.

Over the last 35 years, in addition to his tenure at the ICC, Mr Schwartz has acted as counsel or as an arbitrator in over 100 international arbitration proceedings under all of the principal international arbitration rules and in all of the principal European arbitration venues, as well as in Africa, Asia and the U.S.

He is the co-author (with Yves Derains) of *A Guide to the ICC Rules of Arbitration* as well as dozens of other publications on international arbitration law and practice.

S.I. Strong

Professor of Law, University of Missouri, United States

S.I. Strong specializes in international and comparative law, with a particular emphasis on international commercial arbitration and large-scale (class and collective) suits. She has taught at the Universities of Cambridge and Oxford in the United Kingdom as well as Georgetown Law Center and the University of Missouri in the United States.

Ms Strong is an experienced practitioner, having acted as Counsel at Baker & McKenzie after working as a dual-qualified lawyer (U.S. attorney and English solicitor) in the New York and London offices of Weil, Gotshal & Manges. She has published numerous award-winning books and articles in Europe and the Americas, including *Class, Mass, and Collective Arbitration in National and International Law* (2013) and *Research and Practice in International Commercial Arbitration: Sources and Strategies* (2009), both from Oxford University Press, as well as *International Commercial Arbitration: A Guide for U.S. Judges* (2012) from the Federal Judicial Center.

Ms Strong's scholarly work has also been cited as authority to the U.S. Supreme Court and in ICSID awards. Ms Strong, who holds a Ph.D. in law from the University of Cambridge, a D.Phil. from the University of Oxford, a J.D. from Duke University, an M.P.W. from the University of Southern California and a B.A. from the University of California, Davis, sits as an arbitrator on a variety of complex commercial matters.

Index

C

D

E

F

Cases

A

B

C

D

E

F

G

H

The ICC Institute of World Business Law

The ICC Institute of World Business Law, which acts as a think-tank working closely with the ICC International Court of Arbitration, is composed of a Council of 39 members of 25 nationalities, all experienced professionals or academics in international business law or international commercial arbitration, as well as more than 260 members from around the world. Yves Derains is the Chair of the ICC Institute of World Business Law, and Antonias Dimolitsa and Eric Schwartz are the Vice-Chairs. Created over 35 years ago, the Institute provides research, training and information to the legal profession concerned with the development of international business law. In line with its philosophy of excellence, it proposes publications, trainings and conferences on different topics related to international business law.

Member benefits

- 5% reduction on all Institute conferences and some other selected ICC conferences
- 20% reduction on all Institute publications
- An invitation to attend an annual Colloquium of Arbitrators free of charge
- A twice-yearly electronic Newsletter
- The opportunity to propose various subjects for reflection
- A Directory of Institute Members compiling short biographies of all Members
- After 2 years of Institute membership members will be eligible for Council membership, the governing body of the Institute

Members have the opportunity to:

- Contribute to the work of the Institute
- Make known and support the activities of the Institute
- Apply to speak at Institute events
- Provide the Institute with a wealth of expertise in many fields of international law and practice
- Promote Institute activities in their home countries

Membership Fees

All members are required to pay an annual membership fee that runs from January to December.

- Standard rate: €350*
- Under 35 rate: €200*

* excluding VAT

How to become a member

Register for membership directly online **www.iccinstitute.org or contact:**

E **institute@iccwbo.org** | T +33 (0)1 49 53 28 67

ICC Institute of World Business Law
33-43 avenue du Président Wilson, 75116 Paris, France

ICC Arbitration in Practice

ICC Pub. No. 782E, €150

Written from a practical perspective, this book is an essential resource for company lawyers who wish to familiarize themselves with ICC arbitration, assess the pros and cons of entering into an arbitration clause referring to the ICC Rules, or obtain information and guidance on how to proceed in a given situation. Arbitration practitioners will find useful information on the practice of ICC arbitration, including various notes of the ICC Court Secretariat and reports of the ICC Commission on Arbitration and ADR.

The Secretariat's Guide to ICC Arbitration

A Practical Commentary on the 2012 ICC Rules of Arbitration from the Secretariat of the ICC International Court of Arbitration

ICC Pub. No. 729E, €119

The authors, former senior members of the ICC Secretariat, give an exclusive, behind-the-scenes look into how the 2012 Rules work in practice. With this Guide you will be better equipped to navigate through the ICC arbitral process.

Addressing Issues of Corruption in Commercial and Investment Arbitration

Dossier XIII of the ICC Institute of World Business Law

ICC Pub. No. 768E, €75 (2015 edition)

This publication addresses the issue of corruption in arbitration in a systematic way. The topics covered include the impact of corruption on "gateway issues" of arbitrability, jurisdiction, admissibility and procedure; the arbitrator's rights and duties to investigate and report corruption. It also addresses the most recent thinking and case law on the burden and standard of proof for allegations of corruption as well as the consequences and effects of allegations or positive findings of corruption on the dispute on the merits and the enforceability of the award respectively.

Jurisdictional Choices in Times of Trouble

Dossier XII of the ICC Institute of World Business Law

ICC Pub. No. 755E, €75

Written by arbitrators, academics and practitioners, this dossier addresses the multiple challenges facing the jurisdiction clause through an expert in-depth comparison of syndromes and proposed solutions in both arbitration and court proceedings.

The Application of Substantive Law by International Arbitrators

Dossier XI of the ICC Institute of World Business Law

ICC Pub. No. 753E, €65

This book examines issues that can arise when international arbitrators apply the rules of a national legal system. It provides a thorough picture of the practical issues raised when there is contradiction between the applicable law and the needs of international business.

Third-party Funding in International Arbitration

Dossier X of the ICC Institute of World Business Law

ICC Pub. No. 752E, €75

This publication gives an overview of the various funding techniques specific to international arbitration. It also analyzes some of the legal issues raised by such funding and the reactions it may arouse amongst practitioners. To give you a complete picture of challenges and opportunities of third-party funding, this vital reference for any practitioner and academic includes points of view of financiers, funders, arbitrators and counsel.

Players' Interaction in International Arbitration

Dossier IX of the ICC Institute of World Business Law

ICC Pub. No. 737E, €75

Arbitral procedures are becoming longer, costlier and more complex. How can the different 'players' involved in a case ensure that the proceedings remain efficient, harmonious and at the same time respectful of the parties' rights? Some of today's leading experts discuss this and other questions, taking into account the points of view of all 'players' concerned: arbitrators, counsel, corporate lawyers and arbitral institutions. A must-read for anyone involved in international arbitration.

Is Arbitration Only as Good as the Arbitrator?

Dossier VIII of the ICC Institute of World Business Law

ICC Pub. No. 741E, €75

Invaluable companion for practitioners and scholars alike, this publication looks at the relationship between the qualities of the arbitrators and the arbitrators' "work-products", namely the award and the arbitral process itself. Leading experts discuss issues such as clashes between arbitrator and litigants, arbitral discrimination under English and EU law or the arbitrator's relation with third parties.

Multiparty Arbitration

Dossier VII of the ICC Institute of World Business Law

ICC Pub. No. 701E, €75

Arbitral procedures are becoming more complex as commercial transactions begin to take place in an ever-increasing interdependent world. How can the several parties involved in multiparty contracts and proceedings be harmonized and handled in the interests of the best administration of justice? This Dossier seeks to encourage reflection on complex multiparty, multicontract arbitrations.

Written Evidence and Discovery in International Arbitration

Dossier VI of the ICC Institute of World Business Law

ICC Pub. No. 698E, €125

This Dossier seeks to encourage reflection on future practice in relation to documentary evidence in international arbitration, looking for transnational solutions capable of striking a proper balance between efficiency and fairness. It tackles relevant issues including fraud, forgery, confidentiality and privilege.

Interest, Auxiliary and Alternative Remedies in International Arbitration

Dossier V of the ICC Institute of World Business Law

ICC Pub. No. 684E, €75

How can the quick and effective enforcement of awards be guaranteed in arbitral practice? The aim of this publication is to provide the reader with solutions on how to control the impact of time between the occurrence of the damage and its full compensation. Renowned arbitration professionals Antonias Dimolitsa, John Beechey, Andrea Giardina, John Yukio Gotanda, Grabrielle Kaufmann- Kohler, Alexis Mourre and V.V. Veeder, amongst others, give their own perspective on a wide range of topics related to remedies (contractual remedies, judicial penalties, specific performance) and interest (issue of applicable law, comparative approaches, interest in arbitration practice).

Evaluation of Damages in International Arbitration

Dossier IV of the ICC Institute of World Business Law

ICC Pub. No. 668E, €67.50 e-book

This publication provides the reader with a comprehensive overview of the difficulties encountered by arbitrators, governments and international organizations in calculating the amounts of recoverable damages in cases of international arbitration. Written by expert arbitrators and practitioners, the book covers vital issues arising from determining recoverable damages and proposes practical solutions for resolving them.

Agreed!

Negotiation/Mediation in the 21st century

By Thierry Garby

ICC Pub. No. 777E, €65   Also available in French

In the second half of the 20th century, scientific research unveiled the psychological mechanisms which contribute towards the forming of agreements. Mediation started to break impasses that negotiation could not resolve. This book shows how these findings result in an incredibly powerful method to negotiate contracts and treaties and resolve conflicts of all sorts. Written in an easy-to-read manner and citing many well-known references, this book will appeal to all professionals of negotiation and mediation, lawyers, corporate counsels, business managers, unions and association representatives, project managers, mediators etc.

Mediation Practice

8 Cultures, 16 Cases, 128 Creative Solutions

Edited by Greg Bond

ICC Pub. No. 783E, €65

Mediation Practice is a dialogue between experienced mediation professionals of different nationalities and backgrounds, sharing their ideas on cases from across the globe. The eight mediators provide 16 cases and 128 responses and conclusions to these cases with hundreds of ideas on what mediators might do in specific situations. Each case focuses on a "mediation moment" when mediators ask themselves what to do next. Full of stories and insights, Mediation Practice is an enriching and entertaining read for all mediation practitioners, students, trainees, and trainers, and for anyone wishing to learn about the real world of mediation.

www.ingramcontent.com/pod-product-compliance
Lightning Source LLC
Chambersburg PA
CBHW071440230926
51846CB00001B/296
9789041183859